Speech Sounds and Features

Current Studies in Linguistics Series
Samuel Jay Keyser, general editor

1. *A Reader on the Sanskrit Grammarians*
   J. F. Staal, editor
2. *Semantic Interpretation in Generative Grammar*
   Ray S. Jackendoff
3. *The Structure of the Japanese Language*
   Susumu Kuno
4. *Speech Sounds and Features*
   Gunnar Fant

Speech Sounds and Features

Gunnar Fant

The MIT Press
Cambridge, Massachusetts, and London, England

Copyright © 1973 by
The Massachusetts Institute of Technology

All rights reserved. No part of this book may be reproduced in any form or by any means, electronic or mechanical, including photocopying, recording, or by any information storage and retrieval system, without permission in writing from the publisher.

This book was printed on 60# Decision Offset
and bound in Whitman P.O.C. "Blue Streak"
by The Colonial Press Inc.
in the United States of America.

Library of Congress Cataloging in Publication Data

Fant, Gunnar.
  Speech sounds and features.

  Bibliography: p.
  1. Phonetics—Collected works. 2. Grammar,
Comparative and general—Phonology—Collected works.
I. Title.
[DNLM: 1. Linguistics. 2. Phonetics. 3. Speech.
P 121 F216s 1973]
P215.F3   414   73–4288
ISBN 0-262-06051-5
ISBN: 0-262-56158-1 (Paperback)

Contents

Foreword vii

Introduction ix

Part I
Speech Analysis

Chapter 1
The Acoustics of Speech 3

Chapter 2
Descriptive Analysis of the Acoustic Aspects of Speech 17

Chapter 3
Acoustic Description and Classification of Phonetic Units 32

Chapter 4
A Note on Vocal Tract Size Factors and Nonuniform F-Pattern Scalings 84

Chapter 5
Formant Frequencies of Swedish Vowels 94

Chapter 6
Consonant Confusions in English and Swedish 100

Chapter 7
Stops in CV-Syllables 110

Part II
Features: Theory and Systems

Chapter 8
Structural Classification of Swedish Phonemes 143

Chapter 9
The Nature of Distinctive Features 151

Chapter 10
Sound, Features, and Perception — 160

Chapter 11
Distinctive Features and Phonetic Dimensions — 171

Chapter 12
Notes on the Swedish Vowel System — 192

Chapter 13
Automatic Recognition and Speech Research — 202

Supplementary Bibliography — 217

Index — 223

Foreword

We are pleased to present this book as the fourth volume in the series Current Studies in Linguistics.

As we have defined it, the series will offer book-length studies in linguistics and neighboring fields that further the exploration of man's ability to manipulate symbols. It will pursue the same editorial goals as its companion journal, *Linguistic Inquiry*, and will complement it by providing a format for in-depth studies beyond the scope of the professional article.

By publishing such studies, we hope the series will answer a need for intensive and detailed research that sheds new light on current theoretical issues and provides a new dimension for their resolution. Toward this end it will present books dealing with the widest range of languages and addressing the widest range of theoretical topics. From time to time and with the same ends in view, the series will include collections of significant articles covering single and selected subject areas and works primarily for use as textbooks.

Like *Linguistic Inquiry*, Current Studies in Linguistics will seek to present work of theoretical interest and excellence.

Samuel Jay Keyser

Introduction

The purpose of this volume is to bring together a collection of my articles from the last 15 years contributing to experimental data from speech analysis and discussions on feature systems, exclusively the "inherent" features. Prosodic features are thus not treated. Some of the material, for example that from *Ericsson Technics* (paper 3), is less well known and other articles have appeared in our quarterly reports only.

Except for a basic presentation in paper 1 and the discussions and simulations in papers 4 and 7 it has not been my intention to expand on acoustic theory, Fant (1960). Paper 1 serves an introductory purpose for speech analysis and synthesis techniques. A more comprehensive treatment of this subject with applications to phonetics is found in my monograph in the *Manual of Phonetics,* Fant (1968). Paper 2 discusses the general relations between phonological and phonetic segments with an emphasis on the temporal distribution of acoustic cues.

The data on Swedish vowels and consonants in paper 3 were originally collected during the years 1947–1948 at the Ericsson Telephone Co. in Stockholm. These and the classical study of Peterson and Barney (1952) are the main sources available for both frequency and amplitude data on vowel formants. Female-male differences are studied in detail and a comparison is made with American data. Aspects of vowel perception are also discussed. Those who want to follow up more recent work along these lines are referred to an article by Carlson, Granström, and Fant (1970), not included in this volume. Some short notes on statistical measurements of speech waveform factors and spectrum as a function of voice effort terminate the excerpts from publication 3. These include frequency-intensity distributions of vowel and consonant formants which found their way into the audiological literature at an early stage, Wedenberg (1953).

The physiological origin of male-female-child differences in formant patterns is the topic of paper 4 and more recent data on Swedish vowel formants are presented in paper 5. Consonant confusions induced by low-pass filtering and noise are studied in paper 6 with reference to spectrographic patterns. The last paper (7) in Part I provides a rather detailed study of Swedish stops with respect to segment durations, formant frequency patterns, and coarticulation effects.

The second part of the volume reflects my personal attitudes to feature theory as they have developed from my early cooperation with Roman Jakobson and Morris Halle (1952). These papers deal with general issues associated with developing phonological feature systems that match phonetic facts and discuss the relative merits of specific solutions.

In paper 8 with some minor modifications the Jakobson-Fant-Halle (1952) feature system is applied to the classification of Swedish vowels and consonants. Paper 9 contains a general discussion of the Jakobson-Fant-Halle system and paper 10 presents a discussion of feature theory on a wider phonetic basis and with special regard to perception. My reactions to the Chomsky-Halle (1968) feature system are expressed in paper 11 together with some suggestions and general comments on basic issues such as uniqueness, psychological reality, binarity, and orthogonality. Consequences of a more perceptually oriented and multilevel scaling of vowel features are discussed with reference to Swedish vowels. Paper 12 is altogether devoted to Swedish vowels with a review of how classificatory solutions have developed under the last 20 years, ending up with feature matrices specifically designed to provide compact statements of pronunciation rules.

The concept of distinctive features is both powerful and elusive: powerful in operational efficiency but elusive if the claims of uniqueness and relevance of a single set to both language structure and to speech communication processes are pushed too far. Although a large part of traditional phonetics can be mapped into features, there still remains a lack of data and insight in the human encoding and decoding mechanisms necessary for a realistic choice of features and specification of their correlates. Experiments in formulating new features cannot replace experiments on speech production and speech perception. This is a dilemma but also a challenge for future research. It is not within the scope of this volume to review the most recent development in discussions around distinctive features. Among more general surveys I would like to refer to those of Peter Ladefoged (1971) and Björn Lindblom (1971).

Distinctive feature theory has an important role in the theoretical foundations of automatic speech recognition (ASR) but should not be applied rigorously. The choice of features best suited for ASR is generally not the same as that for general linguistic theory. In paper 13 I have suggested a rather unorthodox conventional set of features, the subdivision of which may have a more general interest than in ASR.

As a concluding remark I would like to emphasize that the second part of this volume is a personal contribution to a general topic where my competence is limited. I hope it can aid students of linguistics and phonetics in developing a critical view of the developments of feature theory and in facilitating the translation from one feature system to other systems which are continually being added to the ever growing jungle of propositions.

Acknowledgments

The many deep and engaging discussions with Roman Jakobson, Morris Halle, Kenneth N. Stevens, Björn Lindblom, and Sven Öhman around the topics of sounds and features belong to my most stimulating experiences.

I would like to thank Professor William S.-Y. Wang for reading through the material and encouraging me to publish it. I would also like to acknowledge my indebtedness to my coauthors in the case of a few of the published papers, the never failing editorial aid of Si Felicetti, and the assistance of Robert McAllister.

Stockholm, 5 October 1972

G. F.

References

Carlson, R., B. Granström, and G. Fant (1970). "Some Studies Concerning Perception of Isolated Vowels," STL-QPSR 2–3/1970, pp. 19–35.

Chomsky, N. and M. Halle (1968). *The Sound Pattern of English,* New York.

Fant, G. (1960). *Acoustic Theory of Speech Production,* 's-Gravenhage; second edition, 1970.

Fant, G. (1968). "Analysis and Synthesis of Speech Processes," in *Manual of Phonetics,* ed. by B. Malmberg, Amsterdam, pp. 173–277.

Fant, G., K. Ishizaka, J. Lindqvist, and J. Sundberg (1972). "Subglottal Formants," STL-QPSR 1/1972, pp. 1–12.

Jakobson, R., G. Fant, and M. Halle (1952). "Preliminaries to Speech Analysis," MIT Acoustics Lab., Techn. Rep. No. 13; 7th ed. publ. by The MIT Press, Cambridge, Mass., 1967.

Ladefoged, P. (1971). *Preliminaries to Linguistic Phonetics,* Chicago.

Lindblom, B. (1971). "Phonetics and the Description of Language," in *Proceedings of the VIIth International Congress of Phonetic Sciences,* Montreal, 1971, ed. by A. Rigault and R. Charbonneau, The Hague, pp. 63–97.

Peterson, G. E. and H. L. Barney (1952). "Control Methods Used in a Study of the Vowels," *J. Acoust. Soc. Am.* 24, pp. 175–184.

Wedenberg, E. (1953). "Auditory Training of Severely Hard of Hearing Pre-School Children," *Acta Oto-Laryng.,* 1953.

Part I
Speech Analysis

Chapter 1
The Acoustics of Speech

The acoustics of speech includes in a broad sense both the theory of speech as wave motion and how speech waves are produced and heard. This is a field of study which has intrigued researchers of various specialities during the last centuries and it has ancient traditions.

Classical phonetics has been and is still articulatory phonetics dealing with an inventory of speech sounds defined from their production within the vocal tract. The speech research of communication engineers is more concerned with the speech wave which we will define by the sound pressure variations at a point in front of the speaker.

With modern sound recording and analysis techniques it is possible to undertake rather complete specifications of the speech wave. However, a maximally detailed description is unmanageably complex and the great problem is to find useful approximation. The physiology of the speaking mechanism on the other hand cannot be studied and described with the same exactness. When it comes to hearing, there are even less possibilities to make complete specifications. The neurophysiology of speaking and hearing are the least accessible links of the complete communication system but they carry the key to many interesting problems.

The following presentation concentrates on the structure of speech waves and the theory of speech production.

SPECTROGRAPHIC ANALYSIS

The "Visible Speech" spectrographic techniques [1], introduced by the Bell Telephone Laboratories some fifteen years ago, are still our most important means of studying the characteristics of speech waves. The most useful records are the well-known spectrograms with time in horizontal direction, frequency in vertical direction, and intensity of time-frequency bounded areas displayed by the relative blackness or brightness of the picture marking.

The spectrograms of Fig. 1 were obtained with the Sona-Graph-analyzer which is a commercial development of the original Bell Telephone Laboratories speech spectrograph. This is a heterodyne analyzer with a fixed filter of alternative 45 c/s or 300 c/s bandwidth. A piece of speech maximally 2.4 sec long is analyzed by repetitive analysis with frequency increments of 15 c/s between successive closed loop repetitions of a stored piece of speech. A doubling of the broad or narrow bandwidths can be accomplished by the trick of replaying the speech material from a tape-recorder to the Sona-Graph storage loop at half the normal speed as is exemplified in Fig. 1. Adjustments have been made in the frequency scale in order to retain the same frequency scale (expanded) as in the normal speech processing.

This article originally appeared in *Proceedings of the Third International Congress on Acoustics, Stuttgart, 1959*, edited by L. Cremer (Amsterdam: Elsevier Publishing Company, 1961). Reprinted with permission.

4   Speech Analysis

The overall intensity as a function of time has to be recorded by means of supplementary instrumentation to the spectrograph, in the form of an amplitude display curve on the same sheet as the spectrogram or as a separate display on an oscillograph[2].

The spectral distribution of intensity or energy within a specific short time interval of the speech wave is defined by an intensity (db amplitude) vs. frequency curve. A

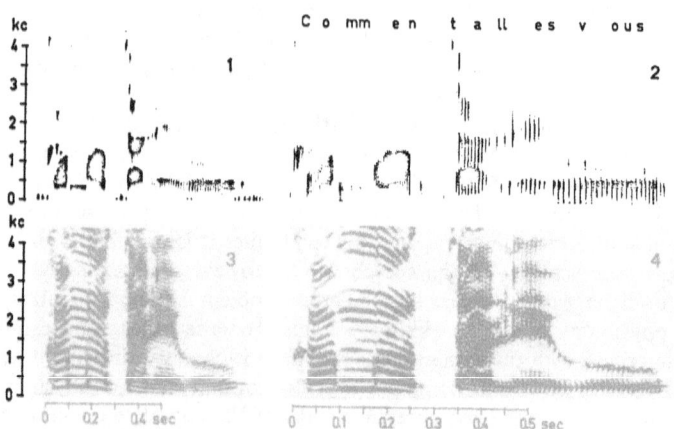

Fig. 1. Time–frequency–intensity spectrograms illustrating the effects of various analysis bandwidths 300 c/s in 1,   600 c/s in 2,   45 c/s in 3,   90 c/s in 4.

spectrum section of this type may be produced on a spectrograph by synchronous sampling of the separate frequency channels. In case the sound to be analyzed is produced in a sustained form it may be convenient to utilize a sweep-frequency method of analysis. The spectra of Fig. 2 pertain to synthetic and human vowels each of 3 sec duration analyzed by means of a filter of 32 c/s width moving at constant speed of 1.3 kc/s through the frequency range of 0–4000 c/s.

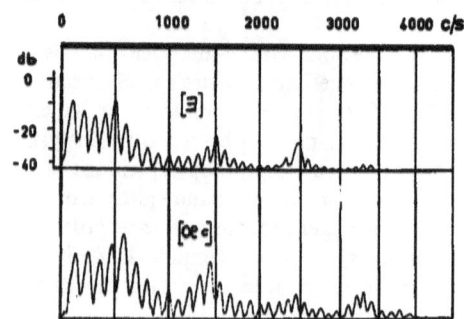

Fig. 2. Harmonic spectra obtained from narrow bandwidth sweep frequency analysis of sustained sound œ, and of the synthetic reference sound [ɜ].

Vowels and other voiced sounds possess periodic or rather quasi-periodic wave forms and accordingly display harmonic spectra. This fine structure originates from the opening and closing movements of the vocal cords periodically modulating the volume of the exhaled air during phonation at a rate of F_0 c/s, which is the voice fundamental frequency[3,4]. In narrow-band spectrograms F_0 is the harmonic spacing and in broad-band spectrograms $1/F_0$ is the time interval between successive striations each reflecting a single voice cycle. The time variation of F_0 is the physical basis of intonation.

The train of successive airpulses emerging from the vibrating glottis is the primary source of voiced sounds. The air cavities within the vocal tract act as a multiresonant filter on the transmitted sound and impress upon it a corresponding formant structure superimposed on the harmonic fine structure. This can be clearly seen in Fig. 2. The frequencies of the three lowest formants, F_1, F_2, F_3, are the main determinants of the phonetic quality of a vowel.

The resonance frequencies of the vocal tract F_1, F_2, F_3, F_4, conceptually contained in the term F-pattern, vary more or less continuously across the often sharply time localized breaks in the spectrographic time-frequency-intensity picture. Such breaks may for instance indicate shifts from voice to noise source or vice versa. Each position of the articulatory organs has its specific F-pattern. Some ambiguities do exist due to compensatory forms of articulation but these are not very important in normal speech. The time-variation of the F-pattern across one or several adjacent sound segments, which may be referred to as the F-formant transitions, are often important auditory cues for the identification of a consonant supplementing the cues inherent in the composition of the sound segments traditionally assigned to the consonant.

In general, the continuous elements of speech are due to the continuity of the position of the articulators. The discrete breaks are mainly due to a shift in manner of production, that is a change in type of source (fine structure), or a radical change in the active resonator system through which the sound is filtered (open/closed mouth passage with and without a lateral or a nasal by-pass of the sound). A sudden shift in the F-pattern and in the overall intensity following the step from a closed to an open mouth passage may thus be regarded as a discontinuity.

Spectrographic pictures convey an overflow of data which are non-essential for descriptive purposes. This redundancy is in part a matter of interrelations, repetitions, and continuities within the signal structure, in part the presence of a fine structure the details of which carry very little or no information. Any description of the speech wave, for speech typewriter coding purposes or for speech bandwidth compression applications or merely for the study of acoustic correlates to phonetic categories, must be based on approximations. Binary coded pattern aspects as well as quantized parameter data belong to the inventory of such specifications.

When processing the spectrographic data on connected speech the first object is to identify the boundaries of successive sound segments. A sound segment generally carries information on more than one phoneme of a sequence. Conversely, each phoneme may be physically encoded to a smaller or greater extent in the pattern aspect of several adjacent sound segments. The number of successive sound segments of a piece of connected speech is generally larger than the number of phonemes. Stop sounds, for instance, can be considered to be made up of at least two typical sound segments, the occlusion and the burst, and the latter phase may in some instances be split up into three successive and partly overlapping phases, the explosion transient, a short fricative, and an h-sound. The description of a sound segment for the purpose of identification may be based on the following parameters, previously mentioned and summarized below.

1. Duration
2. Intensity
3. Energy (Area under the intensity-time curve)
4. Voice fundamental frequency, F_0
5. The F-pattern ($=F_1, F_2, F_3, F_4$, etc.)
6. The formant structure (Frequency-intensity distribution)
7. The fine structure; referring to speech production, the source (Voiced, unvoiced, mixed, or silence)

In addition there enter the dynamical aspects of speech patterns[5] in terms of the time variation of each of the variables 2-7. The identification of a phoneme from the physical data contained in successive sound segments involves first a phonetical categorization, essentially with regard to "manner of production", and then within each category, a choice related to "position of articulators", for instance the choice of one of [b], [d], [g] when the phoneme has been identified as a voiced stop.

The techniques of automatic speech recognition are still in an initial phase of development. Instrumental problems are severe and specificational theory is not fully established. The main difficulty in any speech writing coding scheme[6] is the variability of human speech. However, this area of research is developing rapidly.

THEORY OF SPEECH PRODUCTION

Acoustic theory of speech production[7, 8] in its present form is largely based on equivalent circuit concepts. As visualized in Fig. 3 any speech sound is regarded as the filtered output of a network in which a sound source is inserted. The characteristics of any

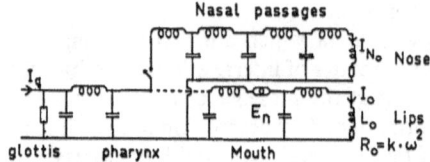

Fig. 3. Equivalent circuit representation of human and synthetic speech production applied to voiced sounds. The coils and condensers of the circuit should be regarded as distributed elements rather than lumped elements pertaining to specific cavities.

quasi-stationary sound segment thus contains the characteristics of the source and those of the network, the latter referred to as the vocal tract transfer function or filter function. In terms of Laplace transforms

$$P(s) = S(s)T(s) \qquad (1)$$

where $P(s)$ pertains to the radiated sound. $S(s)$ to the source, $T(s)$ to the vocal tract transfer function, and $s = \sigma + j\omega$ to the complex frequency variable.

The transfer function $T(s)$ of voiced sounds is defined as the ratio of the Laplace transforms of the sound pressure at a distance l cm from the speaker to the volume velocity of the pulsating airflow passing the vocal cords. If the coupling to the nasal cavities is negligible this function has no other zero than that at the origin of the complex frequency plane. This differentiation approximates the transfer from volume velocity at the lips to the sound pressure in the radiated wave. The ideal transfer function of voiced sounds,

$$T(s,l) = \frac{s}{4\pi l} \cdot \frac{1}{\prod_{n=1}^{\infty}(1 - s/\hat{s}_n)(1 - s/\hat{s}_n^*)} \qquad (2)$$

is thus essentially an infinite pole product, where

$$\hat{s}_n = \sigma_n + j\omega_n \quad \text{and} \quad \hat{s}_n^* = \sigma_n - j\omega_n$$

are conjugate complex poles. For synthesis applications the infinite product is substituted for a finite (3, 4, or 5) number of poles and a "higher pole correction"[8].

The air-filled cavities within the vocal tract constitute a continuously inhomogeneous transmission line with low losses, and the equivalent network may thus be described in terms of the distributed series inductance and parallel capacitance per length unit along the vocal tract. Series and parallel resistances representing finite losses enter a complete representation. A lumped element representation of a series inductance for a constriction and a capacitance for the volume of a specific cavity is not permissible, except for very low frequencies.

Each resonance of the vocal cavities may be described in terms of its frequency F_n and bandwidth B_n which are related to the conjugate complex poles of $T(s)$ as follows

$$\left.\begin{array}{l} F_n = \omega_n/2\pi \\ B_n = -\sigma_n/\pi \end{array}\right\} \qquad (3)$$

The average spacing within the frequency scale of these resonances is of the order of 1000 c/s or more specifically $c/2l_v$ were l_v is the effective length of the vocal tract and c the velocity of sound. This inverse dependency of formant frequencies on vocal cavity length dimensions explains the higher formant frequencies of females compared to males, and of children compared to adults.

The two constituents of a pole, the frequency and the bandwidth, may be studied by various means of exciting the vocal cavities. One is merely to thump the outside of the throat with a finger and measure the damped exponential, the decay characteristics of which provide a measure of the bandwidth according to (3). The vocal tract response to any transient excitation must contain as a component a damped oscillation

$$p_n(t) = A_n e^{-\pi B_n t} \cdot \cos(2\pi F_n t + \varphi_n) \qquad (4)$$

which is the inverse transform of a formant number n.

The same frequencies and bandwidths may be obtained from the sine-wave response of the vocal tract as determined experimentally from driving the vocal tract with a larynx microphone utilized as a sound source and a pickup microphone close to the lips. This is exemplified by Fig. 4. Typical values of resonance bandwidths are shown in Fig. 5. They are of the order of 50 c/s in the frequency region occupied by the first and second formant. Formant bandwidths are slightly greater than resonance bandwidths due to additional losses through the glottis slit.

The equivalent circuit theory of speech production suggests a convenient method[9] of deriving the properties of the vocal source[4] without bringing any probes into the vocal cavities. This is the inverse filtering technique of passing the speech wave

8   Speech Analysis

through anti-resonance circuits, one for each formant. The first step is to integrate the speech wave thus removing the radiation zero of $T(s)$.

Some results of this technique are illustrated in Fig. 6*. It may be observed that integration alone provides a first approximation to the voice flow. The apparent starting point of the damped oscillations appears to coincide with the offset of the flow, *i.e.* the closing phase. These curves display the well-known facts that increased

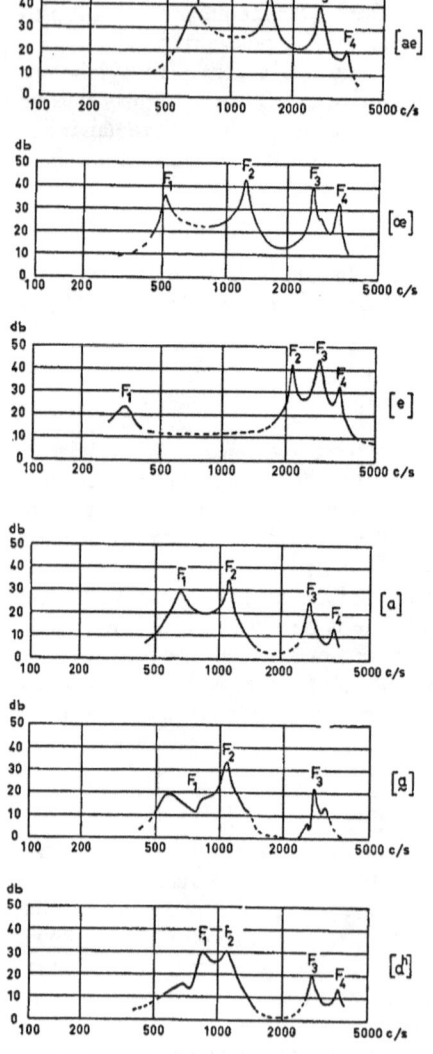

Fig. 4. Sine-wave response curves of the vocal tract driven externally from the pharynx and measured 2 cm in front of the lips. The effect of lowering the soft palate as in a nasalized vowel and of opening the vocal cords as in h-sounds is illustrated for the vowel [ɑ].

---

* These illustrations of inverse filtering originate from a thesis work by C. CEDERLUND of the Speech Transmission Laboratory, Royal Institute of Technology, Stockholm (Sweden).

Acoustics of Speech 9

voice efforts sharpen the wave shape of the vocal airpulses. At low voice intensities the closure phase is relatively short and the wave form is rounded. A tendency of a double peaked voice flow period has been found for one of the subjects.

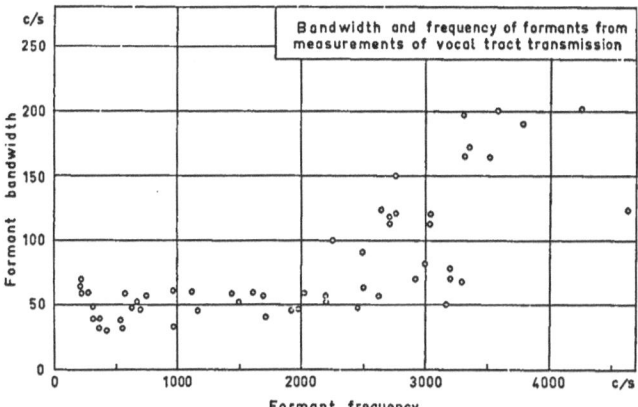

Fig. 5. Frequency dependency of the bandwidth of vocal resonances under conditions of closed glottis.

Another aspect of the Laplace transform representation is the frequency domain decomposition of vowels into elementary resonance curves. This is illustrated in Fig. 7, which pertains to idealized vowels. A shift of F_1 one octave up in frequency is apparently followed by an increase in the spectrum envelope level of 12 db at all frequencies well above F_1. When any two relatively close lying formants approach in frequency there occurs an increase in intensity of each which is 6 db per halving of their distance. These and other rules relating spectrum shape and spectrum levels to formant frequencies, *i.e.* to the F-pattern may be observed from Fig. 8, which illustrates the effects of changing F_1 and F_2 and also F_3 within the spectra of synthetic

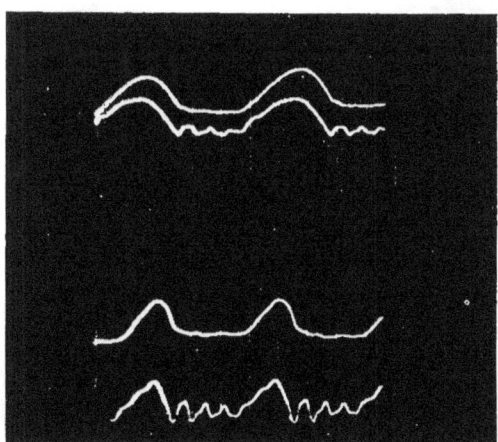

Fig. 6. Wave forms of the regenerated voice flow and, for comparison, the merely integrated speech wave. The upper pair of curves pertains to the vowel [æ] produced with a low voice effort and the bottom pair pertains to the same vowel produced with a high voice effort. The first four formants were filtered out in the top curve of each pair, but appear as damped oscillations in the merely integrated wave.

10 Speech Analysis

vowels. Most of these are close to Swedish vowels, the articulatory positions of which are shown in Fig. 9. Here as well as in Fig. 8 the vowels are arranged in terms of increasing F_1 to the right and increasing F_2 upwards in the diagram.

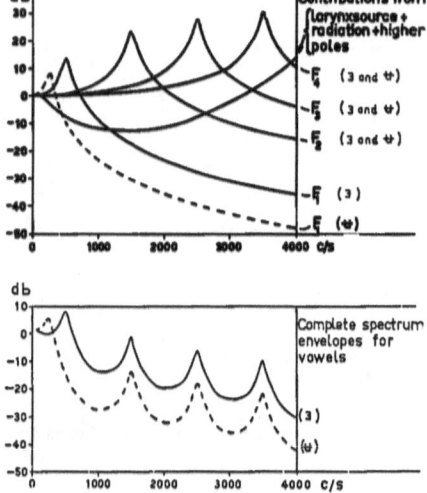

Fig. 7. Spectrum decomposition of ideal vowels in terms of elementary resonance curves, one for each formant plus additional constant characteristics. The latter include a voice source spectrum sloping —12 db/octave and a high frequency emphasis representing the residual contribution from formants higher than the fourth. The effect of shifting F_1 down one octave is indicated by the broken line. Each elementary resonance curve is analogous to a low-pass filter of 12 db/octave attenuation above its cutoff frequency.

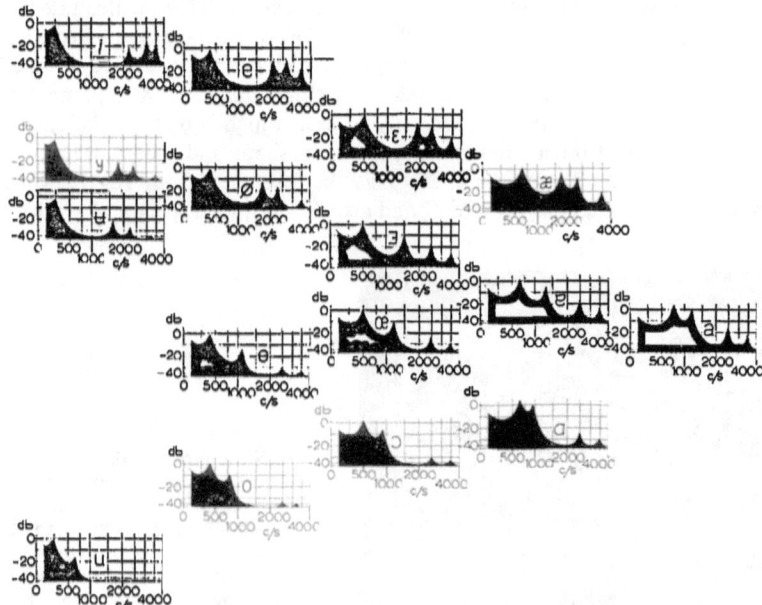

Fig. 8. Spectra on an approximate mel scale of synthetic vowels ordered according to the particular F_1 and F_2. The changes in spectrum shape and in formant levels following a shift in one or more of the formant frequencies should be observed.

The main articulatory variables are
1. the location,
2. the degree of constriction of the main narrowing between the tongue and the opposite wall of the vocal cavities, and
3. the degree of constriction and lengthening of the lip passage. The generalized relation suggested in older phonetics literature, that F_1 is due to the cavity behind the tongue constriction and F_2 to the cavity in front of the constriction is an impermissible oversimplification, sometimes contradicting actual relations. All parts of the vocal cavities have some influence on all formants and each formant is dependent on the entire shape of the complete system[7, 10]. The general rules are that a tongue constriction located in the middle of the mouth cavity is optimal for a high F_2 and that a maximally high F_1 requires the main constriction to be located just above the larynx and the mouth cavity to be wide-open. A constriction location slightly advanced from that of maximum F_2 provides maximal F_3.

A decrease of the lip-opening area or increase of the length of the lip passage

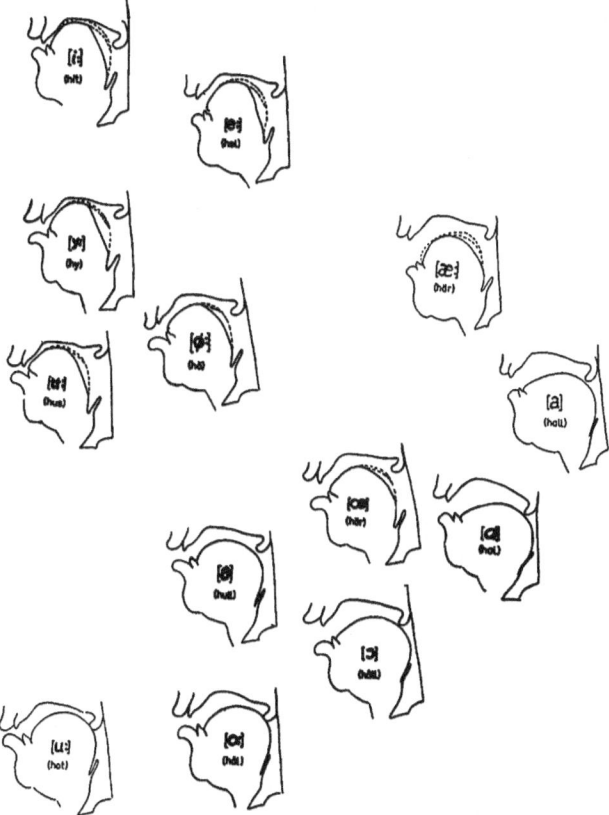

Fig. 9. X-ray tracings of Swedish vowels arranged as in Fig. 8 according to increasing F_1, right, and increasing F_2, up.

causes a lowering of the frequencies of all formants. F_1 is maximally low when the mouth cavity is constricted and F_2 is maximally low when the tongue constriction is in the upper part of the pharynx.

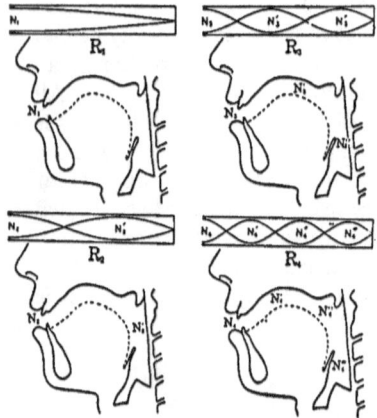

Fig. 10. Distribution of volume velocity at the frequencies of each of the first four resonances of an ideal neutral articulation in which the vocal tract simulates a tube of constant cross-sectional area. (After CHIBA and KAJIYAMA[12].)

All these relations observed when correlating articulatory and spectrographic data and corroborated model experiments[7, 11] may be inferred from a simple consideration of the distribution of pressure of volume velocity inside a neutral state idealized model of the vocal tract defined by a tube of constant cross-sectional area open at the lip end and closed at the larynx end. As shown in Fig. 10 there is a volume velocity maximum at the lips and a minimum at the glottis independent of the particular resonance frequency. The second resonance has an additional volume velocity maximum at $1/3$ of the vocal tract length above the glottis and a volume velocity minimum at a place $1/3$ of the total tube length from the lip end. The homogeneous tube has resonance frequencies at 500, 1500, 2500, 3500 c/s, etc.

If this neutral tube is constricted at a volume velocity maximum, *i.e.* at a pressure minimum, there results a shift down in the frequency of the particular resonance[12, 13]. This is to be expected since the minimum pressure at the constriction implies that the distributed capacitance in this region is small compared to the inductance and that an area change thus is effectively an inductance change[7]. The simple rule may thus be stated that a constriction of the vocal cavities at the place of a volume velocity maximum causes a shift down in the particular resonance frequency and that a constriction at a volume velocity minimum causes a shift up of the particular resonance frequency.

CONSONANT SPECTRA AND THEIR DETERMINANTS IN SPEECH PRODUCTION

Some of the sounds referred to as consonants, *e.g.* [j],[w], [v], [r], and [1] are often produced as voiced continuants with little or insignificant noise added. Sound segments of the speech wave belonging to this category, except [1] in a strict sense, may be analytically treated as vowels, *i.e.* formant intensities are only dependent on the F-pattern of resonance frequencies (poles) and on the particular source spectrum. In all other categories of sound segments, *i.e.* nasal consonants, unvoiced stops, fricatives and affricates, and the unvoiced parts of the corresponding "voiced" sound segments, there enters in addition a 0-pattern of anti-resonances (zeroes) as an additional determinant of formant levels. This is also true of [l] but to a lesser extent.

The common denominator of all non-nasal speech sounds, voiced or not, is the F-pattern defining the frequencies where formants may be found. In some instances the bandwidths of the higher resonances are so broad that adjacent formants merge into a single formant area. Thus, typically for the [s]-sound, the formants $F1$, $F2$, $F3$, $F4$ are very weak and the main spectral energy is contained in $F5$, $F6$, $F7$, $F8$, $F9$ generally seen in the spectrogram as a single or two formant areas. In the sound segment of nasal consonants there are more resonances (poles) than those of the F-pattern in which case the F-pattern is defined to comprise those frequencies which show the greatest continuity with the F-positions of orally open, adjacent sound segments. The F-pattern of nasalized vowels is similarly defined from a continuity to non-nasalized sound segments disregarding those resonances introduced by the nasal coupling.

The zero function of a vocal tract transfer function is due to the cavity system behind the source (typical for all noise sounds) or to the presence of a cavity system in front of the source shunting the main path of wave propagation (typical for nasal consonants, nasalized vowels, and laterals).

When discussing the spectral effects of poles and zeroes, it is convenient to distinguish between free poles and zeroes and bound poles and zeroes, the latter comprising pairs of a pole and a close lying zero, providing small combined spectral contributions only. In a frequency region of low coupling between a front cavity and a back cavity or between a shunting cavity and a main outlet, all the poles of the back cavities or of the shunt are bound. This is the reason for the low intensity of formants lower than $F5$ in the spectrum of the [s]-sound and the low intensity of $F2$

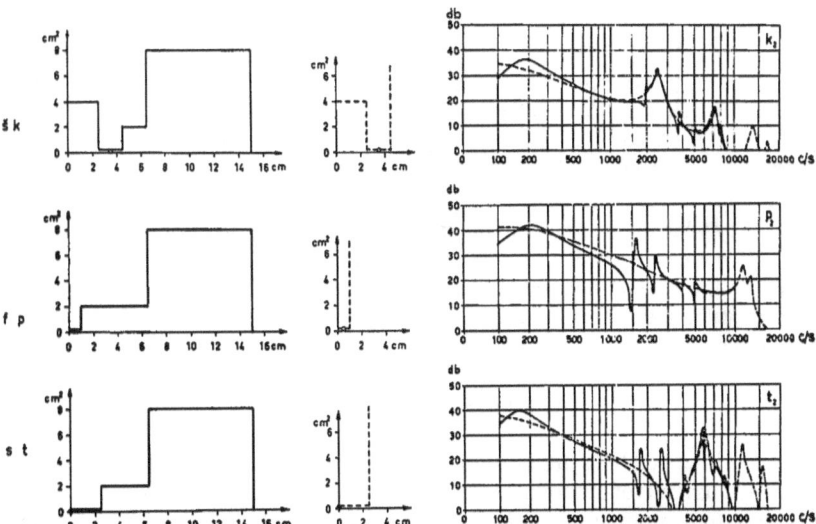

Fig. 11. Simple idealized vocal tract models and corresponding spectra of the sounds [k], [p] and [t]. Coarticulation with a front vowel is suggested by the relatively narrow mouth cavity. Broken line figures and curves pertain to models involving front resonators only and the corresponding spectra.

in the spectrum of most nasal consonants. The free poles are generally due to the cavities in front of the source and have a considerable association with the back cavities only when the coupling is great. When approximating a sound spectrum in terms of poles and zeroes it is evidently possible to discard the bound poles and zeroes. Those bound poles entering the F-pattern are, however, of specificational importance as the starting points of formant transitions towards adjacent sound segments.

Pole-zero patterns of palatal, labial, and dental sounds, derived from idealized cavity configurations, are shown in Fig. 11. The spectrum of the stop [k] is dominated by a free pole which is the first resonance of the front cavity. The labial consonant [p] has no free poles and no free zeroes unless the tongue is in a high palatal position, and the dental consonant [t] has a free zero in the region of 3000 c/s and a free pole at 6000 c/s originating from the narrow tongue passage which contribute to the relative emphasis of the spectrum above 4000 c/s. In natural speech there is an additional free pole originating from the resonance of the cavity in front of the teeth.

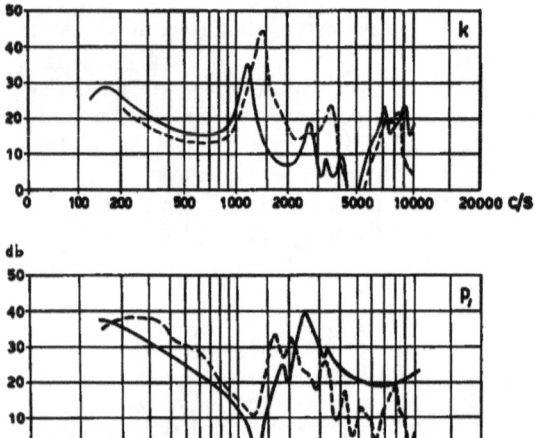

Fig. 12. Calculated spectra (solid lines) derived from X-ray studies of vocal tract dimensions, and spectra of the same sound sampled from the subject's connected speech (broken lines). The tongue articulation of [k] was postvelar and for [p] palatal. The sampling pertains to the first 10 msec of the explosion.

The accuracy which can be achieved in predicting the spectrum of a stop consonant of a subject's connected speech from X-ray pictures of his stationary articulation of the "same" sound is illustrated by Fig. 12 which pertains to the explosion phase of a [k]-sound of velar articulation and a palatalized [p]-sound. The predictability is good considering the apparent difficulties.

SPEECH SYNTHESIS*

Depending on how well the synthesis instrumentation preserves the general properties of speech, various levels of naturalness may be reached from very machine-like qualities to a rather natural sounding speech. Synthesis is made either to simulate a human model or to generate an impersonal speech by rule. Systematic synthesis experiments

---

* A review of synthesis methods may be found in ref. 2 (chapter 3.3).

are generally directed towards the evaluation of the relative importance of various pattern aspects. An important contribution to our understanding of the distinctive sound cues stems from the investigations at the Haskins Laboratories[14]. Their classical investigations were based on a constant pitch harmonic synthesizer, which provides a high degree of approximation of the speech wave. The results obtained from their studies should be checked by similar experiments with formant coded synthesizers capable of producing a more natural speech. Such studies are under way or are planned now in several laboratories in U.S.A., England, and in Sweden. Much of this work is directed to the realization of analysis-synthesis telephone systems enabling bandwidth reductions greater than those of a channel vocoder[15]. The signals extracted at the transmitting end and controlling the synthesis at the receiving end are of a parametric nature and have a low information rate. The formant coding implies an extensive use of Laplace transforms for the parametric decomposition. One example of such a synthesis scheme is shown in Fig. 13.

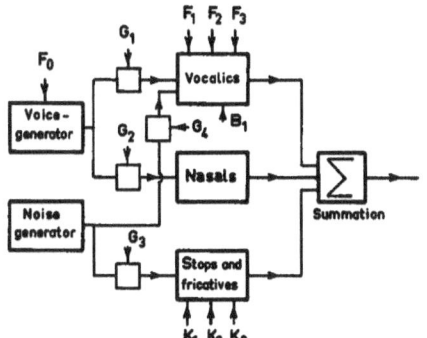

Fig. 13. Block diagram of the Swedish formant coded speech synthesizer OVE II.

Formant coded speech synthesis may be adopted as a supplement to analysis for expressing speech spectra in terms of pole-zero patterns providing a synthetic copy approximating the natural sample. This procedure has been called analysis by synthesis and is a promising approach to descriptive problems.

REFERENCES

1. R. K. POTTER, A. G. KOPP AND H. C. GREEN, *Visible Speech*, Van Nostrand, New York, 1947.
2. G. FANT, *Acta Polytechnica Scand.*, 246 (1958) 1.
3. J. W. VAN DEN BERG, *J. Speech and Hearing Research*, 1 (1958) 227.
4. J. L. FLANAGAN, *J. Speech and Hearing Research*, 1 (1958) 99.
5. H. M. TRUBY, *Acta Radiol.*, (1959) Suppl. 182.
6. D. B. FRY AND P. DENES, *Language and Speech*, 1 (1958) 35.
7. G. FANT, *Acoustic Theory of Speech Production*, RIT Div. of Telegraphy-Telephony, Report No. 10, 1958; to be published by Mouton & Co., 's-Gravenhage, 1960.
8. G. FANT, *Ericsson Technics*, 15 (1959) 3.
9. R. MILLER, *J. Acoust. Soc. Am.*, 31 (1959) 667.
10. H. K. DUNN, *J. Acoust. Soc. Am.*, 22 (1950) 740.

11. K. N. STEVENS AND A. S. HOUSE, *J. Acoust. Soc. Am.*, 27 (1955) 484, and 28 (1956) 578.
12. T. CHIBA AND M. KAJIYAMA, *The Vowel, its Nature and Structure*, Kaiseikan Publ. Co., Tokyo, 1941.
13. G. UNGEHEUER, *Z. Phonetik allgem. Sprachwiss.*, 11 (1958) 35.
14. A. M. LIBERMAN, P. DELATTRE AND F. S. COOPER, *J. Acoust. Soc. Am.*, 29 (1957) 117.
15. M. R. SCHROEDER, *Recent Progress in Speech Coding at the Bell Telephone Laboratories*, this book, p. 201.

Chapter 2
Descriptive Analysis of the Acoustic Aspects of Speech

Speech Research Objectives

The scientific study of speech is at present in a transitional stage of development. The classical articulatory or rather physiological phonetics dealing mainly with a description of the speech mechanism and with articulatory correlates of phonetic symbols is still the basic source of knowledge in phonetics courses at linguistic faculties, although acoustic phonetics is gaining ground. Acoustic phonetics, dealing with the structure of speech as sound waves and the relations of this structure to any other aspects of the speech communication act, does not lack traditions either. This field is developing rapidly as a result of the last few years' intensified investments in speech research from communication engineering quarters.

One aim of the technical speech research is to lay a foundation for techniques of producing artificial speech and of machine identification of spoken words. Applications such as more efficient speech communication systems, book-reading aids for the blind, and means of visual and tactile recording of speech for communication with the deaf, as well as specific voice controlled automata, are within reach of present technology or may be expected to be so in a not too distant future.

The perfect speech typewriter, representing the engineering criterion of a profound knowledge of the acoustic nature of speech and of dialectal, individual, and contextual variations, is a more distant object — it is rather a symbol of combined efforts in speech research. This profound knowledge does not exist yet.

Speech Analysis in Theory and Practice

The techniques of synthesizing speech are already quite advanced. Analysis techniques have not been developed to the same extent, and this is especially true of the analysis directed towards teaching a machine to recognize spoken items. This is not due to lack of research efforts. On the contrary, there is a considerable amount of work undertaken on the use of large digital computers for machine identification of speech, but this work is still in an initial instrumental phase of methodological studies[1]. Phoneme recognizing machines of a simpler analog type have been constructed but their performance has not been very advanced. The possible vocabulary or phoneme inventory has been restricted, and the machines have not responded very well to any one else than "his master's voice"[2,11].

What we really lack is a descriptive study of the visible sound patterns of speech providing an acoustic mapping of the spectrographic correlates to phonetic signs and categories with due regard to particular language, dialectal, individual, and contextual variations. A speech re-

---

This article is based on a paper presented at the Wenner-Gren Foundation for Anthropological Research Symposium on Comparative Aspects of Human Communication at Burg Wartenstein/Austria, September 1960. It originally appeared in *Logos*, Volume 5, pp. 3–17 (April 1962). Reprinted with permission.
The research reported was in part carried out under contract USAF 61(052)–342 and with support by the Swedish State Council of Technical Research.

searcher may be well acquainted with the art of synthesizing speech by general rules but the same man is probably not able to decipher the text of a spectrographic record of which he has no a priori information*.

The difficulties may in part be due to technical shortcomings of commercially available spectrographs, but there are other reasons, such as the lack of a rationale for going through the necessary learning process. Small deviations of the visual pattern may be highly significant for phonemic discriminations whereas quite apparent pattern features may be primarily related to accidental voice characteristics of the speaker. A spectrogram provides an overdetailed reference for the formal contents of a speech message. A basic problem in speech analysis is to formulate the complex transforms whereby the phonetically significant aspects may be extracted from the mass of data available. The pioneering work on the establishment of the metalanguage of Visible Speech is that of Potter, Kopp, and Green[31]. This is a valuable reference but it has shortcomings such as the restriction of the frequency range to that of telephony, i.e., to approximately 3200 c/s upper limit.

The lack of quantitative data on acoustic correlates of phonetic units is especially great for consonants and the more extensive vowel studies available refer to single stressed test words[2] or to sustained forms[8]. What about the distinctive feature approach by Jakobson, Fant and Halle[18]? Is it not possible to learn to read Visible Speech simply by reference to a maximum of 12 distinctive pattern aspects within any sound? The answer is no. Not without the addition of a considerable amount of linguistically redundant information. The particular choice of features* is supported by the main systematizing principles of classical phonetics. The distinctive features[7,18,19] are described in terms of the articulatory and the corresponding acoustic and perceptual correlates of linguistically relevant spectrographic studies of speech.

The limitations of the preliminary study of Jakobson, Fant and Halle[18] are that the formulations are made for the benefit of linguistic theory rather than for engineering or phonetic applications. Statements of the acoustic correlates to distinctive features have been condensed to an extent where they retain merely a generalized abstraction insufficient as a basis for the quantitative operations needed for practical applications. It should also be remembered that most of the features are relational in character and thus imply comparisons rather than absolute identifications. The absolute references vary with the speaker, his dialect, the context, the stress-pattern, etc., according to normali-

---

*As a matter of fact I have not met one single speech researcher who has claimed he could read speech spectrograms fluently, and I am no exception myself. I only know of the group of subjects at Bell Telephone Laboratories who participated in a Visible Speech learning experiment in 1945. Speech researchers would, however, benefit from going through this learning process. It would, aid them in teaching machines to do the same job.

*A few words may be apropos here to explain the nature of distinctive features. If a minimal difference is found between two phonemes, it is highly probable that the same distinction will recur in several other phoneme pairs. Thus, the difference between /s/ and /f/ is the same as between /z/ and /v/, and between /t/ and /p/, and /d/ and /b/, and between /n/ and /m/. This is the acute/grave distinction according to the terminology of Jakobson, Fant, and Halle. It is similar to and stands in complementary distribution with the distinction between /i/ and /u/, /e/ and /o/, and /ae/ and /a/, which motivates the usage of the same term acute/grave also for vowels. Within the consonants referred to above it is apparent that the relation of /z/ to /s/ is the same as of /v/ to /f/, /b/ to /p/, and /d/ to /t/. The main advantage of the distinctive features approach is that the number of basic signs is minimized. Maximally 12 distinctive features are sufficient for defining any phoneme of most languages.

zation principles which have not been fully investigated.

It should be noted that a specification of speech wave data may be translated to any of an infinite number of alternative forms, each based on a different choice of variables. This is true of instrumental techniques as well as of the technical and conceptual operations performed on the raw material from analysis. A linguist may radically change a specificational system in order to gain a small saving in specificational costs. The minimum redundancy of the system becomes the holy principle and a purpose in itself. The engineer is more interested in the application of the system and will generally accept some redundancy in order to facilitate automatic recognition procedures or to clarify the nature of a distinction. However, in several respects the linguistic and engineering systems should be identical. The more rigidly and unambiguously a linguistic distinction can be correlated to quantitative speech wave data, the more useful it will be for engineering applications. Investigations into the quantitative aspects of formulating distinctive features are much needed. Some experimental work in this direction has been undertaken by Halle and associates[12,15,17].

Speech synthesis is an important tool for testing the relative importance of various aspects of the sound patterns contributing to a distinction. Valuable empirical information on these "cues" and on the general rules for synthesizing speech stems from the well-known work at the Haskins Laboratories[4,24,25]. Similar work is now also under progress at various other places*.

One of the achievements of acoustic speech research is the study of the analytical ties between the physiological and the acoustic aspects[7,33,34]. Given the evidence of the dimensions of the vocal cavities, it is possible to calculate the essentials of the spectral properties of the corresponding speech sound. There is also a reverse predictability, though to a lesser extent due to the fact that compensatory forms of articulation can provide rather similar speech wave patterns.

The rules relating speech waves to speech production are in general complex since one articulatory parameter, e.g., tongue height, affects several of the parameters of the spectrogram. Conversely, each of the parameters of the spectrogram is generally influenced by several articulatory variables. However, to establish and learn these analytical ties is by no means a hopeless undertaking. Some elementary knowledge in acoustics is valuable, but the main requirement is a sound knowledge of articulatory phonetics.

TRANSCRIPTION OF SPEECH SPECTROGRAMS

A common observation when spectrograms of ordinary *connected* speech are studied is that modifications and omissions of speech sounds are frequent. Carefully pronounced single testwords and phrases may differ considerably from ordinary speech. These effects may cause transcription difficulties. Shall the investigator transcribe the spectrograms according to the phonemic structure or shall he, according to phonetical principles, write the phonetic symbols of what he hears? A third possibility might be to infer from the spectrogram how the speech has been produced and adapt the transcription thereafter. The latter method is quite feasible in view of the apparent articulatory significance of phonetic symbols, but the technique will have to rely on the use of an extended set of phonetic signs just as the phonetic transcription by ear utilizes a

---

*Phonetics Department, University of Edinburgh; Massachusetts Institute of Technology, Cambridge/Mass., U.S.A.; Royal Institute of Technology, Stockholm, Sweden.

greater inventory of signs than the phonemic transcription. The choice of system, phonemic, perceptual, or articulatory, is primarily a matter of the purpose of the investigation. The articulatory transcription is a powerful method of checking the

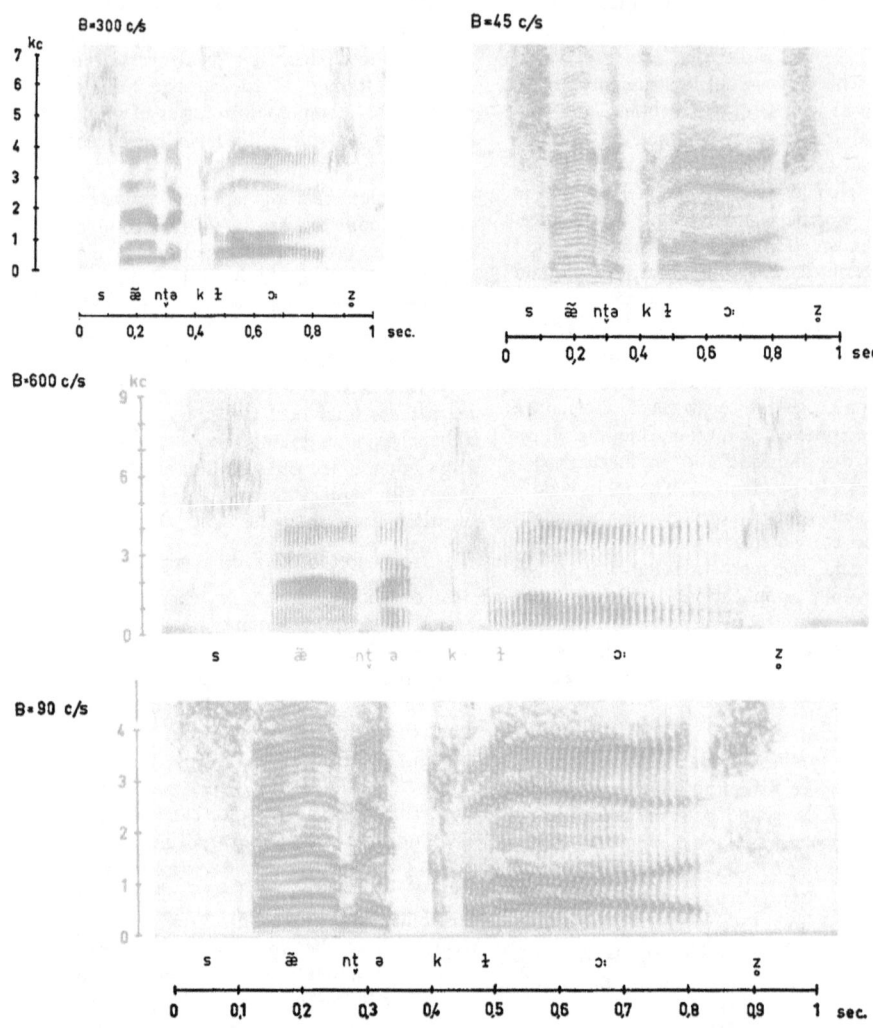

Fig. 1. Spectrograms illustrating the effects of varying the bandwidth of the spectrum analyzer. In "narrow"-band (B = 45 c/s) analysis (upper right) the harmonics are resolved. In the "broad"-band (B = 300 c/s) analysis (upper left) the formants are resolved. When the speech material is played into the analyzer at half speed, the time-scale is stretched by a factor of 2 and all frequencies are divided by the same factor. The apparent bandwidths of the analyzer then becomes B = 90 c/s and B = 600 c/s respectively. All spectrograms pertain to one and the same utterance, "Santa Claus".

perceptual transcription and can be utilized once the investigator has become sufficiently accustomed to reading spectrographic patterns.

Fig. 1 exemplifies Visible Speech spectrograms produced with a Sona-Graph analyzer. The text was "Santa Claus" spoken by an American subject*. On the top of the figure there appears the normal broad-band (300 c/s) and the narrow-band (45 c/s) spectrogram. The middle and the bottom spectrograms were made after a speed reduction by a factor of 2 which implies an effective doubling of the filter bandwidths, i.e., 600 c/s and 90 c/s respectively. Normally a broad-band spectrogram shows the formant structure whereas the narrow-band analysis displays a harmonic spectrum. In case of high-pitched voices, however, the 600 c/s-analysis is needed in order to avoid harmonic analysis and retain the formant structure. At a low-pitched interval of speech, on the other hand, the 90 c/s-filter provides an optimal frequency resolution of the formant structure.

The auditive transcription of the utterance was [sænţə klɔːz]. A segmentation of the spectrum in terms of successive sound intervals, or in other words sound segments, should be performed from the broad-band display and not from the narrow-band display since the latter will tend to smooth out rapid shifts of the spectral composition. The very distinct boundary between the [s] and the [æ] in the form of a shift of the spectral energy distribution and the shift from a voiced to an unvoiced sound is typical. Most of the other sound boundaries are also distinct.

As seen from the split first formant the speaker has apparently nasalized the entire [æ] in anticipation of the /n/ and there is no separate [t]-segment except for

___
*General American. The subject was born in Texas.

a weak high frequency burst in the latter part of the [n]-segment. Alternatively, it might be argued that there is no separate [n]-segment, the intended /n/ being signaled by the nasalization of the [æ] and of the following voiced nasalized dental stop [d]. Another observation of some interest is that the [z]-segment is devoiced, i.e., no traces of vocal cord vibrations appear within the fricative.

The stop sound [k] of Claus has first a period of silence, the occlusion. Then comes the explosion in the form of a transient and then a continuant noise structure, the latter part of which is merely an unvoiced beginning of the [l]. It has been shown by Truby[35] that the [l] of a cluster [kl] is often fully articulated even before the explosion is released.

THE DISCRETE VERSUS THE CONTINUOUS
VIEW OF SPEECH

Divergent opinions have been expressed on the nature of speech. The concept of speech as a sequence of discrete units with distinct boundaries joined together as beads on a string is contrasted to the view of speech as a continuous succession of gradually varying and overlapping patterns. This divergency has been discussed by Joos[20], Hockett[16], Halle[13,14], Pike[30], and others. What evidence do we have in favor of one or the other view? Fig. 2 illustrates various concepts. These are from the top:

a) A sequence of ideal non-overlapping phonemes.
b) A sequence of minimal sound segments, the boundaries of which are defined by relative distinct changes in the speech wave structure.
c) One or more of the sound features characterizing a sound segment may extend over several segments.
d) A continuously varying importance function for each phoneme describing the extent of its dependency of particular events within the speech wave. Overlapping curves without sharp boundaries.

The models above may appear to repre-

22 Speech Analysis

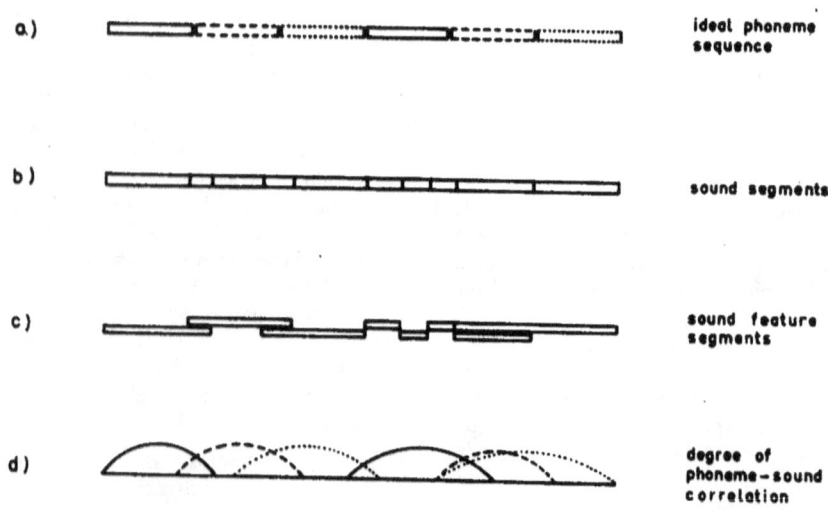

Fig. 2. Schematic representation of sequential elements of speech. a) is the phonemic aspect, b) and c) represent acoustic aspects, and d) shows the degree of phoneme-sound correlation.

sent quite different views of the nature of speech. They are, however, not contradictory in any way. The overlap in the time domain according to d) does not invalidate the concept of the phonemes as discrete and successive in a)[13]. The representation in a) relates to the message aspect of the speech communication whereas representation b) and c) pertain to the speech wave and d) more to the perception of speech.

It is of interest to note that spectrographic pictures of speech often display quite distinct boundaries between successive parts along the time axis. These boundaries are related to switching events in the speech production mechanism such as a shift in the primary sound source, e.g., from voice to noise, or the opening or closing off of a passage within the vocal cavities, the lateral and nasal pathways included. Less distinct sound boundaries may be defined from typical changes in the pattern of formant frequencies. A common aspect of spectrographic records not shown in Fig. 2 is the more or less continuous variation of some of the formants with respect to their frequency locations. Formant frequency patterns may vary within and across sound segment boundaries.

The number of successive sound segments within an utterance is greater than the number of phonemes. Fully developed unvoiced stops, for instance, contain at least two sound segments, the occlusion and the burst, and the latter may be subdivided into an explosion transient and a short fricative. The first part of a vowel following the burst generally assimilates the voicelessness of the preceding sound. It is a matter of convention whether this sound segment is to be assigned to the vowel, or to the preceding "aspirated" consonant.

Sound segments defined from the procedure above may be decomposed into a number of simultaneously present sound features. Boundaries between sound segments are due to the beginning or end of at least one of the sound features but one and the same sound feature may extend over several successive sound segments. One example seen in the spectrogram of Fig. 1 is the nasalization of a vowel adjacent to a nasal consonant. The most common example would be the continuity of vocal cord vibrations over a series of voiced sounds.

Sound segment boundaries should not be confused with phoneme boundaries. Several adjacent sounds of connected speech may carry information on one and the same phoneme, and there is overlapping in so far as one and the same sound segment carries information on several adjacent phonemes. The typical example is the influence exerted by a consonant on a following vowel. The extent to which a phoneme of the message has influenced the physical structure of the speech wave often varies continuously along the sound substance as indicated by Fig. 2 d. One practical method of investigating these dependencies is by means of tape-cutting techniques whereby the removal of a part of the sound substance is correlated with the phonemic discrimination loss*.

---

*See for instance Truby[35] and Öhman[36,37].

POLE-ZERO DESCRIPTIONS OF SPEECH SPECTRA

The engineer's concept of speech is very much influenced by an analytical methodology which has been called analysis-by-synthesis[32]. Any short segment or sample of natural speech may be described in terms of the parameters of a synthesis procedure providing a piece of artificial speech approximating the natural sample with an accuracy which depends on the complexity of the specification.

In one specificational system the spectral energy of a sample is quantitized in terms of the frequency, intensity, and bandwidths of the major energy peaks, the formants. This is the "parallel synthesizer" system in which each formant is fabricated separately and fed in parallel to a mixer. The second system is referred to as the "series synthesizer" scheme in which the output from an electrical analog to the primary sound source is led through a number of consecutive resonance and antiresonance circuits, the combined filtering effect of which is a good approximation to the filtering of the vocal cavities. Providing the bandwidths of these spectral determinants, in mathematical terminology poles and zeros, are made a unique function of their frequency locations, it follows that formant intensities as well as the intensities at any part of the spectrum will be predictable from the frequency locations of the resonances and the antiresonances supplemented by the additional information on the intensity and spectral composition of the source[8].

A complete specification thus comprises a statement of the frequencies and bandwidths of each of the poles and zeros of the vocal tract, and the frequencies and bandwidths of each of the poles and zeros of the source. In addition a scale factor representing source-intensity is needed and a statement concerning the nature of the source, whether of voice or noise character and, if voiced, the frequency of the voice fundamental, F_0. Sounds comprising both a noise source and a voice source are regarded as the superposition of two sounds, one voiced and one of noise character.

The filter function of an ideal non-nasalized vowel does not contain any zeros, i.e., anti-resonance effects. The resonance frequencies of the vocal tract, i.e., the pole frequencies, are labeled F_1, F_2, F_3, F_4, etc. The term F-pattern has been suggested as the compound term for a specification of these frequencies[6,7,8].

As viewed from X-ray moving film, articulation is a continuity of movements. The resulting continuous variations in the dimensions of the vocal cavities determine uniquely the variations of the vocal tract resonance frequencies, the F-pattern. There is thus a continuity of F-pattern within any length of utterance and across any sound segment boundary. However, some boundaries are set by a rapid shift of the F-pattern.

The transitional cues whereby a consonant vowel may in part be identified by its influence on an adjacent vowel may thus be described in terms of F-pattern variations. The term "hub" from the book *Visible Speech*[31] is thus identical with F_2.

Only in non-nasalized, non-lateral sounds produced from a source located at a vibrating or a narrow glottis can the F-pattern up to F_3 be seen with optimal clarity. Under these circumstances the vocal tract filter function does not possess any zeros. When the source is located higher up in the vocal tract there will appear zeros at approximately the same frequencies as the poles representing the resonances of the cavities behind the consonantal constriction. The spectral contribution of a pole and a zero of the same complex frequency amounts to nothing,

i.e., the pole-zero pair may be removed from the specification without any effect on the spectrum of the sound to be synthesized. In these instances the pole and the zero are "bound". Those poles which represent the resonance frequencies of the cavities in front of the source, on the other hand, are "free" from adjacent zeros and thus appear as formants in the spectrum of the sound. There are also "free zeros" which depend on the geometry of the back cavities including those parts of the constriction which lie behind the source. The free zeros may under favorable conditions be seen as spectral minima in an amplitude-frequency display.

The alternative condition for the appearance of zeros in the specification of the vocal tract filter function, is that the sound propagated from the vocal cord source to the lips is shunted by the nasal cavities. Similarly, the nasal output of a sound segment of nasal murmur is submitted to the shunting effects of the mouth cavity as a side chamber. A third possibility is in the production of an [l]-sound. The laterally propagated sound is submitted to some degree of frequency selective shunting by the mouth cavity behind the tongue.

The addition of a shunting cavity system introduces not only zeros but also extra poles. The first nasal resonance indicated by FN1 in the spectrogram of Fig. 1 is thus an extra formant. The associated zero probably located between FN1 and F1 causes a marked decrease of the intensities of both these formants. The other pole-zero pairs of the nasalization do not radically change the phonetic value of the vowel.

If the mouth and nose outlets are closed, there is still some sound propagated through the vibrating walls of the vocal cavities. This is the case of the voiced occlusion of stop sounds. The second and third formants of the voiced occlusion are generally very weak and thus below the reproduction threshold of the spectrograph. If the mouth passage is gradually opened from the closed state to a merely constricted state as in voiced fricatives, there is a gradual rise in the intensities of the higher formants. This rise continues with an increasing mouth-opening and is followed by a shift up in frequency of the first formant. An octave increase in F_1 is correlated with $+12$ dB increase in the whole spectrum level above F_1[21].

Spectral descriptions in terms of poles and zeros are the results of a processing of the primary data from spectrum analysis which is performed either by means of a digital computer or by means of a series connected speech synthesizer. A third method would be to perform the matching by paper and pencil and an inventory of resonance and anti-resonance curves.

It should be noted that the analysis-by-synthesis approach even without a detailed matching procedure allows a reader of spectrograms to avoid errors in the identification of the particular type and order number of a formant and increases the accuracy in the estimation of formant frequencies. The mere knowledge of the interrelations between frequencies of formants and the relative levels to be expected within a spectrum is an insurance against errors*.

In most studies for phonetic descriptive purposes, vowels and other zero-free sounds can be described by an F-pattern alone. The source characteristics are generally of very small interest. An exception is F_0, the frequency of the voice fundamental. When zero-functions are to be avoided, the spectra of other sounds are specified in terms of frequencies and intensities of major formants or by some other approximation. The F-pattern should be stated in addition. If the F-pattern formants are not directly observable in the spectrum of the particular sound segment it might be possible to interpolate these frequencies from the F-pattern variations in adjacent sound segments.

A TENTATIVE SYSTEM OF SPEECH SEGMENT CLASSIFICATION

Speech can be divided into a sequence of sound segments the acoustic boundaries of which are definable either from specific articulatory events or from the corresponding time-selective changes in the spectral composition of the speech wave. The following is an attempt to describe the possible structure of these elementary constituents of the speech wave as a basis for phonetic descriptive work and automatic recognition schemes. The classification of sound segments and their sound features should be detailed enough to provide correlates to any category of interest, thus not only to phonemic units. This is the difference of the present approach to that of the earlier work by Jakobson, Fant and Halle[18].

As discussed above, a sound segment is of the dimension of a speech sound or smaller and there may occur several successive sound segments within the time interval of the speech wave traditionally assigned to the phoneme. The number of successive sound segments within an utterance is therefore generally larger than the number of successive phonemes, as conceptually indicated in Fig. 2.

When sound segments are decomposed into bundles of simultaneous sound features it is often seen that a single sound feature carrying a minimal distinction may extend

---

*I know of several vowel studies providing data on formant frequencies which are invalidated by an inability of the investigator to keep track of one and the same formant within a series of vowel sounds. Nasal formants are often confused with the F-pattern formants. Similar difficulties exist in automatic formant-tracking schemes.

over all sound segments of importance for a phoneme, including sound segments which essentially belong to adjacent phonemes. A typical example of this is the GA /r/ phoneme the retroflexion (acoustically low frequency F_3) of which generally modifies neighboring sounds. In other instances, such as the voiced/voiceless distinction, it can be the sound segment of adjacent phonemes that carry the major part of the relevant sound feature (the lengthening of a preceding vowel is a voicing cue of intervocalic consonants).

The acoustic basis for identification of sound features and for the establishment of fine gradations and subdivisions within a sound segment of arbitrary composition can be stated in terms of the following parameters, most of which are time variable within a sound segment.

Speech Parameters

1. Segment duration.
2. Source intensity (short-time sample of a specified time location within the segment).
3. Source energy (product of segment duration and the time average of source intensity within the segment).
4. Source spectrum (either a short-time sample or the time average of the source intensity-frequency distribution within the segment).
5. Voice fundamental frequency, F_0.
6. F-pattern (= F_1, F_2, F_3, etc.).
7. Sound intensity (short-time sample of a specified location within the segment).
8. Sound energy (product of segment duration and the time average of sound intensity within the segment).
9. Sound spectrum (either a short-time sample or the time average of sound intensity-frequency distribution within the segment).

It has not been attempted to select a set of independent measures in this list, but rather to exemplify what sort of basic data is made use of in acoustic specifications.

The source characteristics have to be determined by removal of the formant structure from the sound. As indicated in the previous section this is done by spectrum-matching or inverse-filtering techniques, in more general terminology by means of analysis-by-synthesis techniques.

The first step in the analysis of a sound segment according to the proposed scheme would be a classification in terms of a set of primary features which will be called the *segment type features*. For convenience, these features are referred to by speech production terminology and are to be considered as binary in nature, i.e., expressing presence versus absence of a specific quality. In this respect they reflect the constraints of the human speaking mechanism and correspond to what is commonly referred to as "manner of production". The second step in the analysis of a sound segment is essentially a classification in terms of the "place of articulation". The term *segment pattern features* is adopted here in order to form a more general concept applicable to both articulatory and speech wave phenomena.

List of Segment Type Features

Feature number	Feature
	Source features
1	voice
2	noise
3	transient
	Resonator features
4	occlusive
5	fricative
6	lateral
7	nasal
8	vowellike
9	transitional
10	glide*

As indicated in the list of segment type features above, there are three possible sound sources supplying the primary acoustic energy of a speech sound segment. These are *voice* (vocal cord vibrations), *noise* (random noise from turbulent airflow through narrow passages and past sharp obstacles), and *transient* (single shock excitation of the vocal cavities). The

---
*In a recent publication it has been considered desirable to omit feature 10 since it may be included in feature 9. See Fant, Lindblom[10].

transient is due to the sudden release of an over-pressure or a sudden checking of an airflow at any obstruction in the vocal cavities, the vocal cords included. In this sense, voice is identical to quasi-periodically repeated transients. In a broad-band spectrogram of a voiced stop the transient is seen as an additional vertical striation which is non-synchronous with the pitch pulses. Additional noise may also be found in this explosion segment, though of less duration than in an unvoiced stop. In an unvoiced stop the transient precedes a noise interval of fricative or aspirative (vowellike) type. The duration of the interval is not the duration of the transient source, which is very small, but the duration of the damped oscillations excited by the transient. When these extend into the following noise interval there is overlap, i.e., co-occurrence of noise and transient. The typical example of co-occurrence of voice and noise is in voiced fricatives. There is a tendency of the voicing to dominate in the early part and the noise in the later part of the fricative. The extreme case of separate sound segments was pointed out in connection with the [z] of Fig. 1.

The resonator features are on the whole independent of the source features. In one and the same sound segment it is possible to find almost any combination of the segment type features. The possible co-occurrences and their statistics have not been studied in detail yet. The resonator features may be described at the level of speech production as follows.

SPEECH PRODUCTION CORRELATES

4. *Occlusive:* Complete closure in the mouth or in the pharynx.
5. *Fricative:* Very narrow passage for the air stream at an obstructed region of the mouth or the pharynx.
6. *Lateral:* Central closure combined with lateral opening in the mouth cavity.
7. *Nasal:* Nasal passages connected to the rest of the vocal system owing to a lowered velum.
8. *Vowellike:* Free passage for the air stream through the pharynx and the mouth cavities.
9. *Transitional:* The articulators moving at a high speed within the segment.
10. *Glide:* The articulators moving at a moderate speed within the segment.

The speech wave correlates of the resonator features may be described as follows:

4. *Occlusive:* The spectrum of a voiced non-nasal occlusive is dominated by a formant F1 of a very low frequency F_1 (the voice bar). However, with considerable high-frequency pre-emphasis it may be possible to detect F2 and F3.
5. *Fricative:* Spectra of voiced fricatives can display the whole F-pattern up to F4 but with less intensity and a lower frequency F_1 than vowellike sounds. A fricative produced with a supraglottal noise source is recognized by a high-frequency noise area in the spectrum. Compared with an unvoiced vowellike sound of a similar articulation, the fricative spectrum displays a larger high-frequency emphasis. The typical fricative is a noise sound, the spectral energy of which is largely contained in formants from cavities in front of the articulatory narrowing.
6. *Lateral:* Sound segments of lateral articulation produced with a voice source possess the vowellike feature except for a reduction of either second, third, or fourth formant intensity due to the first zero of the shunting mouth cavity behind the tongue. An additional high-frequency formant is generally seen. The oral break provides a typical discontinuity in the connection to a following vowel. The lateral sound segment is generally, but not always, of lower frequency F_1 than a following or preceding vowel.
7. *Nasal:* A voiced occlusive nasal (nasal murmur) is characterized by a spectrum in which F2 is weak or absent. A formant at approximately 250 c/s dominates the spectrum, but several weaker high-frequency formants (not always seen in spectrograms) occur, one typically at 2200 c/s. These higher formants are generally weaker than for laterals. The bandwidths of nasal formants are generally larger than in vowellike sounds. Voiced vowellike nasal sounds (nasalized vowels) possess the nasal characteristics as a distortion superimposed on the vowel spectrum. Typical nasalization cues are addition of the first nasal resonance in the region below the first formant of the vowellike sound and simultaneous weakening and shift up in frequency of the first formant, F_1.
8. *Vowellike:* The F-pattern formants are clearly visible in the spectrogram. In the case of voiced or unvoiced vowellike sounds produced with a glottal source it is required that at least F1 and F2 be detectable. F3 should also be seen providing F_1 and F_2 are not located at their extreme low frequency limits. A specific feature of sounds produced with a glottal source is that the relative formant levels are highly predictable from

the particular F-pattern, i.e., from the formant frequency locations*. Vowellike noise sounds produced from a supraglottal source possess a rather weak first formant, F_1. This is especially the case with [h]-segments produced with a tongue articulation of a high front vowel. Unless the fricative feature is superimposed there should not occur a prominent high-frequency noise area in the sound spectrum.

9. *Transitional:* The spectrum changes at a relatively fast rate in the segment. The first part of a vowel following a voiced stop or nasal is characterized by a rapid change in at least one formant frequency, e.g., F_1. The transitional sound segment ends where the major part of the formant transition is completed.

10. *Glide:* The spectrum changes at a relatively slow rate but faster than for a mere combination of two vowels. Variants of [r] [l] [j] [w] sounds occur as glides.

SEGMENT PATTERN FEATURES

ARTICULATION	SPEECH WAVE
11. Tongue fronted a) Prepalatal position b) Midpalatal position	F_2-F_1 large. F_2 high, F_3 maximally high. F_2 maximally high and close to F_3.
12. Tongue retracted	F_2-F_1 small. F_1 comparatively high.
13. Mouth-opening (including tongue section and lips) narrow	F_1 low.
14. Lips relatively close and protruded (small lip-opening area)	F_1+F_2+F_3 lower than with a larger lip-opening and the same tongue articulation. A progressing lip closure alone causes a decrease in each of F_1, F_2, and F_3 but with varying amounts depending on the particular tongue position. The effect on F_3 is pronounced in case of prepalatal tongue positions.
15. Retroflex modification a) Alveolar articulation b) Palatal articulation	F_4 low and close to F_3. F_3 low and close to F_2.
16. Bilabial or labiodental closure	F_2 in the region of approximately 500-1500 c/s depending on the tongue location of the associated vowel or vowellike segment. A palatal tongue position favors high F_2. The noise spectrum of the fricative [f] is essentially flat and of low intensity.
17. Interdental articulation	F_2 1400-1800 c/s. Fricative noise of [θ] much weaker than for [s] and with a more continuous spectrum. Center of gravity is higher than for the labiodental fricative [f].
18. Dental or prealveolar articulation	F_2 in the region of 1400-1800 c/s, F_3 high. Fricative noise strong. The main part of the [s]-energy is above 4000 c/s. This cutoff frequency is lower for alveolar than for dentals.
19. a) Palatal retroflex articulation b) Palatal articulation with tip of tongue down	F_3 low. The fricative noise of [ʂ] is of high intensity and is carried by F_3 and F_4. F_2 and F_3 high. Strong fricative noise centered on F3 and F4 and also on F2 providing the tongue pass is sufficiently wide. The lower frequency limit of [ç] noise is higher than for retroflex sounds.
20. Velar and pharyngeal articulation	F_2 medium or low. A large part of the fricative noise is carried by F2. The F-pattern except F1 is clearly visible.
21. Glottal source	The entire F-pattern including F1 is visible.

---

*An alternative to the *vowellike* feature would accordingly be *zero-free* which on the speech production level implies non-nasalized, non-lateral, glottis source sound, acoustically correlated to the predictability of formant levels from the F-pattern. An apparent F1 would be one necessary condition. A second alternative would be to retain the term *vowellike* but restrict the feature to glottal sources, in which case the first formant F1 must be present. However, in case of both whispered vowels and [h]-sounds articulated with the tongue in an [i]-position it is highly probable that supraglottal sources exist alone or in addition to glottal sources. This would lead to the classification of some whispered vowels and [h]-sounds as vowellike and other as non-vowellike. The best choice among these alternatives has to be determined from experience.

The existence of *complex articulations* should be kept in mind. The most apparent example referred to above is the freedom of the tongue to take any position during lip closure which makes the F-pattern of labials variable. In dentals the back of the tongue is partially free to approach the back wall of the pharynx which lowers F_2 and increases F_1. This is the case of the "dark l". The articulatory contrast between a wide unobstructed and a narrow divided pharynx, resulting in a high versus a low F_2, is the counterpart of the hard/soft distinction in Russian consonants.

THE NORMALIZATION PROBLEM

The phonetic identity of a speech sound is to some extent dependent on the sound context, that is, formant frequencies within a sound segment have to be judged by reference to the average formant frequencies of the speaker and to have his voice fundamental frequency. Variational features are in some respects more essential than the absolute characteristics of the speech wave. This fact is confirmed by experiments with synthetic speech[23].

An international standard of phonetic pronunciation norms could be established by reference to a few selected speakers. For the Cardinal vowels the pronunciation of Daniel Jones has been considered authoritative[21,22]. Another alternative is synthetic speech[3]. The quality of synthetic speech[8] can be made sufficiently high to fulfill the minimum requirements of naturalness. The advantage compared with real speech would be that the acoustic specification could be made more exact.

A more difficult task is to establish a unique code between the measurable parameters of any sample of live speech and its absolute phonetic quality[28]. The analysis-by-synthesis approach[32] would be to specify the sample by the parameters of synthesis providing equal phonetic quality.

We would also like to be able to predict these settings from the available data inherent in the speech wave. However, normalization techniques have not developed far enough yet even for the simpler task of machine identification of the phonemic structure of a spoken message.

One of the most important factors involved in normalization is to take into account the influence of the size of the speaker's vocal tract. The F-pattern frequencies are to a first approximation inversely proportional to the length of the speaker's vocal tract from the glottis to the lips. Children have smaller heads than adults and their formant frequencies are thus on the average higher. The average female-male difference is of the order of 20%. However, normalization is not merely a question of a constant scale factor.

SUMMARY

This article aims at summarizing the present status of speech analysis techniques, specifically spectrographic analysis. Special attention is given to the problems of segmenting speech into successive phonetic elements and to the categorization of such minimal sound segments in terms of segment type (manner of production) and segment pattern (place of articulation). For this purpose the relations between the physiological parameters of speech and corresponding acoustic speech wave characteristics have been summarized in the form of a dictionary.

It is pointed out that segment boundaries are associated with changes in the manner of production (voiced/voiceless, fricative/non-fricative, nasal/non-nasal, etc.) whereas the place of articulation determines acoustic patterns that vary more or less continuously within and across segment boundaries. There are as a rule a larger number of sound segments than phonemes in any utterance. For this reason and because of coarticulation effects any phoneme is generally signalled by several successive sound segments. Conversely, any sound segment is generally influenced by several adjacent phonemes of the speech message transcription.

REFERENCES

1. David, E. E., Jr.: Artificial Auditory Recognition in Telephony. IBM J. 2, 1958, 294-309.
2. Davis, K. H., Biddulph, R. and Balashek, S.: Automatic Recognition of Spoken Digits, in Communication Theory, ed. W. Jackson, London, 1953, 433-441.
3. Delattre, P., Liberman, A. M. and Cooper, F. S.: Voyelles synthétiques a deux formantes et voyelles cardinales. Maître Phonétique, 96, 1951, 30-36.
4. Delattre, P., Liberman, A. M. and Cooper, F. S.: Acoustic Loci and Transitional Cues for Consonants. J. Acoust. Soc. Am. 27, 1955, 769-773.
5. Fant, C. G. M.: On the Predictability of Formant Levels and Spectrum Envelopes from Formant Frequencies. For Roman Jakobson, 's-Gravenhage, 1956, 109-120.
6. Fant, C. G. M.: Modern Instruments and Methods for Acoustic Studies of Speech. Proc. of VIII Internat. Congr. of Linguistics, Oslo. Oslo, 1958, 282-358; and Acta Polytechnica Scandinavica Ph 1 (246/1958).
7. Fant, C. G. M.: Acoustic Theory of Speech Production. 's-Gravenhage, 1960.
8. Fant, C. G. M.: Acoustic Analysis and Synthesis of Speech with Applications to Swedish. Ericsson Technics, 15, No. 1, 1959, 3-108.
9. Fant, C. G. M.: Phonetics and Speech Research, invited paper presented at the International Conference on Research Potentials in Voice Physiology, Syracuse, N. Y., May 29-June 2, 1961; to be publ. in the Proc. from this conference.
10. Fant, C. G. M. and Lindblom, B.: Studies of Minimal Speech Sound Units. Speech Transmission Laboratory, Quarterly Progress and Status Report No. 2/1961, 1-11.
11. Fry, D. B. and Denes, P.: The Solution of Some Fundamental Problems in Mechanical Speech Recognition. Language and Speech, 1, 1958, 35-38.
12. Halle, M.: The Sound Pattern of Russian. 's-Gravenhage, 1959.
13. Halle, M.: The Strategy of Phonemics. Word, 10, 1954, 197-209.
14. Halle, M.: Review of Manual of Phonology by C. F. Hockett. J. Acoust. Soc. Am. 28, 1956, 509-511.
15. Halle, M., Hughes, C. W. and Radley, J. P.: Acoustic Properties of Stop Consonants. J. Acoust. Soc. Am. 29, 1957, 107-116.
16. Hockett, C. F.: Manual of Phonology. Indiana Univ. Publications in Anthropology and Linguistics, No. 11, Bloomington, 1955.
17. Hughes, C. W. and Halle, M.: Spectral Properties of Fricative Consonants. J. Acoust. Soc. Am. 28, 1956, 303-310.
18. Jakobson, R., Fant, C. G. M. and Halle, M.: Preliminaries to Speech Analysis. M.I.T. Acoustics Lab. Tech. Rep. No. 13, 1952; 3rd printing.
19. Jakobson, R. and Halle, M.: Fundamentals of Language. 's-Gravenhage, 1956.
20. Joos, M.: Acoustic Phonetics. Language, 24, 1948, 1-136.
21. Ladefoged, P.: The Classification of Vowels. Lingua, 5, 1956, 113.
22. Ladefoged, P.: The Perception of Vowel Sounds. Edinburgh, 1959, Ph.D. Thesis, Univ. of Edinburgh.
23. Ladefoged, P. and Broadbent, D. E.: Information Conveyed by Vowels. J. Acoust. Soc. Am. 29, 1957, 98-104.
24. Liberman, A. M.: Some Results of Research on Speech Perception. J. Acoust. Soc. Am. 29, 1957, 117-123.
25. Liberman, A. M., Ingemann, F., Lisker, L., Delattre, P. and Cooper, F. S.: Minimal Rules for Synthesizing Speech. J. Acoust. Soc. Am. 31, 1959, 1490-1499.
26. Miller, R. L.: Auditory Tests with Synthetic Vowels. J. Acoust. Soc. Am. 25, 1953, 114-121.
27. Olson, H. F. and Belar, H.: Phonetic Typewriter. J. Acoust. Soc. Am. 28, 1956, 1072-1081.
28. Peterson, G. E.: The Information Bearing Elements of Speech. J. Acoust. Soc. Am. 24, 1952, 629-637.
29. Peterson, G. E. and Barney, H. L.: Control Methods Used in a Study of the Vowels. J. Acoust. Soc. Am. 24, 1952, 175-184.
30. Pike, K. L.: Language as Particle, Wave and Field. The Texas Quarterly II, 1959, 37-54.
31. Potter, R. K., Kopp, A. G. and Green, H. C.: Visible Speech. New York, 1947.
32. Stevens, K. N.: Toward a Model for Speech Recognition. J. Acoust. Soc. Am. 32, 1960, 47-55.
33. Stevens, K. N. and House, A. S.: Development of a Quantitative Description of Vowel Articulation. J. Acoust. Soc. Am. 27, 1955, 484-493.
34. Stevens, K. N. and House, A. S.: Studies of Formant Transitions Using a Vocal Tract Analog. J. Acoust. Soc. Am. 28, 1956, 578-585.
35. Truby, H. M.: Acoustico-Cineradiographic

Analysis Considerations with especial reference to certain consonantal complexes. Acta Radiologica, Suppl. 182, Stockholm, 1959, Ph.D. Thesis, Univ. of Lund.
36. Öhman, S.: On the Contribution of Speech Segments to the Identification of Swedish Consonant Phonemes. Speech Transmission Laboratory, Quarterly Progress and Status Report No. 2, 1961, pp. 12-15.

37. Öhman, S.: Relative Importance of Sound Segments for the Identification of Swedish Stops in VC and CV Syllables. Speech Transmission Laboratory, Quarterly Progress and Status Report No. 3, 1961, pp. 6-14.

Chapter 3
Acoustic Description and Classification of Phonetic Units

Subjects and phonetic material

Seven male subjects and seven female subjects participated in the investigations. The male subjects will be numbered from 1 to 7, and the female subjects from I to VII. Male subject 1, also referred to as Gj-n, was a professor of phonetics at Uppsala University, and his speech is representative of standard Swedish (riksmål) with an influence from the district of Södermanland, and has been regarded as normative in this work. Female subject I, also referred to as M-r, was a well-known Swedish singer and voice specialist. All subjects had lived in Stockholm for more than five years, and most of them were also born in Stockholm. Subject 2, the author, F-t, was born in Nyköping. Subject 5 was born in Lappland, subject III in Nynäshamn, and subjects 7 and IV in Södertälje. All subjects, except subject 5, thus belong to a fairly homogeneous dialectal group, representative of standard Swedish.

For the benefit of a simple transcription of the speech material the phonemes of Swedish have been given the following symbols in close conformity to Swedish orthography. This transcription is referred to as the Swedish Technical Alphabet (STA):

Long vowels		Short vowels	
STA	Key words	STA	Key words
o_1	rot, hot, mos	o_2	rott, bonde
$å_1$	råt, håt, kål	$å_2$	rått, olja
a_1	rat-, hat, mat	a_2	ratt, hatt, matt
$ä_1$	rät, räv, även	$ä_2$	rätt, den
e_1	ret-, rev, ek	e_2	rett,
i_1	rit, riv, is	i_2	ritt, finna
y_1	ryt, fy	y_2	rytt-, hytt, nyck
u_1	Rut, ute	u_2	rutt, hutt
$ö_1$	röt, ösa	$ö_2$	rött, hött, kött
Long pre-r allophones		Short pre-r allophones	
$ä_3$	här, ära	$ä_4$	herr
$ö_3$	hör, för	$ö_4$	förr

This article originally appeared as a reprint from *Ericsson Technics*, No. 1, 1959. Reprinted with permission.

The fact that a commutation of vowels within the frame of an initial r and a final short or long consonant t produces 18 words of different meaning indicates the existence of 9 long vowel phonemes and 9 short vowel phonemes; see further ELERT (1955, 1957), FANT (1954). A few of these words are prefixes but a secondary commutation series employing a different consonantal frame provides supplementary evidence. The notations above refer to vowels in stressed positions only and these were also the only ones investigated.

In traditional phonetical terminology o_1, $å_1$, and a_1 and further o_2 and $å_2$ are called back vowels, referring to a retracted location of the tongue during articulation. It was found in the acoustic analysis that a_2 could conveniently be grouped with the back vowels because its formant pattern is close to that of a_1 and its relation to $å_2$ is the same as that of a_1 to $å_1$.

This classification was also found to be suggested from X-ray studies. The vowels y_1, u_1, $ö_1$, are the long "rounded" front vowels referring to the more narrow lip-opening and/or the lip-protrusion in comparison to the long unrounded i_1, e_1, $ä_1$. Among the short unrounded front vowels no distinction is generally made between $ä_2$ and e_2 in the Stockholm dialect. This is in some instances also true of e_1—$ä_1$. The relation of i_1 to e_1 to $ä_1$, phonetically referred to as a series of progressive opening, is similar in some respects to that within the series o_1 to $å_1$ to a_1, although a progressive delabialization enters. The same is true of the corresponding short vowels and of the relation of y_1 to $ö_1$, or y_2 to $ö_2$. There is some motivation for placing u_1 in between y_1 and $ö_1$ but less for placing u_2 in between y_2 and $ö_2$. This latter solution (FANT, 1954) makes the system simpler but the acoustic analysis more complicated. As shown by MALMBERG (1956, 1957) it is more natural to place u_1 and u_2 as a separate group more rounded than the y and $ö$ vowels. According to FANT (1957 b) it is also possible to classify u_2 as intermediate between the front and back vowels. This vowel is actually very close to $å_2$ in terms of both articulatory and acoustic criteria and is further apart from u_1 than any other short vowel compared to its long mate.

A long vowel in stressed position can only occur before a short consonant and vice versa. In unstressed positions there is no distinction between long and short vowels. The sound quality is closer to that of the short stressed vowel but more neutral. Sometimes the quality of the long stressed vowel is retained; see further GJERDMAN (1950, 1954), MALMBERG (1949), ELERT (1955, 1957).

It is not very hard to make an untrained subject aware of a difference in inherent sound quality of a sustained a_1 compared to a_2 or $å_1$ compared to $å_2$ or u_1 compared to u_2. In all other pairs of long and short vowels the quality difference is rather small, and it is doubtful whether there is any difference between $ä_3$ and $ä_4$ or between $ö_3$ and $ö_4$. The length differences alone may signal the short versus long distinction in connected speech.

It was therefore decided to let all subjects except 1 and I sustain only the long vowels plus $å_2$, a_2, u_2, and the pre-r allophones $ä_3$ and $ö_3$.

The consonant phonemes are given the following STA signs:

h	Liquids	Voiced fricative continuants	Unvoiced fricative continuants	Nasals
h	l	v	f	s	m n
	r̰l		s̰j		r̰n
	r	j	t̰j		ṇg

Voiced stops	Unvoiced stops
b d	p t
r̰d	r̰t
g	k

in addition the sign # could be included for denoting absence of any phoneme. As long as sound boundaries are recognized it is redundant, but its use is motivated when statistical counts of phonemes are undertaken. Except for the liquids and the /h/-phoneme the system underlying the grouping of the consonants is to place the phonemes normally articulated with a palatal or velar tongue position at the bottom of a group. The labial member is placed to the left and the dental to the right. The *rd, rt, rn, rl, rs* symbols apply to alveolar articulation of simple sounds spelled *r* plus *d, t, n, l,* or *s,* (normal pronunciation even when a word boundary falls between the *r* and the dental sign). The phoneme *sj* is regarded as identical to *rs* and either notation may be utilized. Since the STA signs are independent of the specific individual and dialectal sound qualities, there is no unique relation between these signs and the signs of the International Phonetic Association (IPA). When a translation from one system to the other is indicated as in the amplitude-frequency spectra of Fig. 2, it is thus with the understanding that the code is strictly valid for this speaker only. However, pronunciation habits are sufficiently homogeneous that a code (valid, for instance, for standard Swedish "riksmål") may be established, as in the case of Fig. 2 represented by speaker Gj-n, the reference subject.

One object of phonetic analysis is to perform descriptions of average pronunciations. As long as this is an aural transcription of sound qualities in terms of the signs of a particular alphabet an element of subjectiveness enters due to each investigator's particular quality norms, which are easily influenced by his particular language and dialect.

The possibilities of adopting the speech wave characteristics as an absolute reference are of considerable importance. It must be stressed that even though physical data are of great significance there can be no strict one-to-one correspondence. Different acoustic patterns may evoke the same sensations, and approximately the same acoustic pattern can signify different phonemes depending on the particular speaker and context. Vowel qualities may have slightly different absolute values due to degree of stress and speech tempo, even if the other conditioning factors already mentioned are the same. One important aspect of this rule is that the formant frequency data reported here for vowel sounds sustained during a laboratory experiment cannot be utilized as absolute norms for the same sounds in connected speech. Some minor systematic differences should be taken into account.

Independent of the particular conditioning circumstances, the relations between the phonemes stay the same and these relations may be specified in terms of speech wave characteristics. Any speaker who wants to make himself understood must follow this code. A Swedish e_1 may sound as *i* to an Englishman but both make a distinction between the *i* and the *e*, the latter being articulated more openly, i.e., with a wider pass between the tongue and the palate, which invariably results in a higher frequency of the first formant and a lower frequency of the third formant.

A tentative survey of these "distinctive features" has been undertaken by JAKOBSON et al, (1952). There remains much to be learned in these matters and there is specifically a need for more extensive acoustic data. The following sections provide a material contributing to the understanding of the distinctive features of Swedish. It is by no means sufficient for the practical technical or linguistic demands. Large scale acoustic studies of connected speech are at present being undertaken at the Royal Institute of Technology but are not complete enough to be published yet.

A study of Swedish vowels

Formant data on Swedish vowels

The frequency analysis of vowels and all other sustainable sounds was performed by the sweep frequency analysis method. The subject was seated in an anechoic chamber at 12.5 cm speaking distance from a condensor microphone (Siemens) and could receive instructions via a pair of headphones. These were also utilized for supplying the subjects with a reference tone as a guide for sustaining the sounds at a constant predetermined pitch. A vacuum tube voltmeter was within visual reach of the subject as a guide for keeping his voice level constant. In the external laboratory the experimenter could control the produced sound by means of a monitoring loudspeaker and a VU-meter.

The sound spectrum was recorded on a galvanometer oscillograph (Siemens) simultaneously with an intensity curve and with the harmonic output from a second wave analyzer connected to the limited and differentiated output of a frequency standard generator. These precautions provided a reliable frequency calibration and a possibility to correct the recorded spectra with regard to small voice-level variations.

The time needed for analysis was 5 seconds. Each subject was instructed to speak out the key word containing the vowel to be analyzed, and then to prolong the vowel more and more. After a short period of training the subjects were able to sustain the vowels at sufficiently even voice conditions.

The condensor microphone was absolute-calibrated and all spectral levels were expressed in dB with a reference sound pressure of 1 dyne/cm². The amplitude characteristics of the recording were highly compressed enabling a measurement range of 45 dB. It is of some interest to note that the broadest and narrowest filter bands of the specially constructed wave analyzer were independently chosen the same as those of the Bell Telephone Laboratories sound spectrograph. Only the narrow-band, 45 c/s-wide filter, was utilized for the vowel analysis. An intermediate filter bandwidth of 140 c/s was adopted for the analysis of fricatives, which enabled the analysis time to be shortened to 1 second.

Table 1 shows the frequency and formant intensity levels of the first four formants below the upper frequency limit 4000 c/s. In addition the frequency and level of the voice fundamental are given. The individual data for each subject may be found in the earlier publication (FANT, 1948). Data are given here for subjects 1 = Gj-n, and I = M-r, and for the average of the male group (7 subjects) and for the female group (7 subjects):

Table 1. Formant data of vowels

Vowel	Subject	F_0 c/s	L_0 dB	F_1 c/s	L_1 dB	F_2 c/s	L_2 dB	F_3 c/s	L_3 dB	F_4 c/s	L_4 dB
o_1	Gj-n....	125	0.5	325	3	640	2.5	2,400	—40	3,500	—40
	M-r.....	256	6	270	6	740	— 5	2,550	—37	(3,200	—35)
	Male....	127	—0.5	307	4.5	730	— 8	2,230	—37	3,300	—38
	Female..	222	2	340	5	690	— 6	2,900	—43	(4,000	—45)
o_2	Gj-n....	125	1	370	4	680	— 2	2,600	—27	3,200	—25
$å_1$	Gj-n....	125	2	405	6	700	— 1	2,450	—32	3,200	—29
	M-r.....	256	5	380	8	850	—10	2,800	—38	—	—
	Male....	132	—0.5	402	6	708	— 2	2,460	—31	3,150	—33
	Female..	223	1	433	7	815	— 9	2,840	—38	(3,600)	—37)
$å_2$	Gj-n....	125	1.5	500	7	800	— 1	2,530	—26	3,150	—25
	M-r.....	257	5	510	8	900	0	2,800	—35	(3,000	—35)
	Male....	123	—0.5	487	6	825	1	2,560	—26	3,250	—28
	Female..	217	—2	518	5	840	— 6	2,825	—36	(3,500)	—40)
a_1	Gj-n....	125	1.5	600	7	935	0	2,620	—18	3,150	—22
	M-r.....	250	4	650	6	1,125	0	2,800	—18	—	—
	Male....	126	—1	582	7.5	940	4	2,480	—21	3,290	—20
	Female..	225	—1	682	4	1,075	4	2,930	—22	(3,800)	—28)
a_2	Gj-n....	125	2.5	680	6	1,075	— 1	2,720	—18	3,350	—18
	M-r.....	255	3	770	8	1,250	1	2,800	—15	—	—
	Male....	124	—1	680	6	1,070	1	2,520	—10	3,345	—20
	Female..	215	—1	860	4	1,195	4	2,830	—23	—	—
$ä_3(ä_4)$	Gj-n....	125	2.5	560	6	1,740	— 7	2,470	—12	3,200	—16
	M-r.....	257	3	600	6	1,740	— 7	2,900	—20	—	—
	Male....	125	0.5	606	7	1,550	— 3	2,450	—12	3,400	—15
	Female..	213	0	785	5	1,820	— 6	2,950	—18	(3,600)	—17

Acoustic Description and Classification of Phonetic Units 37

Vowel	Subject	F_0 c/s	L_0 dB	F_1 c/s	L_1 dB	F_2 c/s	L_2 dB	F_3 c/s	L_3 dB	F_4 c/s	L_4 dB
$å_1$	Gj-n....	125	2.5	480	5	1,870	−7	2,480	−9	3,250	−18
	M-r.....	255	4	535	7	1,870	−8	2,600	−18	—	—
	Male....	125	0	438	6	1,795	−9	2,385	−12	3,415	−19
	Female..	214	0	545	5	2,140	−11	2,860	−20	—	—
$å_2 = e_2$	Gj-n....	125	2	385	4	1,960	−7	2,450	−8	3,400	−17
	M-r.....	256	3	425	9	1,950	−12	2,600	−17	—	—
e_1	Gj-n....	125	1	325	4	2,210	−11	2,650	−12	3,400	−20
	M-r.....	256	7	320	7	2,200	−13	2,700	−12	—	—
	Male....	124	0	334	6	2,050	−12	2,510	−13	3,400	−16
	Female..	215	1	365	6	2,540	−15	2,950	−18	—	—
i_2	Gj-n....	125	1.5	300	1.5	2,170	−13	2,700	−13	3,500	−22
i_1	Gj-n....	140	2	275	2	2,205	−17	3,100	−12	3,500	−17
	M-r.....	256	7	270	7	2,200	−23	3,100	−15	—	—
	Male....	128	0	256	3	2,066	−23	2,960	−20	3,400	−23
	Female..	218	3	278	5	2,520	−24	3,450	−24	(3,900	−28)
y_1	Gj-n....	140	3	275	2	2,050	−12	2,300	−15	3,325	−21
	M-r.....	257	8	260	8	2,070	−22	2,820	−17	3,300	−24
	Male....	128	1	257	4.5	1,928	−17	2,421	−19	3,300	−24
	Female..	215	5	270	6	2,480	−21	2,920	−23	3,575	−26
y_2	Gj-n....	125	2.5	300	2.5	1,985	−12	2,360	−13	3,250	−18
u_1	Gj-n....	125	1	290	3	1,690	−12	2,170	−15	3,300	−22
	M-r.....	256	6	300	6	1,760	−14	2,270	−14	3,100	−34
	Male....	126	0	283	5.5	1,633	−13	2,140	−17	3,314	−26
	Female..	217	4	300	5	1,910	−18	2,600	−22	3,450	−34
u_2	Gj-n....	125	2.5	375	4	1,070	−12	2,500	−20	3,500	−27
	M-r.....	257	9	370	10	1,050	−14	2,400	−22	—	—
	Male....	125	−0.5	416	6	1,070	−7	2,315	−24	3,300	−29
	Female..	216	2	410	7	1,175	−11	2,700	−31	3,600	−35
$ö_1$	Gj-n....	125	2.5	345	5	1,735	−10	2,250	−12	3,400	−22
	M-r.....	257	8	350	8	1,800	−2	2,250	−8	—	—
	Male....	126	0	363	6.5	1,690	−9	2,200	−11	3,390	−20
	Female..	215	2	372	5	2,000	−14	2,610	−18	3,650	−28
$ö_2$	Gj-n....	125	2.5	370	5	1,570	−10	2,300	−14	3,300	−24
	M-r.....	257	4	410	11	1,550	−7	2,220	−11	—	—
$ö_3(ö_4)$	Gj-n....	125	2.5	470	5	1,195	−7	2,550	−16	3,300	−24
	M-r.....	257	4	500	10	1,300	−11	2,600	−22	3,500	−35
	Male....	124	−0.5	524	6	1,103	−4	2,430	−22	3,250	−19
	Female..	217	1	565	8	1,290	−6	2,730	−21	3,700	−29

The accuracy of a formant frequency measurement is primarily dependent on the frequency spacings between harmonics, i.e., F_0. When F_0 is high the formant envelope is less clearly defined and there results an apparent tendency of the investigator to estimate the peak as falling close to the highest level harmonic within the resonance area. When the pitch is low

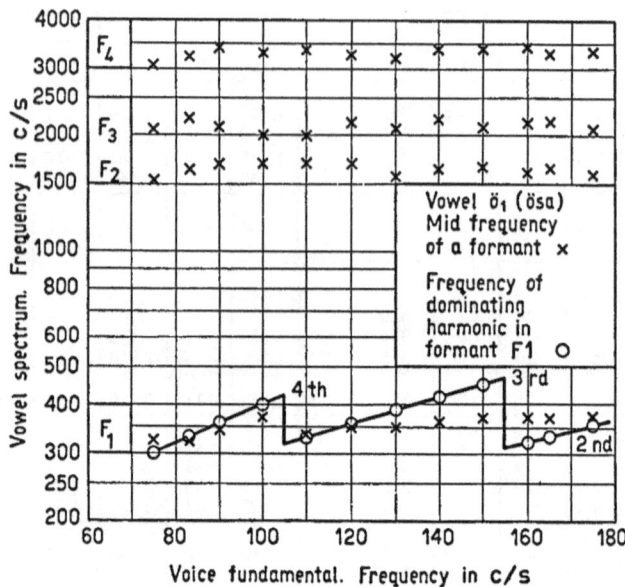

Fig. 1. Formant frequency determinations of a vowel sustained at a series of different voice fundamental frequencies.

this area is filled in with harmonics and a visual interpolation may be undertaken with greater ease. Figure 1 demonstrates a series of formant frequency measurements of a vowel sustained at fundamental frequencies $F_0 = 75$—175 c/s. Even in this comparatively low F_0-range the investigator has been somewhat influenced by the particular leading harmonic. In other respects the figure illustrates the general law of independency of formant frequencies and harmonic numbers.

To measure an F_1 of a low frequency is often more complicated than to measure the frequency of a higher formant since $F1$ tends to be asymmetric, the high frequency end of $F1$ sloping off at a faster rate than the low frequency end of the spectrum. Configurations are possible where the first two harmonics are of equal amplitude in which case it will be necessary to rely on the information contained in the second, third, and fourth harmonics. A single formula, for instance, providing a center of gravity measure of a formant from all harmonics of any importance is not recommendable since the systematic differences between various types of formants are too large.

The frequency region up to 250 c/s containing one or two of the first harmonics is often intense enough to be regarded as a minor fixed formant. In the frequency region of 800 c/s to 1200 c/s there is also seen a "spurious formant", especially in so-called open vowels $å$ and a. These are probably due to some degree of nasal coupling and/or subglottal coupling

(FANT, 1958 a). For male voices the third formant is located at a mean frequency of 2,500 c/s and there is often an additional weaker formant above F_3 and in addition to F_4 or just below F_3. All these extra formants can be held apart from those of the F-pattern by an inspection of the continuous changes of the whole spectrum envelope from one sound to the next. The spectra of Fig. 2 pertain to subject 1, Gj-n. It can be observed how the spectrum level of the valley in between F_1 and F_2 rises within the series from i_1 to $ä_3$, or y_1 to $ö_3$ following the approach of F_1 to F_2. Within the series from o_1 to a_2 it may be seen how the simultaneous upward shift of F_1 and F_2 has an overall effect on the spectrum similar to that of raising the cutoff frequency of a low-pass filter. The total pass band is made wider and the level of the higher formants increases. The close proximity of F_2 to F_1 is typical for this series. The main systematic difference between the spectra of Fig. 2 and those of connected speech is the tendency of F_1 and F_2 of sustained $å_1å_2a_1a_2$ to be 50—100 c/s too low.

In general, the ordering principle of Fig. 2 is that F_1 rises in a direction from the top to the bottom of the assembly, and F_2 and/or F_3 shift to higher frequencies from a vowel spectrum to the left to one of a location more to the right. These relations will be studied closer in the next section.

The relations between formant frequencies and the particular configuration of the vocal tract have been dealt with in detail in a separate publication (FANT, 1958 a). It should be kept in mind that because of the relatively large dimensions of the vocal tract there are seldom pure "Helmholtz" resonances involved. All three first formants are more or less influenced by standing wave resonances (DUNN, 1950). F_1 and F_2 are not invariably related to a back and front cavity. Those circumstances under which this relation does hold are rather particular involving a clear separation of a medium size front cavity from a back cavity, and further some degree of lip-rounding. In back vowels both F_1 and F_2 are substantially dependent on front and back parts of the vocal tract. The same is true of F_2 and F_3 of front vowels. F_1 of front vowels is dependent on the whole of the vocal tract and the pharynx acting as a capacitance and the whole of the mouth as an inductance. When the tongue is in the *i*-position, there will be a clear dependency of F_2 on a standing wave resonance effect in the back cavity, i.e., in the pharynx. F_3 is then mainly influenced by the mouth cavity.

The effect of a lip-rounding is invariably to lower all three first formant frequencies, providing the articulation is kept constant in other respects. An advanced tongue position such that the upper part of the tongue-blade is close to the palate provides maximally high F_2 and low F_1. F_2 and F_1 come, on the other hand, maximally close when the back part of the tongue approaches the pharynx wall. When the narrowest passage is in the front of the mouth, the effect of making this pass wider is to increase F_1 and decrease F_2 until the limiting conditions of a neutral articulation have been reached. When the tongue-pass has a retracted position, the effect of an increasing tongue-pass cross-sectional area is to increase F_2, and F_1 is maximally high at an optimal degree of narrowing, and thus varying less than F_2.

40 Speech Analysis

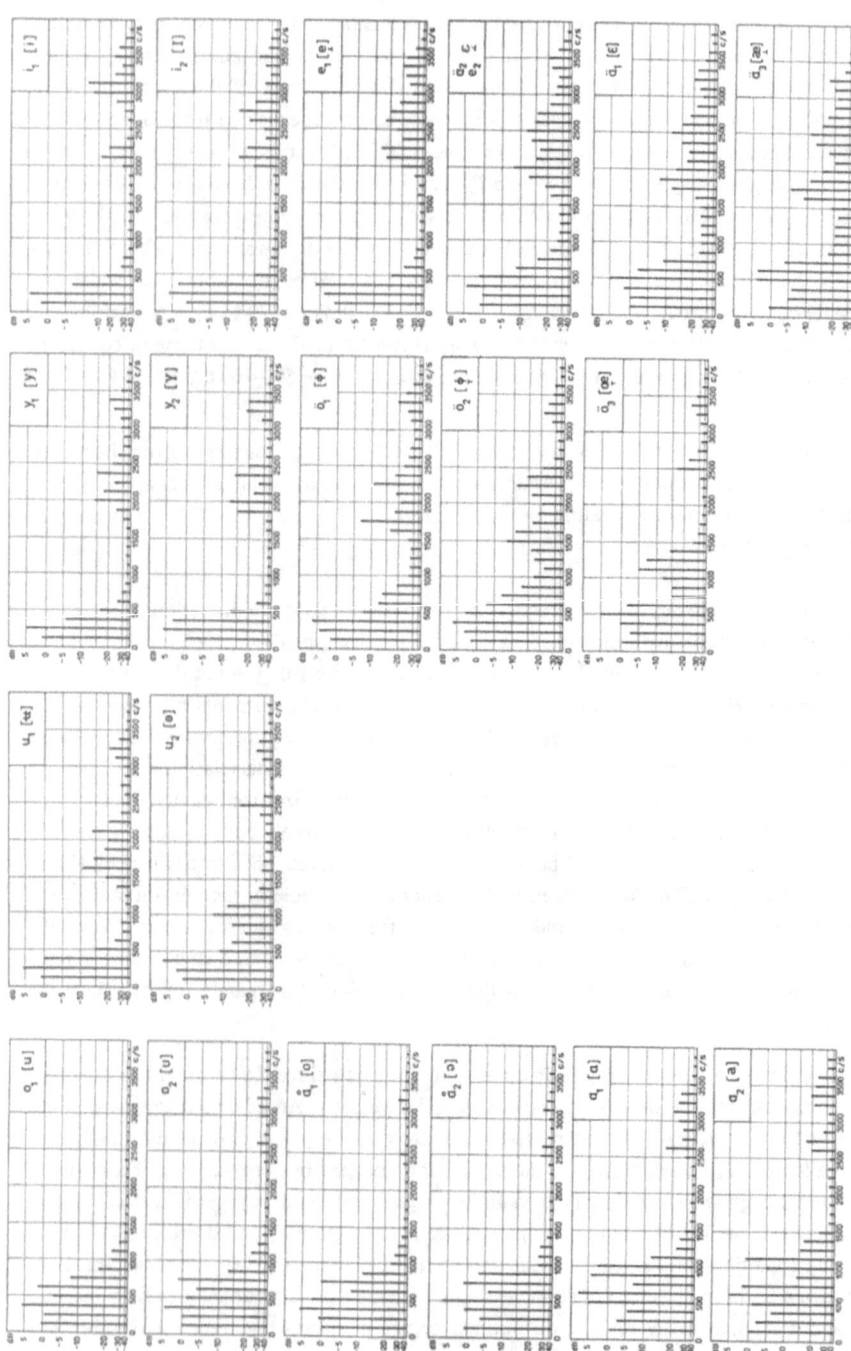

Fig. 2. Harmonic spectra of sustained vowels, subject Gj-n.

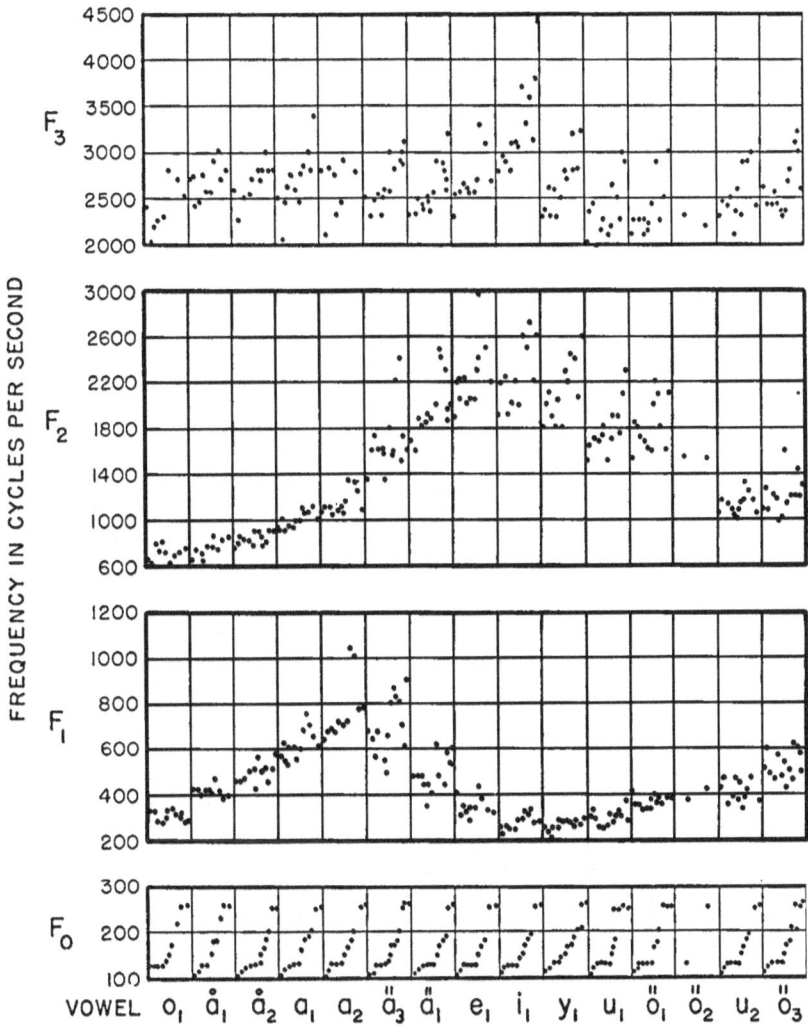

Fig. 3. The formant frequency data of all subjects for a sequence of vowels.

The compound formant frequency data from all the subjects may be studied in Fig. 3 showing F_0, F_1, F_2, and F_3 of a sequence of vowels. Most of the observable spread is due to characteristic speaker differences. The standard deviation of a formant frequency within a repeated series of measurements with subject Gj-n was 25 c/s in F_1, 50 c/s in F_2, and 80 c/s in F_3 which compares well with the data of POTTER and STEINBERG (1950), who stated 20—40 c/s in F_1, 40—70 c/s in F_2, and 60—90 c/s in F_3. It is of some interest to observe that the

42   Speech Analysis

minimum perceptible differences (DL) in formant frequencies reported on by FLANAGAN (1957 a) are very close to the standard deviation for our subject Gj-n. The DL:s are ± 20 c/s in F_1, ± 50 c/s in F_2, and ± 75 c/s in F_3. The accuracy of a single measurement due to instrumental limitations was estimated to be of the order of $[(15)^2 + (0.2F_0)^2]^{1/2}$. It may be of interest to note that the reproducibility of subject Gj-n's formant frequencies from one day's measurements to a day one month later was of the order of 15 c/s in F_1 and 20 c/s in F_2 and F_3. These data pertain to the average of a series of 7 determinations at approximately the same pitch. Observed differences were not statistically significant indicating a considerable consistency of articulation. The standard deviation within the group of male speakers was 35 c/s in F_1, 90 c/s in F_2, and 130 c/s in F_3. Corresponding data for the female group were 45 c/s in F_1, 130 c/s in F_2, and 240 c/s in F_3. These figures represent speaker variability due to differences in vocal tract dimensions and pronunciation.

Acoustic vowel diagrams based on formant parameters

The most extensive vowel measurements ever reported on are those performed at the Bell Telephone Laboratories by POTTER and STEINBERG (1950) and by PETERSON and BARNEY (1952). An attempt has been made to map Potter and Steinberg's data on to the Swedish vowel data, represented by the subject Gj-n. The main purpose of this matching was not to make phonetic comparisons on an acoustic basis but to check the general similarity of

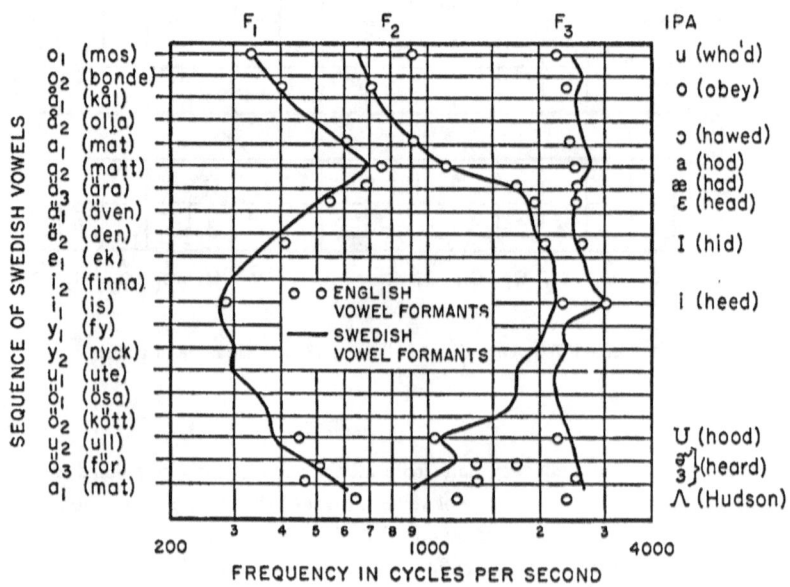

Fig. 4. Sequential diagram of Swedish and American English vowels.

Acoustic Description and Classification of Phonetic Units 43

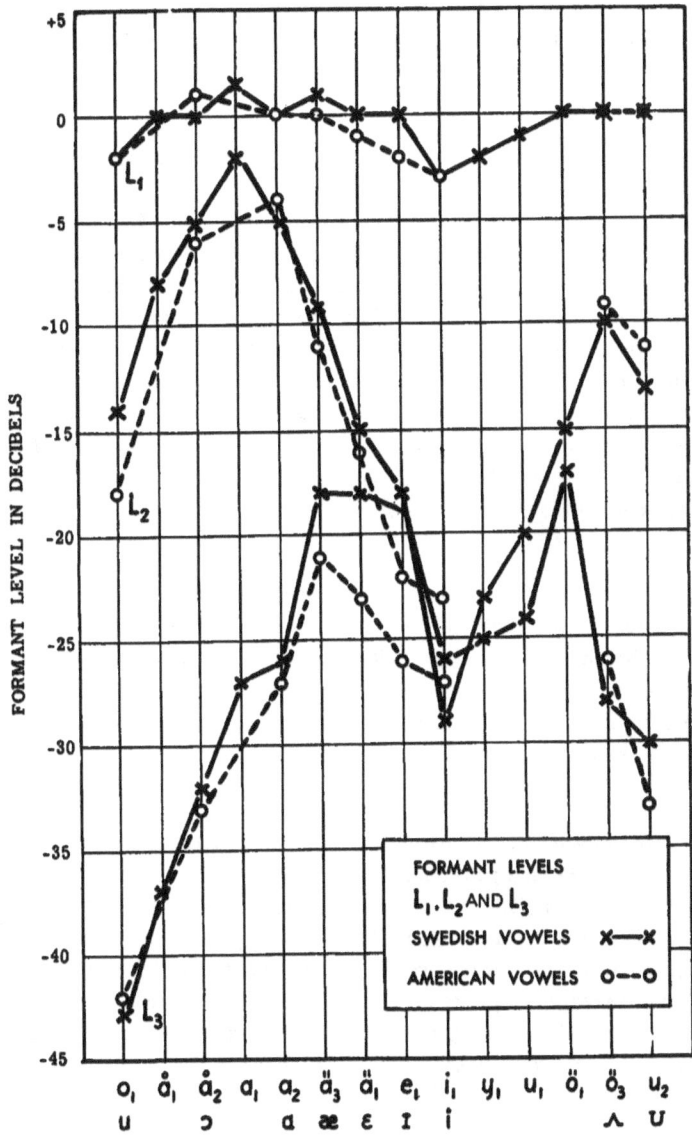

Fig. 5. First, second, and third formant amplitudes of a sequence of Swedish and American English vowels.

the formant patterns. As seen from Fig. 4, the fit is good enough in phonetically similar pairs as [o] $å_1$, [ɔ] a_1, [æ] $ä_3$, [i] i_1, that it may be concluded that F_1, F_2, and F_3 refer to the same formants and that there accordingly exists a basis for future detailed comparisons.

The investigation of PETERSON and BARNEY (1952) is the only survey providing data on both formant frequencies and formant levels besides the earlier Swedish measurements (FANT, 1948), discussed in this chapter. The sequence diagram of Fig. 5 (earlier discussed by FANT, 1956) is intended to show that providing two vowels, one Swedish and one American English vowel, have approximately the same formant frequencies, they will also have approximately the same formant levels. This agreement exists in spite of the systematic differences involved; the Swedish vowels being sustained, the American English vowels sampled from mono-syllabic test words. Both sets of data pertain to the average figures for a group of males; several general observations of interest may be made from Fig. 5, e.g., the rapid increase of L_2 and L_3 within the series o_1 to a_2. L_2 and L_3 of front vowels are found to be of the same order of magnitude. Exceptions are $ö_3$ and u_2 which behave more like back vowels.

The relative formant levels within a spectrum determine the main shape of the spectrum envelope. Because of the analytical relations between formant frequencies and formant levels, there exists the theoretical possibility of phonetic classification of vowels according to relative formant levels. However, the formant level information is related not only to articulation, but also to phonation, i.e., to the voice source characteristics, whereas the formant frequencies are related to articulation alone.

The spread of formant levels comparing different speakers is of the order of 4 dB in L_2—L_1 and 5 dB in L_3—L_1. From a perceptional point of view these numbers are not very large. According to FLANAGAN (1957 a) the minimum perceptual difference, DL, in second and third formant level is $\pm$ 3 dB and $\pm$ 5 dB respectively. The DL of the first formant level is 1 dB, which also is valid for the overall loudness sensation of the vowel. It can thus be concluded that the range of L_2-variation, 25 dB, covers approximately 5 of the $\pm$ 3 dB DL, whereas the range of F_2 frequency variation, 1,500 c/s, contains approximately 15 of the $\pm$ 50 c/s frequency DL; see further FLANAGAN (1957 a).

There is one additional conformity comparing the American and Swedish data that should be mentioned. As shown by FANT (1953), the female versus male average differences in formant frequencies are similar even when a specific vowel is studied. Table 2 summarizes the results of this study in terms of the frequency percentage relation of each of F_1, F_2, and F_3 of the female average data to corresponding male data. The 9 selected vowels are paired on an F-pattern matching basis. Numerical data on the male formant frequencies are also given below.

Table 2. Average male F-patterns and the female/male frequency percentage

$$k = 100 \left(\frac{F_{\text{female}}}{F_{\text{male}}} - 1\right) \%$$

American English data (A) 33 subjects
Swedish data (S) 7 subjects

IPA	STA		F_1 c/s	k_1 %	F_2 c/s	k_2 %	F_3 c/s	k_3 %
[i]		(A)	270	10.0	2,290	22.0	3,010	10.0
	i_1	(S)	260	8.5	2,070	22.0	2,960	16.5
[ɪ]		(A)	390	10.0	1,990	24.5	2,550	20.0
	e_1	(S)	330	9.5	2,050	24.0	2,510	17.5
[ɛ]		(A)	530	15.0	1,840	26.5	2,480	20.0
	$ä_1$	(S)	440	24.5	1,800	19.0	2,390	20.0
[æ]		(A)	660	30.0	1,720	19.0	2,410	18.5
	$ä_3$	(S)	610	29.5	1,550	17.5	2,450	18.5
[ɑ]		(A)	730	16.5	1,090	12.0	2,440	15.0
	a_2	(S)	680	26.5	1,070	12.0	2,520	16.0
[ɔ]		(A)	570	3.5	840	9.5	2,410	12.5
	$å_2$	(S)	490	6.0	820	2.0	2,560	10.5
[ʊ]		(A)	440	7.0	1,020	14.0	2,240	19.5
	u_2	(S)	420	−1.0	1,070	10.0	2,320	16.5
[u]		(A)	300	23.0	870	9.0	2,240	19.0
	o_1	(S)	310	10.5	710	−3.0	2,230	30.0
[ʌ]		(A)	640	19.0	1,190	17.5	2,390	16.5
	$ö_3$	(S)	520	8.0	1,100	17.0	2,430	12.5

The agreement is appreciable in some instances, e.g., comparing the front vowels i_1, e_1, and $ä_3$ with the corresponding American vowels. The overall correlation is significant. It suggests that the female-male differences are greater for formants of a standing wave origin, e.g., F_2 and F_3 of front vowels, and F_1 of the very open $ä_3$. The differences are smaller for F_1 and F_2 of back vowels, e.g., $å_1$, and for F_1 of close front vowels, e.g., i_1. This could be conceived of in the light of the partial applicability of the double or single Helmholtz resonator formula in these instances. A reduction of cavity volume can be compensated for by a narrowing of the associated orifice. In the case of standing wave resonances on the other hand, the length dimensions alone are crucial.

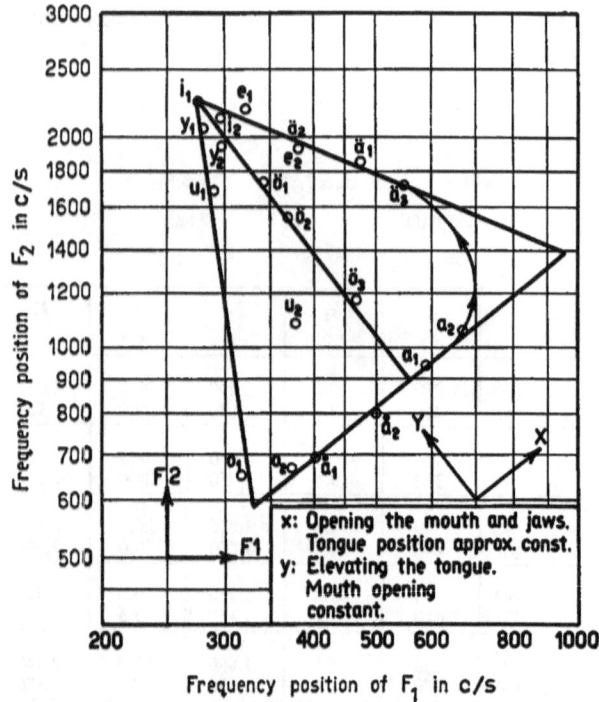

Fig. 6. First formant versus second formant representation of Swedish vowels. Subject Gj-n. A "vowel triangle" is indicated.

According to CHIBA and KAJIYAMA (1941), the total length of an average female vocal tract is 15 per cent shorter than an average male vocal tract. The corresponding value for the boy of 9 was 25 per cent, and for the girl of 8 years of age 42 per cent. A larger part of the male-female vocal tract length difference lies in the pharynx. The tendency of F_2 of front vowels to be more or less related to a pharynx standing wave resonance conforms with their high k_3-factor. More detailed information on vocal tract dimensions is needed as a foundation for closer studies of these relations. The number of subjects of the Swedish survey is rather small, and the average data thus not as reliable as those of PETERSON and BARNEY (1952).

The acoustic representation of vowels in terms of F_1 versus F_2 diagrams has come to extensive use; see for instance POTTER and STEINBERG (1950), PETERSON (1951, 1952), PETERSON and BARNEY (1952). A number of different variations of this basic representational form will be investigated here.

Logarithmic frequency scales have been chosen for the F_1 versus F_2 diagram of Fig. 6 pertaining to the vowels sustained by the reference male subject. A triangle has been constructed to enclose the data in accordance with the classical concept of the vowel triangle. The upper right corner, however, is far beyond the closest vowels a_2 and $ä_3$. It can be seen that the high front vowels e_1, i_1, y_1, u_1, crowd together in the upper left corner. This lack of differentiation is due to the logarithmic scale and to the lack of the information on formant frequencies higher than F_2. The main articulatory variables have been condensed into two variables defining a coordinate system rotated 45 degrees versus F_1 and F_2. The two extreme sounds in the y-dimension are a_1 representing pharyngeal location of the main tongue constriction and i_1 representing palatal articulation. The x-axis combines delabialization with increased jaw-opening[1].

The logarithmic frequency scale is not preferable to a linear scale. The optimum scale appears to be something like the mel scale which is essentially linear at low frequencies and logarithmic at higher frequencies. The mel scale has been constructed on the basis of subjective pitch evaluations involving the determination of the frequency intervals corresponding to halving and doubling of the pitch and equal increments of the pitch as sensed by naive listeners. At very low frequencies such an interval is approximately one octave. At higher frequencies it is more than two octaves and at 1,000 c/s approximately one and a half octave. A conversion of a frequency to a mel value is roughly identical with an estimate of the spatial position of the corresponding point of maximum excitation on the basilar membrane.

A translation from frequency to mels may be undertaken with the aid of interpolations from the following tabulation given by BERANEK (1949):

Frequency c/s	Pitch mels
20	0
160	250
394	500
670	750
1,000	1,000
1,420	1,250
1,900	1,500
2,450	1,750
3,120	2,000
4,000	2,250
5,100	2,500
6,600	2,750
9,000	3,000
14,000	3,250

---

[1] (It is of some interest to note that Fig. 6 was constructed in 1948. Compare a similar discussion by FANT, 1958 a).

A technically useful approximation to the mel scale is shown in Fig. 7. It is of the form

$$y = k \log (1 + f/1000) \qquad (1)$$

where f is the frequency in c/s and y the positional coordinate. This formula, discussed in more detail earlier (FANT, 1949), is a better mel approximation than the Koenig scale which is exactly linear below 1,000 c/s and logarithmic above 1,000 c/s. The significance of the mel scale for incremental pitch judgments, masking, and intelligibility is discussed by KOENIG (1949), MUNSON and GARDNER (1950). Equal increments along the mel scale or one of its technical approximations above correspond closely to equal increments of auditory sensation.

In the sequence diagram of Swedish vowels, Fig. 8, the formant frequencies have been expressed in mels. It can be seen that the first two formants of back vowels retain an approximately constant mel difference within the sequence $å_1$ to a_2, and their mel sum is approximately constant along the a_2 to i_1 sequence. The incremental pitch change in each of the first two formants comparing two adjacent sounds of the diagram has an average value of 90 mels and this quantal step is typical for several of these minimal pairs of comparison.

One additional motivation for converting the numerical data of a formant pattern, F_1, F_2, F_3, etc., into corresponding pitch values M_1, M_2, M_3, etc., is that the minimum perceptible shift in formant pitch turns out to be of the same order of magnitude for all three

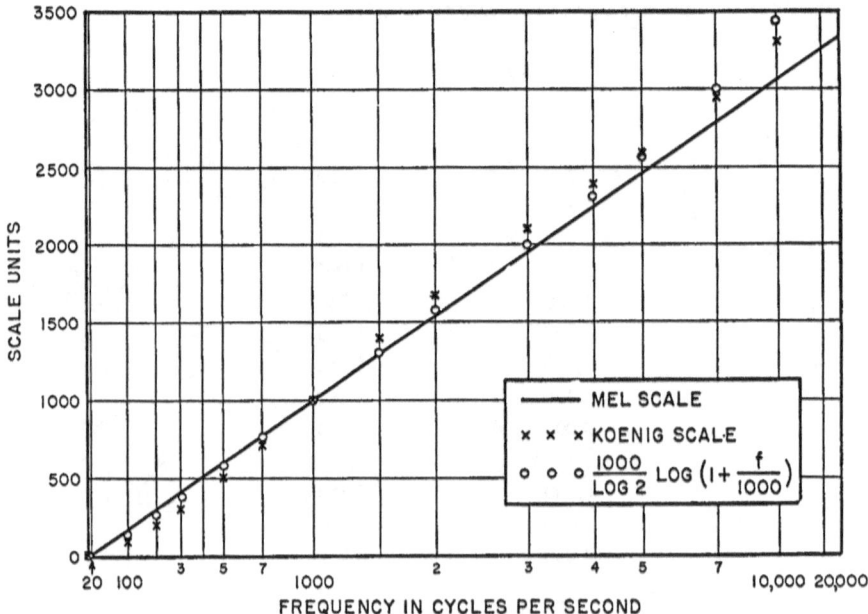

Fig. 7. Mel scale approximations.

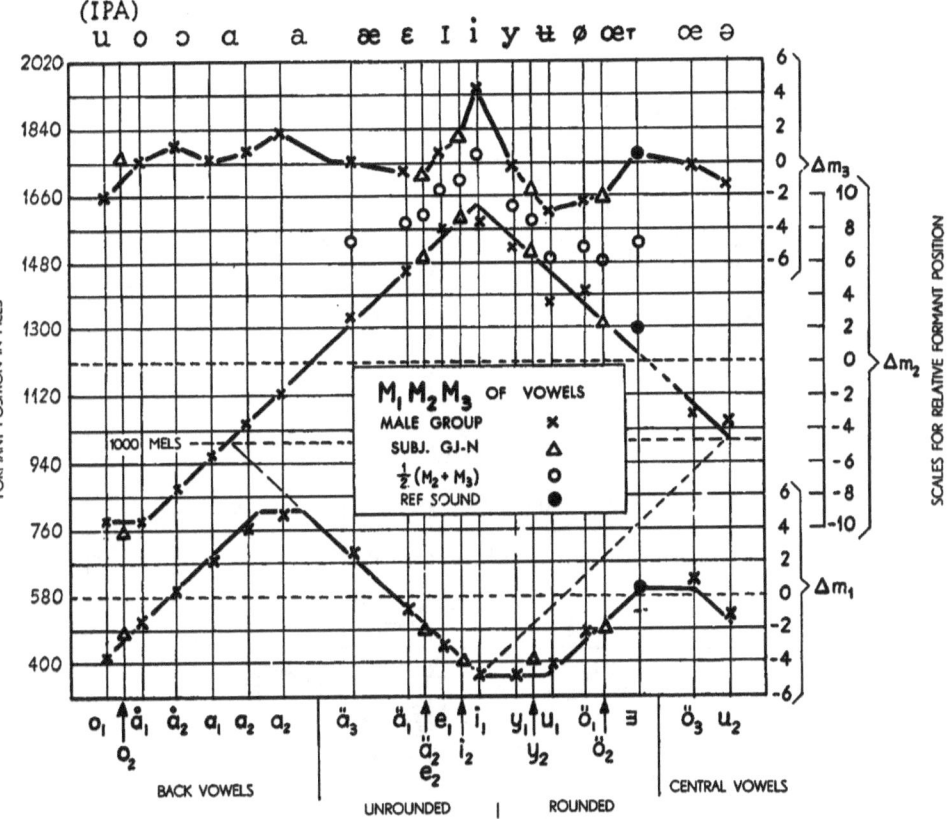

Fig. 8. Sequential vowel diagram on a mel scale basis.

first formants. The earlier quoted DL data from FLANAGAN (1957 a) may thus be expressed as 23 mels in M_1, 27 mels in M_2, and 31 mels in M_3.

Figure 9 shows the formant one versus formant two data for the total ensemble of male and female measurements. It should be remembered that $ä_3$ and $ö_3$ are pre-r variants and that $ä_2$, e_2, i_2, y_2, and $ö_2$ were not included. There is no overlap whatsoever between o_1, $å_1$, a_1, $ä_3$, and $ö_3$, or between $å_2$, a_2, and u_2 but considerable overlap in the region of i_1, e_1, y_1, u_1, $ö_1$.

The average male and female formant one versus formant two data may be observed in Fig. 10, where two corresponding vowel loops are indicated. It may be seen that the male a_2 is very close to the female a_1, and that a female $ö_1$ falls on the line connecting male e_1 and $ä_1$. None of these overlaps has phonetic reality. The a_1 and a_2 of connected speech are in addition differentiated by the length feature and by the higher F_0 of the female voice.

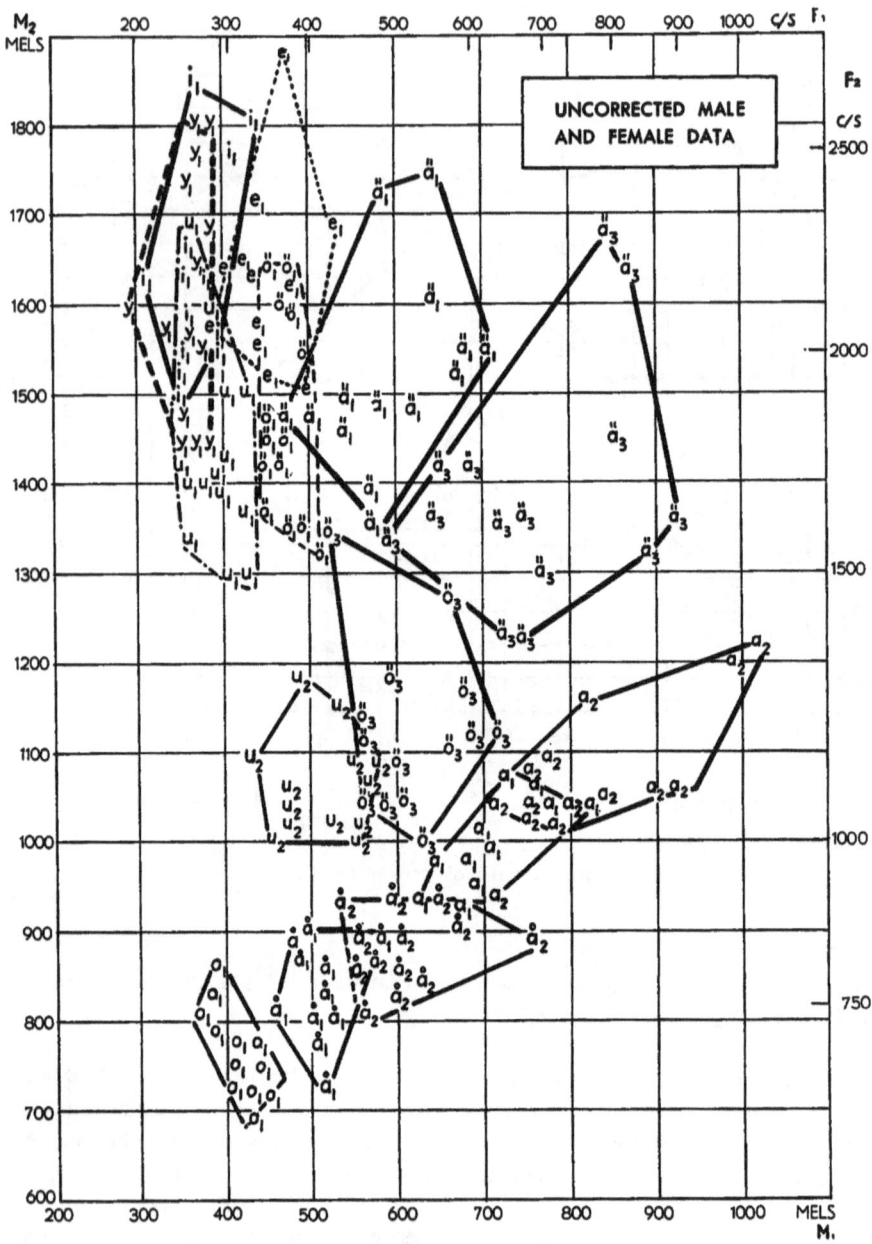

Fig. 9. M_2 versus M_1 plot of the unnormalized formant data of all subjects.

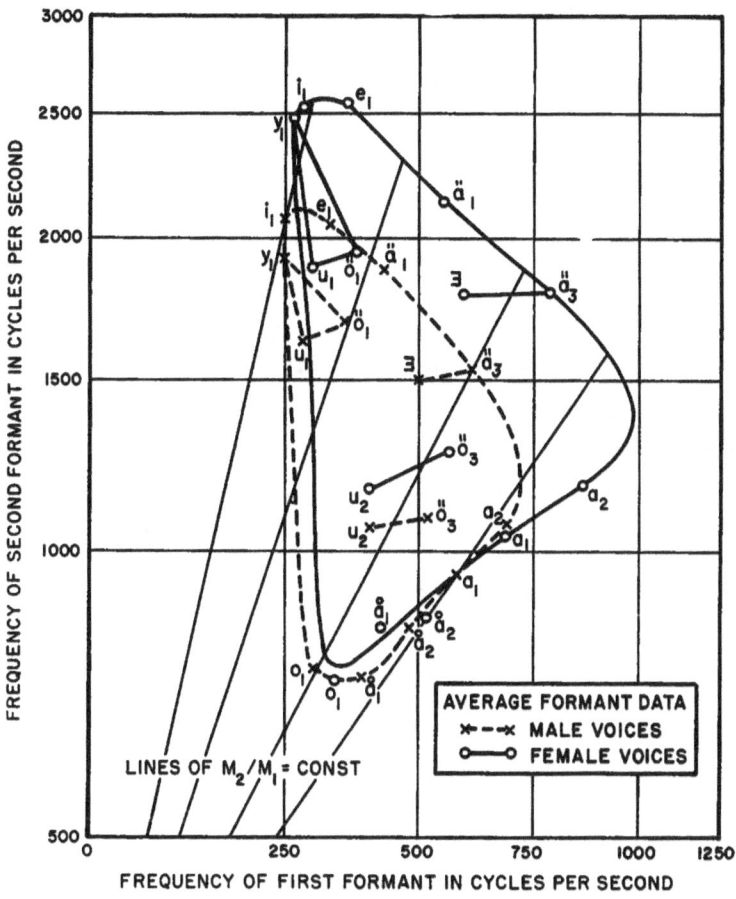

Fig. 10. F_2 versus F_1 diagram of the unnormalized average male and average female data.

The overlap between female $\ddot{o}_1$ and an unrounded male front vowel is due to the missing information on F_3 and the voice fundamental frequency.

From experiments with synthetic speech (MILLER, 1953), it is known that a shift in voice fundamental frequency from e.g., $F_0 = 144$ c/s to $F_0 = 288$ c/s, the spectrum envelope held constant, causes a small shift in phonetic quality towards that of a sound of slightly lower F_1 and F_2. The size of this shift is of the order of 75 mels, i.e., it is barely noticeable. Our own experiments confirm in part these observations but indicate the need of further studies before this effect can be taken into account in formulas for the normalization of formant data.

All vowels can be fairly well synthesized from two formants of independently variable frequency and intensity, as judged from experiments at the Haskins Laboratories (DELATTRE ET AL., 1952). Our own experiments on Swedish vowels have confirmed the well-established rules that back vowels, i.e., those vowels where F_1 and F_2 come close, may be approximated fairly well by the natural F_1 and F_2. This was found to be the case not only for o_1, $å_1$, $å_2$, a_1, a_2, but also for $ö_3$, u_2, and u_1, $ö_1$. In the case of $ä_3$ and y_1, a position halfway between F_2 and F_3 was preferred for the upper formant, and for e_1 a position close to F_3. A position in the region of F_4 or F_5 was chosen for i_1. These experiments were performed with two resonance circuits in parallel and need to be supplemented by studies of the influence of formant intensity level and the particular spectral shape of each formant. It should be noted that the two-formant [i] produced by DELATTRE et al. (1951, 1952) had an upper frequency close to F_3. The difference depends on the synthesis technique.

It is apparently motivated for the presentation of data from speech analysis to perform two-dimensional mapping of vowels in terms of F_1 and an upper effective second formant frequency, here labeled F'_2, chosen so as to take into account a gradual increase in the importance of the third formant as F_2 is raised in frequency. One specific formula made use of here is

$$F'_2 = F_2 + \frac{1}{2}(F_3 - F_2)\frac{(F_2 - F_1)}{(F_3 - F_1)} \qquad (2)$$

or

$$M'_2 = M_2 + \frac{1}{2}(M_3 - M_2)\frac{(M_2 - M_1)}{(M_3 - M_1)} \qquad (3)$$

if the mel scale is preferred.

The limiting value of F'_2 for an F_2 very close to F_1 equals F_2, and when F_2 comes close to F_3, it is apparent that F'_2 is close to a position halfway between F_2 and F_3. Other formulas providing greater F_3-emphasis could alternatively be adopted.

In order to normalize the data with regard to the physiological speaker differences, the following attempt has been made. A speaker's average M_3 is computed and denoted M_{3a}. The reference M_{3a} is called M_{30}. The factor

$$k_s = M_{3a}/M_{30} \qquad (4)$$

is referred to as the speaker's scale factor. A value of $M_{30} = 1{,}750$ mels corresponding to an $F_{30} = 2{,}450$ c/s typical for male voices was adopted. It should be noted that if the scale factor is expressed by a frequency ratio

$$k_s = F_{3a}/F_{30}, \qquad (5)$$

this should approximate the average vocal tract length divided by the length of the speaker's tract. The F_{3a} or M_{3a} of a speaker has been calculated as an average for all vowels, except those of the lowest F_1, thus excluding i_1, y_1, u_1, o_1.

Figure 11 contains the formant data of the male speakers in an M_1 versus M'_2 diagram, and an M_1/k_s versus M'_2/k_s diagram. It may be seen that the k_s-normalization does not

Acoustic Description and Classification of Phonetic Units 53

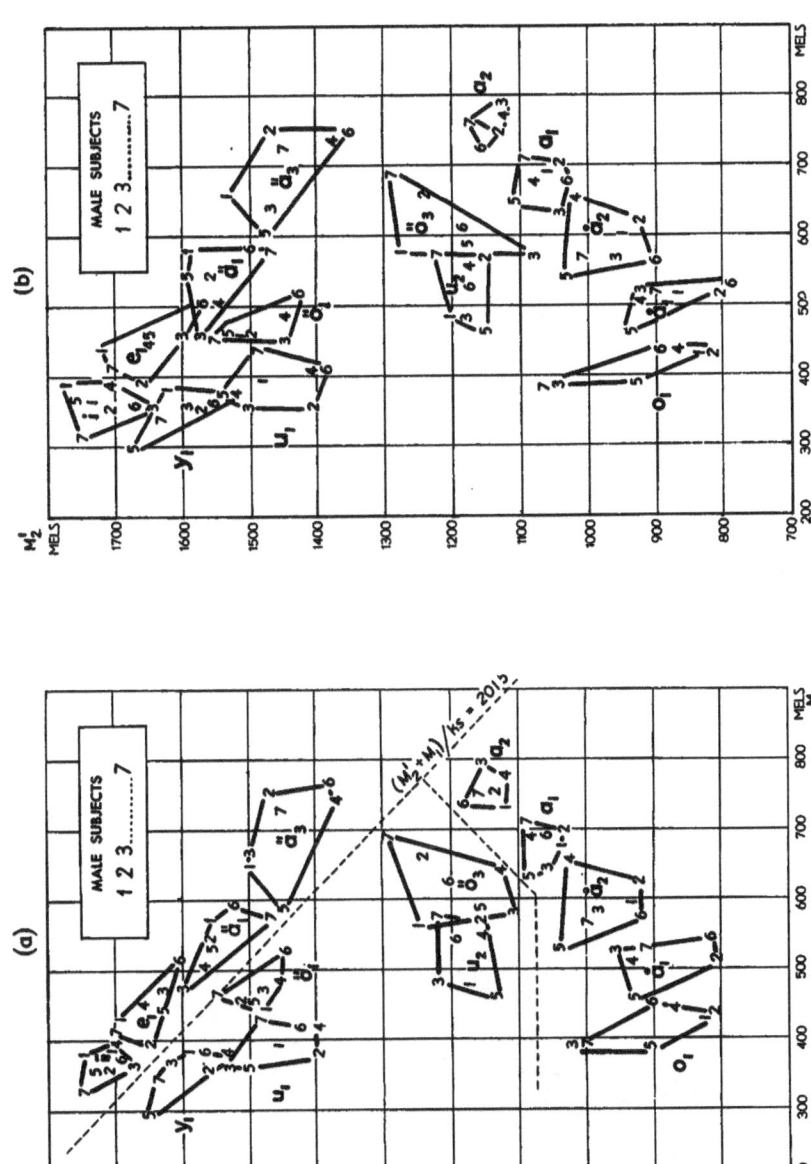

Fig. 11. The effective second formant frequency versus the frequency of the first formant on a mel scale basis for the separate male subjects.
a. Size factor correction applied.
b. No size factor applied.

54 Speech Analysis

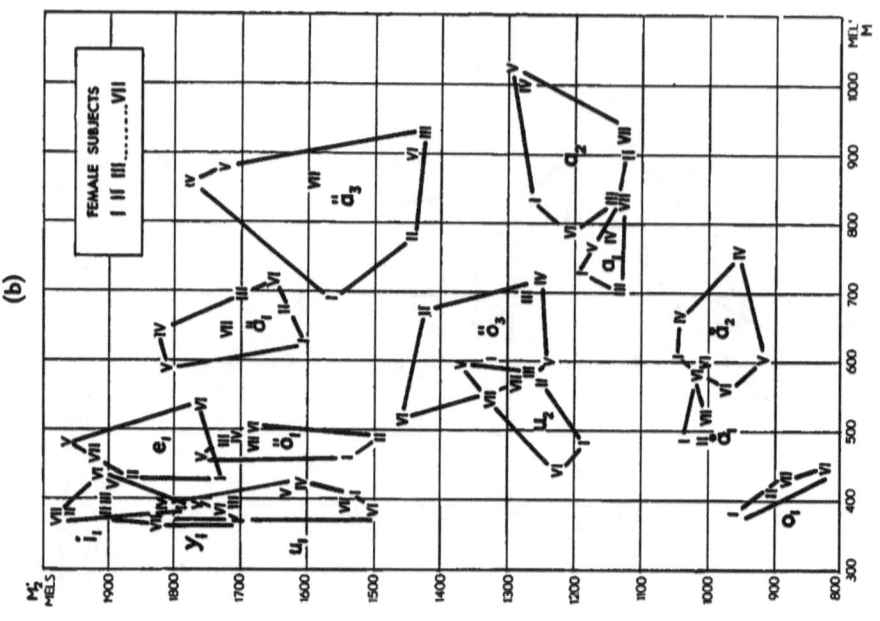

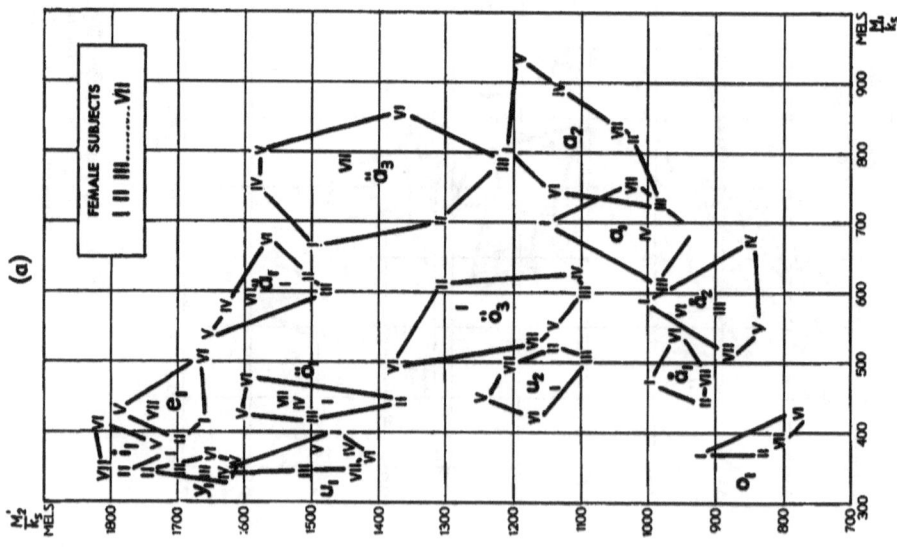

Fig. 12. Vowels diagram for the separate female subjects. The variables of presentation are the same as in Fig. 11.

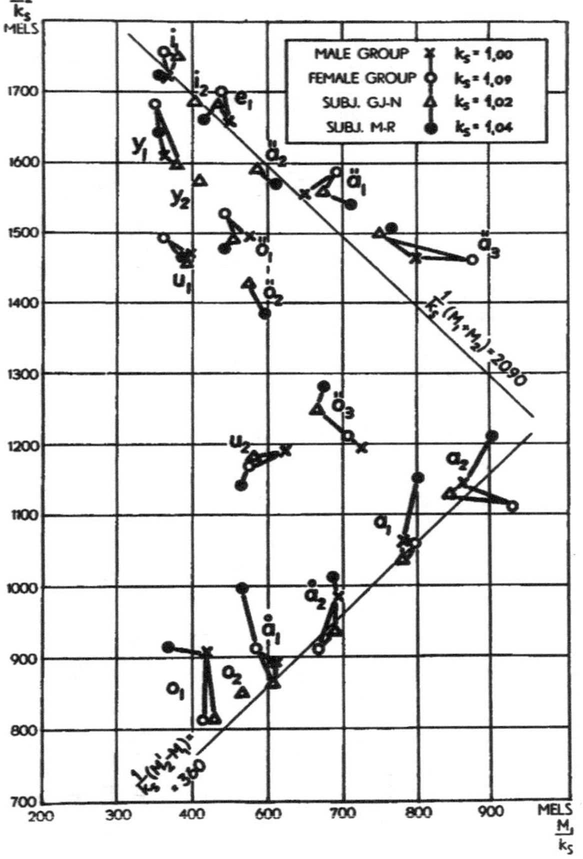

Acoustic Description and Classification of Phonetic Units

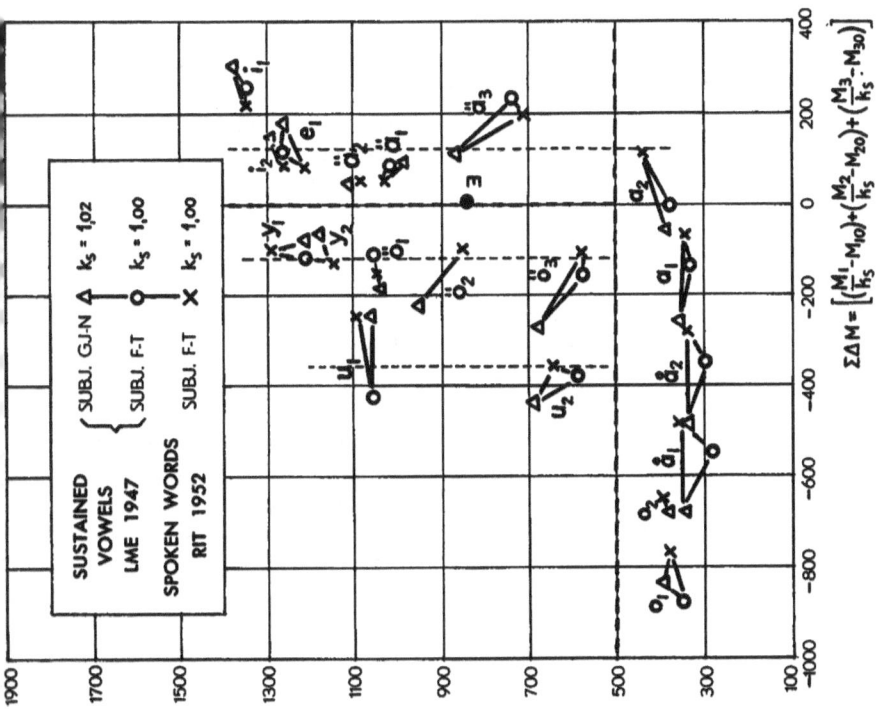

Fig. 13. Size factor normalized, effective second formant frequency versus the first formant frequency for the average male and the average female data. Mel scale representation.

Fig. 14. Size factor normalized, effective second formant frequency minus first formant frequency versus the sum of the frequencies of the first three formants minus the sum for the reference neutral vowel. Mel scale representation.

affect the apparent speaker spread in the lower part of the diagram. There is an improvement in the upper part of the diagram, enabling a better separation of rounded from unrounded front vowels, here represented by the space between y_1, u_1, $ö_1$, and i_1, e_1, $ä_1$. The tendency is similar in Fig. 12 pertaining to female data. It can be seen that the overlap in the high front vowel area is reduced. However, the individual spread is increased within the back vowels, when the k_s-factor is applied. This observation conforms with the insignificance of the third formant for the perception of back vowels.

The k_s-correction removes, however, some of the tendency of back vowel overlap as long as average female data are plotted together with average male data, as in Fig. 13, where in addition the reference male and the reference female subject are included. The figure is based on the parameters M_1/k_s and M'_2/k_s. Even here it is apparent that the form of representation chosen favors front vowels.

From the vowel diagrams based on the frequency of the first formant and the frequency of the second formant or an effective second formant frequency, it is evident that the back vowels are characterized by a fairly constant low frequency difference, and that the rounded front vowels differ from the unrounded front vowels by a smaller sum of the two frequencies. The latter parameter is also effective for classifying the separate back vowels o_1, $å_1$, a_1, or o_2, $å_2$, a_2.

An effective version of the formant frequency difference versus sum specificational system may be studied in Fig. 14. The ordinate is the k_s-normalized difference between M'_2 and M_1, and the abscissa is the k_s-normalized sum of M_1, M_2, and M_3, minus the corresponding sum for the neutral vowel [ə] of formant frequencies $F_1 = 500$ c/s, $F_2 = 1,500$ c/s, and $F_3 = 2,500$ c/s, which in pitch units is $M_1 = 600$ mels, $M_2 = 1,300$ mels, and $M_3 = 1,770$ mels.

The data of Fig. 14 pertain to two male subjects, one of these represented by two sets of measurements, (1) from sweep frequency analysis of sustained sounds as the rest of these diagrams, and (2) Sonagraph analysis of vowels from monosyllabic test words. The higher formant frequencies of o_1, $å_1$, $å_2$, a_1, a_2 within the latter set of data may be seen. The same effect is also apparent for u_1 but not in other front vowels. The phonetic classification of various groups of vowels comes out clearly. The vowels u_1 and u_2 differ from the rest of the rounded front vowels y_1, y_2, $ö_1$, $ö_2$, $ö_3$ in the same manner as the latter differ from the unrounded front vowels i_1, e_1, $ä_2$, $ä_1$, $ä_3$. This apparent order supports the recognition of three degrees of rounding as being relevant in Swedish, as suggested earlier by MALMBERG (1956) and discussed by FANT (1957 b).

The formant difference parameter separates not only back vowels from front vowels but also the individual front vowels of various degree of opening, e.g., i_1, e_1, $ä_1$, or y_1, $ö_1$. It would have been even more effective to utilize the normalized $(M_2 + M_3 - M_1)$ for this purpose, as shown by Fig. 15, containing the average male and the average female data.

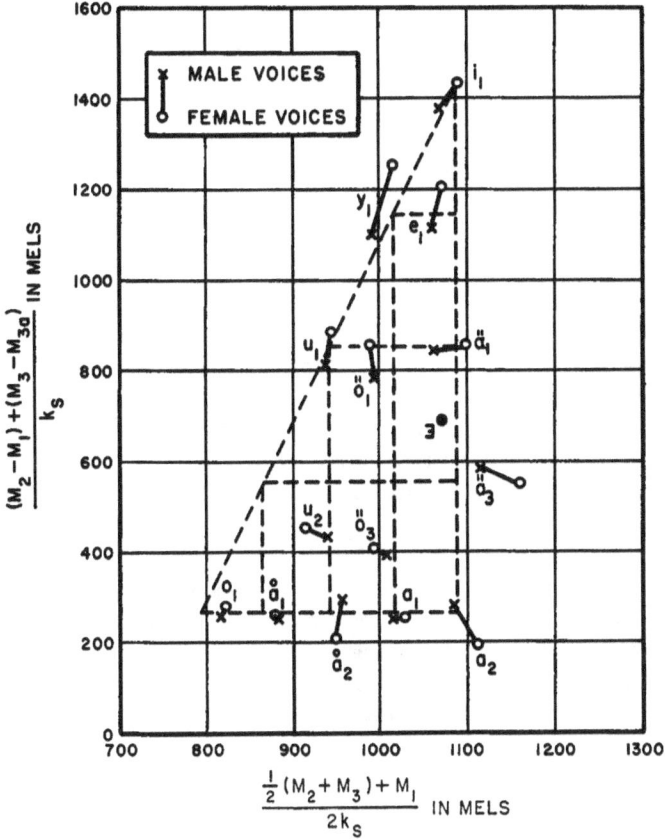

Fig. 15. Size factor normalized diagram of the average male and the average female vowel data. The ordinate is the distance of the second formant to the first plus the elevation of the third formant above the average value. The abscissa provides a center of gravity measure. Mel scale representation.

The abscissa of Fig. 15 is one-half the normalized sum $\frac{1}{2}(M_2 + M_3) + M_1$, which serves essentially the same function as that of Fig. 14, i.e., as a center of gravity measure. It may be seen that the distinction between i_1 and e_1 is improved. The male and female data keep together fairly well. The tendency of the vowels to occupy positions within a net composed of five levels in a vertical and five in a horizontal direction is apparent. Thanks to the mel scale presentation, there are approximately equal intervals for any two minimal distinctions of the same type, i.e., in horizontal or vertical direction.

This is a true orthogonal system. The variables of the two axes, x = center of gravity and y = dispersion, conform essentially but not completely with the gravity and compactness features, as defined by JAKOBSON et al, (1952). The specific function of the dispersion parameter is that it separates back vowels from front vowels in addition to the differentiation of the front vowels of various degree of opening. It has thus four distinctive values which can be expressed in terms of two binary features. The basic of these separates *i, e, y,* from the rest of the system. The second separates *e* from the maximal spread *i*, and also *ä* from the maximally concentrated *a*. In addition, the ternary feature of center of gravity separates *u* from *ö*, and *ö* from *ä*, as well as *o* from *å*, and *å* from *a*. Among the spread vowels *y* is opposed to *i* and *e* by the same distinction reduced to a binary form.

These two distinctions may be projected on the articulatory plane of description by replacing the classical opening variable by one in which palatal constriction and pharyngeal constriction are the two extremes. The shift from one of these places of articulation to an intermediate one or to one of greater cross-sectional area of tongue-pass will cause a reduction of the particular extreme spectral quality—that of maximum or minimum formant separation. As in any phonemic interpretation of acoustic data this is an oversimplification, but it avoids some of the difficulties associated with the earlier proposed systems; see further FANT (1958 a).

None of the vowel diagrams discussed here is ideal. Further research is needed, especially with regard to the demand for a better understanding of the auditory perception of vowel quality. As a rule, the relations between vowels as judged from a two-dimensional diagram stay approximately the same independent of the particular choice of parameters as long as these carry the essential information. An additional example on the formant spread versus sum diagram is that of Fig. 4 of an earlier publication (FANT, 1957 b).

When the voice fundamental frequency is high, or when the analyzing equipment is less selective, it will not be possible to separate the close lying F_1 and F_2 of back vowels. In this connection it is of some interest to review the results of the very first acoustic analysis made at Telefonaktiebolaget L M Ericsson of Swedish vowels (KÅELL, 1943) by means of the Siemens spectrometer (FREYSTEDT, 1935). This instrument provides an instantaneous intensity-frequency display on the screen of a cathode ray tube. Rather unselective one third octave filters provide the frequency analysis.

The following data were obtained for male voices:

Vowel STA	Low formant frequency c/s	High formant frequency c/s
o_1	320	
$å_1$	450	
$å_2$	570	—
a_1	750	—
a_2	900	

Vowel STA	Low formant frequency c/s	High formant frequency c/s
$ä_3$	630	1,600
$ä_1$	500	2,000
e_1	450	2,250
i_1	320	3,200
y_1	320	2,500
u_1	320	2,000
$ö_1$	450	1,700
u_2	570	1,250

The high formant apparently comprises F_2 alone for $ä_1$, u_2, and $ö_1$, and is closer to F_2 than to F_3 for e_1. It lies halfway between F_2 and F_3 for u_1, and close to F_3 of i and y. The low formant frequency is closer to F_1 than to F_2 in o_1, $å_1$, and $å_2$, and it lies halfway between F_1 and F_2 of a_1 and a_2. The data above apparently conform better to a formant concept defined from perception than from speech production; cf. the rules for two-formant synthesis of vowels.

Vowel associations through simple tones

The simplest experiment that can be performed on the acoustic determinants of vowel quality is to present a short sine wave to an audience and ask them to associate the tone with a vowel. The results of such a test given at three separate occasions to three different listener groups, each of about twenty subjects, and with one year's interval between each test, No. 1, 2, and 3, are shown in Fig. 16. The frequencies of the test tones were 250 c/s, 500 c/s, 750 c/s, 1,000 c/s, 1,250 c/s, 1,500 c/s, 1,750 c/s, 2,000 c/s, 2,500 c/s, 3,000 c/s, 3,500 c/s, and 4,000 c/s. The number of listener responses to each of these tones distributed over the nine vowels o_1, $å_1$, a_1, $ä_3$, e_1, i_1, y_1, u_1, $ö_1$, constituting a forced choice ensemble, are shown by one diagram for each vowel. To the left of the figure the mean curve for the three tests is compared with the line spectrum of the corresponding vowel, as produced by subject Gj-n. The main dialectal difference between this subject and the average of the listener group is that F_2 of his $ä_3$ was higher.

Most of the distributional curves cover large frequency regions, e.g., those of e_1, y_1, u_1, $ö_1$, and any tone is generally capable of evoking various vowel responses as well as none. However, there are clear tendencies to be observed, and several of the well-known spectral relations between different vowels, see e.g., i_1 and y_1, are reflected. In some instances, e.g., for the case of o_1 and $å_1$, the distributional curve resembles the spectrum envelope. The

60 Speech Analysis

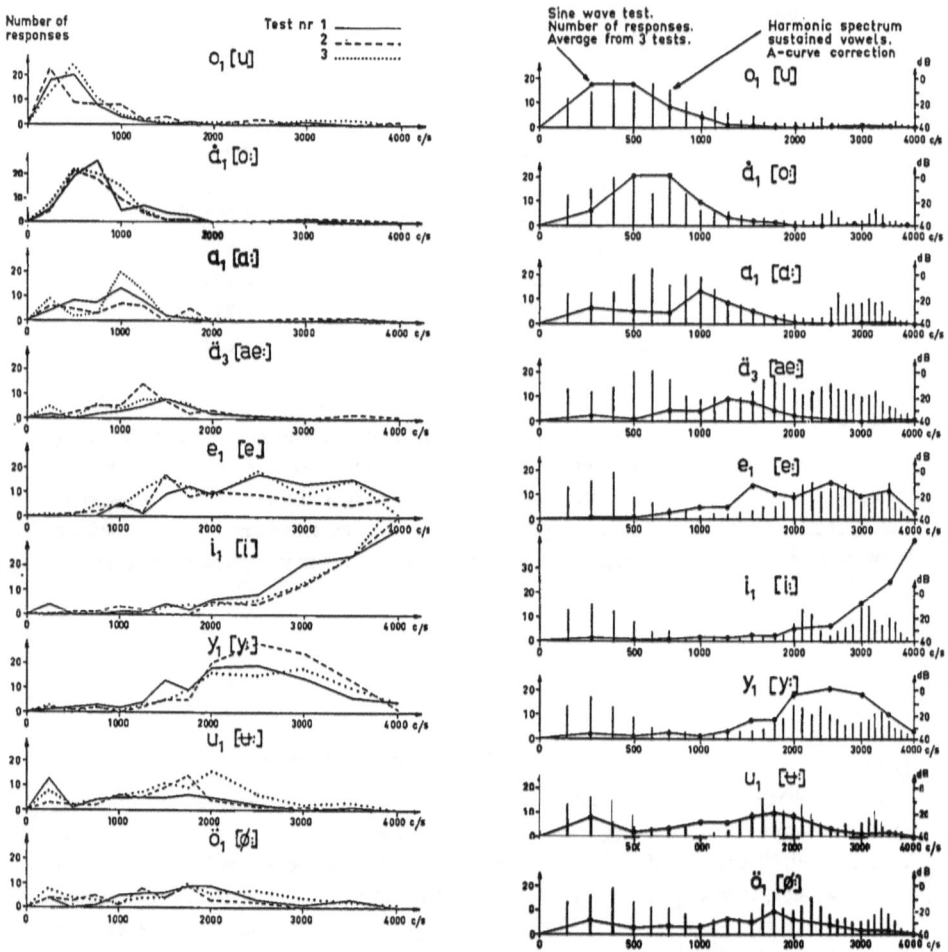

Fig. 16. Results from tone-vowel association tests. The distributional curves are compared with vowel spectra, presented on a technical mel scale and with A-curve sound level correction.

maximum point of a distributional curve has a crude correspondence to the uncoupled resonance frequency of the mouth cavity. The following maxima points may be observed:

	primary c/s	secondary c/s
o_1	400	—
$å_1$	625	—
a_1	1,000	—
$ä_3$	1,250	
e_1	2,500	(1,600) (3,500)
i_1	4,000	—
y_1	2,500	—
u_1	1,750	(250)
$ö_1$	1,750	(250)

The general appearance of the data of Fig. 16 conforms with that of FARNSWORTH (1937); cf. the discussion by CHIBA and KAJIYAMA (1941).

A study of Swedish consonants

Not only vowels but also all sustainable consonants were analyzed by means of the sweep frequency technique which was described elsewhere. Stops were analyzed by means of the multi-band-pass sampling technique. Since a complete discussion of consonants cannot be undertaken without the reference to connected speech, in particular to the transitional characteristics which at present are under investigation and in view of the obvious limitations of sustained speech with regard to naturalness, it has not been considered worthwhile to undertake an extensive review of the material contained in the earlier report (FANT, 1949).

Spectra of consonants sustained by Gj-n are shown in Fig. 17. Harmonic spectra are indicated by line spectra, and spectra of sounds possessing a random fine structure are represented by the envelope only.

There are four unvoiced fricative phonemes of Swedish: *f, s, tj, sj*, of which *tj* occurs only in initial position. The typical feature of *s* is that the major part of the spectral energy is contained above 4,000 c/s. The superimposed formant fine structure of the *s* of Fig. 17 is exceptionally large and should not be regarded as typical. The spectral energy of *f* is more evenly spread, but in some instances there is a clear tendency of a major peak at or above 6,000 c/s. However, compared to *s* the spectrum intensity level of *f* is appreciably lower (generally 15—20 dB lower), especially in the frequency range above 4,000 c/s.

The major energy concentration of *tj* and *sj* is found at frequencies between 1,000 and 4,000 c/s. From experiments with listening to high-pass filtered white noise of gradually lowered

62 Speech Analysis

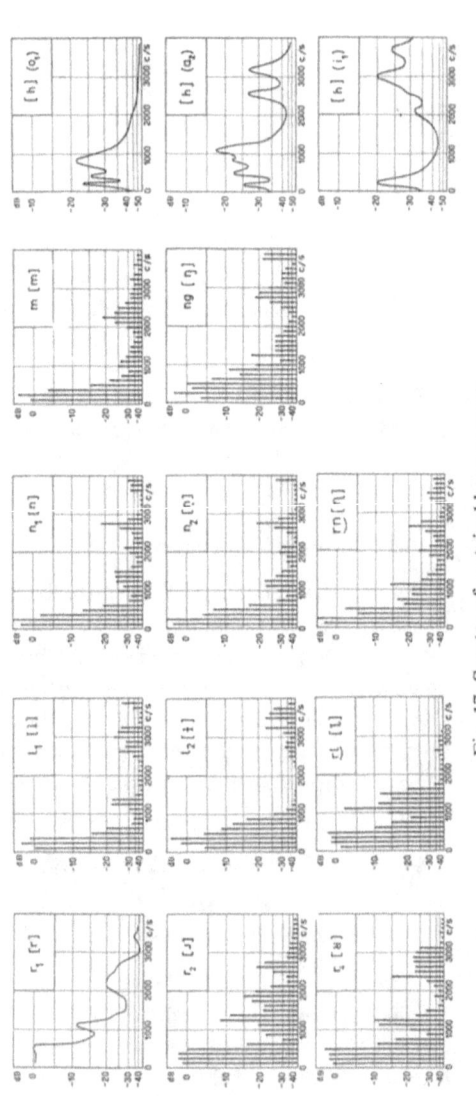

Fig. 17. Spectra of sustainable consonants.

cutoff frequency, it is found that the speech sound association shifts from s to tj to sj to f, but providing this series starts from a cutoff higher than 7,000 c/s, an f may occasionally be heard in the beginning of this series. As judged from the spectrograms, the center of gravity of an s is always higher than tj which in turn is always higher than sj. From experiments with commutation of sound intervals from tape recordings, it is found that the invariably higher F_2-locus within tj compared to sj, approximately 2,200 c/s as compared to 1,600 c/s, contributes to the distinction. However, as a rule a fricative consonant does not need the support from the transitional sound intervals to be identified.

Comparing tj with its voiced mate j it may be seen that F_2 and F_1 are eliminated in tj. This is due to a pole-zero overlap. Both F_1 and F_2 of palatal sounds are mainly dependent on the cavities behind the tongue constriction and so are all zeroes. The observable antiresonances in the tj-spectrum indicating zeroes at 3,400 c/s, 5,000 c/s, and 6,600 c/s, signal a location of the source at $l = c/2\Delta F_2 = 35,300/(2 \cdot 1,600) = 11$ cm from the glottis end of the vocal tract.

In general, the spectrum of a fricative consonant is mainly conditioned by the cavities in front of and in the vicinity of the constriction. Extensive discussions of cavity formant relations may be found in a separate publication (FANT, 1958 a). Reference to Swedish speech is made in an earlier publication (FANT, 1957 a).

The h-sounds show formant patterns that are similar to vowels of corresponding articulation. The coupling to the trachea via the open glottis introduces below F_1 a low frequency formant at 150 c/s and in the case of $h(a_2)$ a split second formant. The very weak second formant of $h(i_1)$ is in part due to the damping through the open glottis but may also be the result of noise generation chiefly from a palatal source. The first formants of h-sounds are rather weak in ordinary spectrographic display depending on the high frequency pre-emphasis.

The first formants of the voiced continuants l, m, and n occupy a low frequency position, somewhat lower in m and n than in l. The intensity level of the higher formants of an m or n at about 2,200 c/s and/or higher frequencies is generally but not always below the level of the higher l-formants. The difference between the m and the n is not very clear from the spectrum of the stationary interval (nasal murmur). As known from synthesis experiments it is the transitional characteristics that are of main importance. The stationary interval of the consonant ng differs from that of m and n by a first formant of somewhat higher frequency and a higher level of the 300—800 c/s region.

Three r-variants are included; $r_1 =$ rolled, apical; $r_2 =$ voiced, continuant, apical; $r_4 =$ voiced, continuant back-tongue r. The variant l_2 is the dark l produced with retracted tongue position and uvular constriction. It can be seen that the second formant is very close to the first.

The observable spectrographic differences between r and l are the lower frequency F_3 and/or F_4 of r, and generally also the lower F_2 of r_1 compared to l_1. The intensity of the second or third formant of l is often reduced by an anti-resonance effect which, however, is combined with emphasis of formants of higher frequencies. The transition from an *l* to a vowel is generally abrupt. The combination of rolled *r* plus vowel is easily recognized in spectrograms by the periodic interruption of the pattern. The fricative or single flap *r*-sounds show transitional intervals of greater length than the combinations of *l* plus vowel.

Some of the results from the measurements of stop sound spectra are shown in Fig. 18. These data were compiled from oscillographic records of the output of a wave analyzer employing a 350 c/s-wide filter. The analyzer mid-frequency was shifted 300 c/s after each completed oscillogram of the text:

»kakk, papp, tatt, kok, pop, tot, kik, pip, tit,
gagg, babb, dadd, gog, bob, dod, gig, bib, did.»

Intensity versus frequency diagrams were tabulated for two samples in the noise interval of the initial consonant and for two samples within the final consonant. The first sample of the initial sound, labeled k_{11}, p_{11}, t_{11}, etc., and the first sample of the final sound k_{21}, p_{21}, t_{21}, etc., pertain to the first 10 msec of the explosion noise. The second sample was taken 20—30 msec later and is labeled k_{12}, p_{12}, t_{12}, and k_{22}, p_{22}, t_{22}, respectively. In case of the initial voiced stops the second sample generally fell in the first or second voice period of the following vowel. The average duration of the stop "burst" from the leading edge of the explosion wave front to the onset of voicing in the following vowel was

	k	p	t	g	b	d
duration of burst in msec.....	60	40	50	20	8	12

In case of *b* and *d* the duration and energy content of the burst is insignificantly low, and the consonant is then merely to be regarded as a transient onset of the following vowel in which the formant frequency transitions play an important role. The distinction *k* to *g*, *p* to *b*, and *t* to *d* in initial positions is thus essentially one of burst duration. The voicing during the closed interval preceding the explosion is acoustically represented by a spectrum entirely dominated by a first formant of very low frequency F_1 close to F_0. This voicing is found primarily in intervocalic positions, and is generally left out in initial positions. It should be observed that when the voicing starts in an "aspirated" Swedish *k*, *p*, or *t*, the articulators have already moved away from the state of closure and a substantial part of the formant frequency transition may then have been completed.

The first interval after explosion seems to be most characteristic of *k* and *p* and the second interval is more important for *t* since the intensity of the fricative noise is at a maximum here. The characteristic differences between the spectral qualities of *k*, *p*, and *t* are generally neutralized in the very last part of the burst just before the onset of voicing. This is especially true of aspirated stops of a long duration in which case this final interval is merely a short *h*-sound with a formant pattern determined by the following vowel.

To the lower left of Fig. 18 the spectral characteristics of *k*, *p*, and *t* are displayed in the form of average curves for the male and the female group. The single formant structure of

Acoustic Description and Classification of Phonetic Units 65

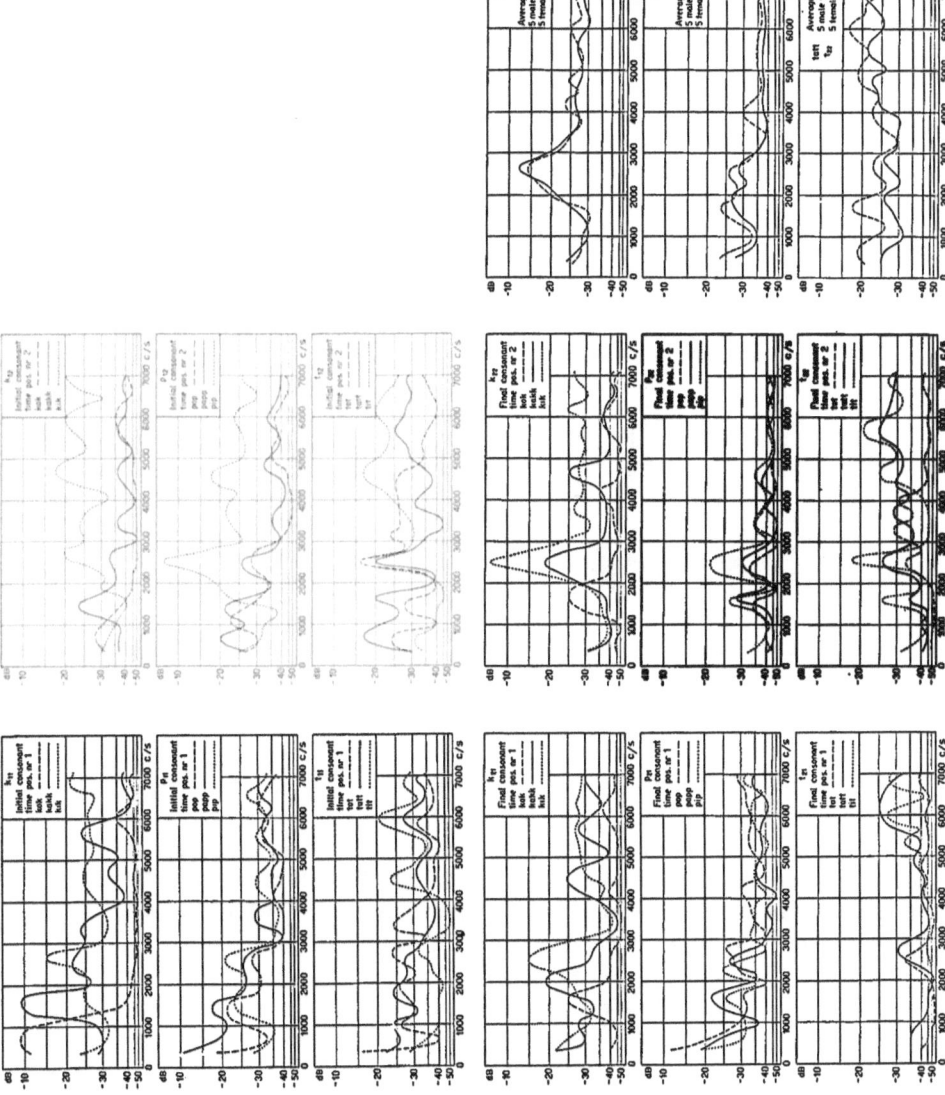

Fig. 18. Spectra of the stop consonants k, p, and t.

66 Speech Analysis

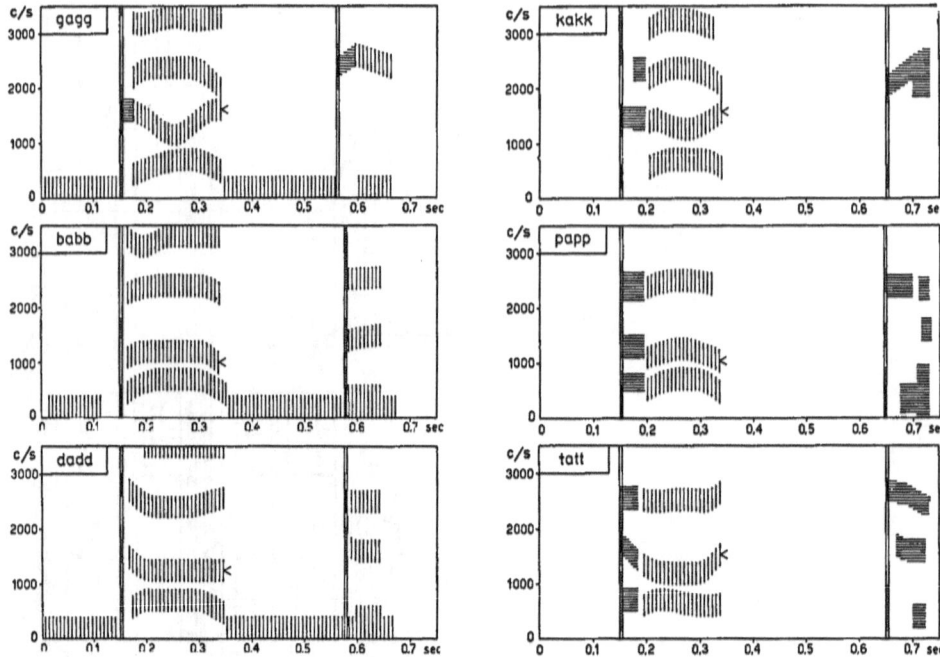

Fig. 19. Stylized spectrograms of "gagg, babb, dadd, kakk, papp, tatt" compiled from band-pass oscillograms.

k is apparent, as well as the falling overall slope of the p and the level or rising overall slope of t. As seen from the other diagrams of Fig. 18, the frequency of the main k-formant follows the frequency of the second or third formant of the adjacent vowel. This is evidently the main formant of the cavity in front of the velar or palatal tongue constriction. The most apparent formants of the p-spectrum are F_1, F_2, and F_3, and these are obviously dependent on the total cavity system of the vocal tract behind the lips. Since an increased lip-opening, everything else held constant, invariably causes a frequency rise of these formants, it is to be expected that the labial transitions are always rising from the consonant to the vowel, and falling from the vowel to the consonant. However, a simultaneous tongue movement may compensate this effect. The main formants of the dental stop t are the same as those of an s-sound, i.e., a fricative noise confined to frequencies above 4,000 c/s caused by the resonance effect of the dental constriction and front cavity. However, F_3 and F_2 are often of apparent intensity.

Figure 19 shows a time-frequency-intensity spectrogram compiled from tabulated data of the intensity as a function of time in the separate frequency bands. The text is "gagg, babb, dadd, kakk, papp, tatt," spoken by subject Gj-n. The frequency range has been given an upper limit of 3,300 c/s. Voiced formants are indicated by a periodic fine structure of vertical lines conforming with broad-band sonagrams.

The formant transitions are typical. It may be seen how F_2 and F_3 of the vowel approach at the boundary towards an initial or final g or k. The F_2 and F_3 transitions from b to a are rising, but they are falling from d to a due to the high F_3-locus of d. The F_2-locus of d is somewhat higher than F_2 of a. One feature to be observed from Fig. 19 is that some of the formants of the aspiratory interval of p occupy higher frequency positions than in the following vowel, the onset of voicing causing a discontinuous drop of about 200 c/s formant frequency. This is due to the closure of the glottis.

The F_1-locus must always start from a low position at an interval of a complete articulatory obstruction and thus at a higher position in k, p, or t, as compared to g, b, or d, because of the relative delay in the onset of voicing.

Providing the burst and the transitions are treated as a single auditory stimulus and further if F_2 and higher formants of front vowels are treated as a single perceptual unit, it can be concluded that k and g provide a neutral transition with regard to the effective upper formant of the beginning of the following vowel. In addition, or perhaps as the main auditory cue, the k and g onset is characterized by a concentration of a larger part of the spectral energy to a single formant, that is, to the frequency region of the front cavity resonances. The higher order resonances of this system occur at appreciably higher frequencies and are weaker. The p, b, t, and d sounds have less concentrated spectra. Normally, the t or d transition, defined as the time variation of the center of gravity of the spectrum, is falling and the p or b transition rising. This statement, however, needs quantitative verification.

When a stop sound precedes another stop sound the former is generally imploded, as exemplified by the schematized spectrogram of the words "jord bort" in Fig. 20. The rd-sound is imploded, i.e., signaled only as a terminating modification of the preceding vowel $o͡$.

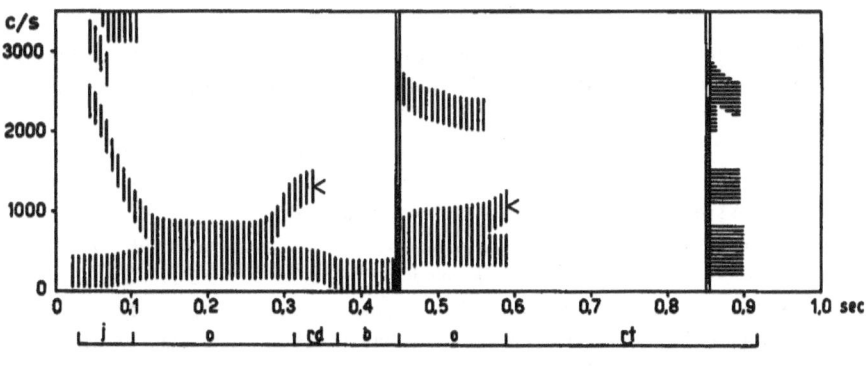

Fig. 20. Stylized spectrograms illustrating implosion of a stop consonant when followed by another stop consonant.

The phonemes r̬d, r̬t, r̬s, r̬n, and r̬l occur only in positions after a vowel. These alveolar modifications differ from the corresponding dentals by a shift down of the lower frequency limit of fricative noise, if present, and further by a shift down in F_3 and/or some of the higher formants.

The general results of the measurements on stops reported on here agree in large with the data provided by FISCHER-JØRGENSEN (1954) and HALLE, HUGHES, and RADLEY (1957). The data on fricatives are comparable to those of HUGHES and HALLE (1956) but are not so extensive.

A summary of formant data

Figure 21 provides a schematized summary of the spectral characteristics of the Swedish phonemes as found in the investigation at Telefonaktiebolaget L M Ericsson, 1945—1949. The vowels have been corrected in order to be valid for connected speech as found from later measurements with the Sonagraph.

Vowels are sufficiently described by their F-patterns. A consonant specification must in addition include the spectral composition of the sound, since the spectral energy is only in part attached to the first three formants. In stops and fricatives an essential part of the sound energy may be confined to formants higher than F_3 and in the interval of nasal murmur there are other formants present while the oral formants of the F-pattern are highly attenuated. This is one possible basis for classifying the liquids *l* and *r* apart from other consonants; see further FANT (1958 a).

A complete consonant study should include the specification of the F-pattern of all consonants in all vowel combinations. In Fig. 21 the positions or "loci" of the four first frequencies of the F-pattern F_1, F_2, F_3, and F_4 are indicated for all sounds, and in the case of consonants in combination with a vowel a_2.

Figure 22 is intended for studies of a more statistical character directed towards an analysis of the gain requirements in speech amplification systems for making specific formants of speech audible. Each formant is plotted as an intensity level versus frequency point. In addition, the threshold of hearing and the 40 phon equal-loudness contour are indicated. The extent of the formant distribution in the intensity dimension is approximately 30 dB. The long-time-average speech spectrum of FRENCH and STEINBERG (1947), adjusted to represent root mean square levels in successive 250 c/s band, is included. With this scale adjustment the average spectrum lies 10 dB below the upper points of the quantized formant data. In spite of the fact that most of the data originate from sweep frequency analysis of sustained sounds, they appear to have an acceptable degree of representability as judged from control experiments of the overall intensity level of each sound.

It should be observed that the relative audibility of any specific sound under any specific reception conditions, e.g., a hearing loss, cannot be inferred quantitatively from this diagram.

Acoustic Description and Classification of Phonetic Units

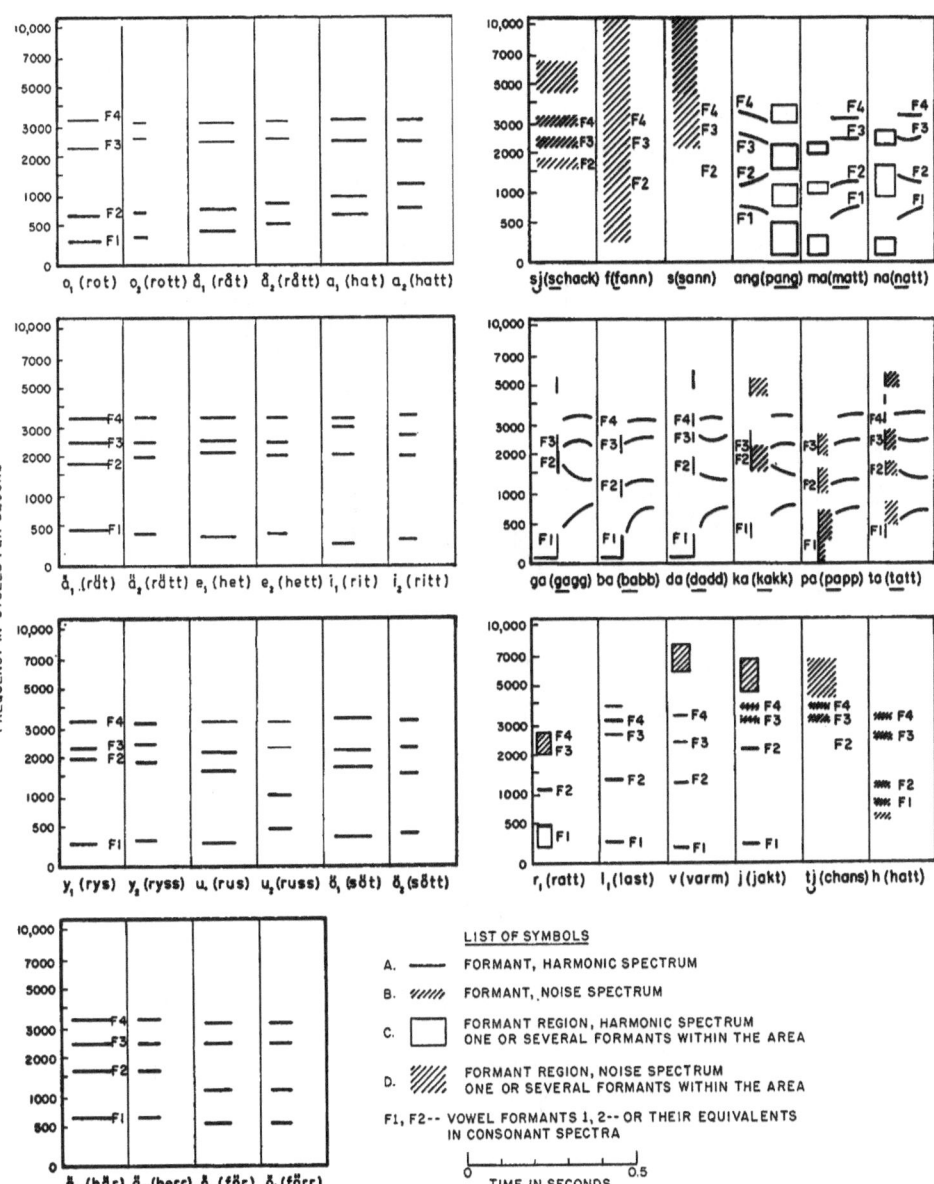

Fig. 21. Schematized spectrographic assembly of Swedish vowels and consonants. The F-patterns of the consonants are indicated.

70 Speech Analysis

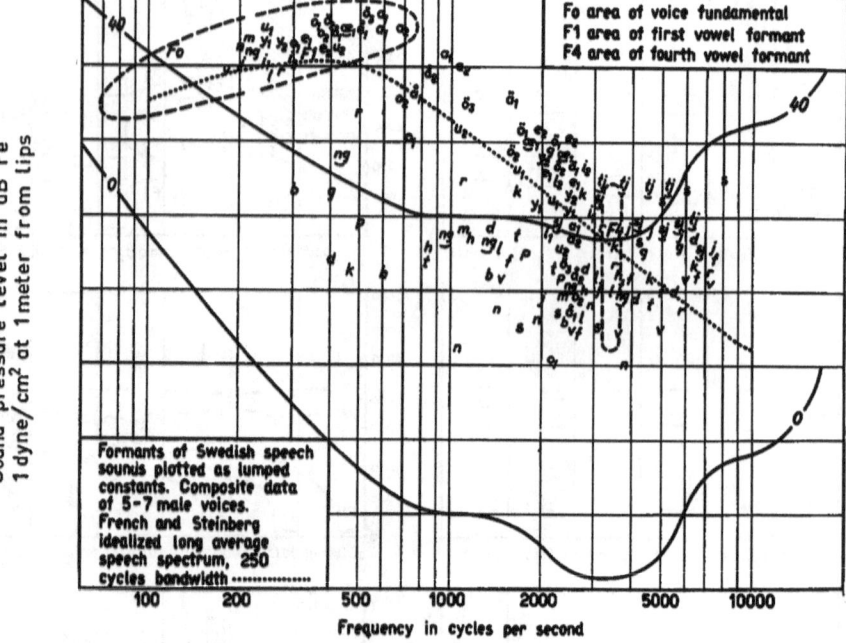

Fig. 22. Sound pressure level versus frequency plot of the vowel and consonant formant data.

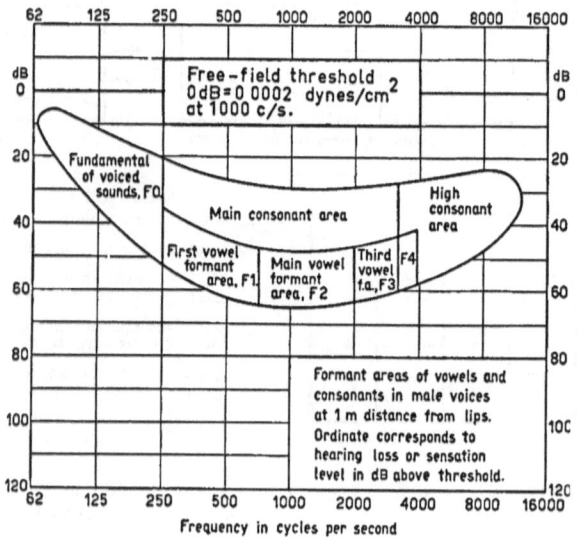

Fig. 23. Schematized presentation of the average speech spectrum within an audiogram in terms of main formant areas. Sensation levels (down) are relative to the standardized free-field threshold.

An obvious limitation is the information on consonants carried by preceding and following vowels; cf. the threshold determinations for each separate phoneme performed by FLETCHER (1953). The diagram is merely intended for estimates of whether certain speech quanta lie above a specific threshold or not.

For several practical applications, detailed information concerning individual sounds may be of secondary interest, and a simplified figure like that of Fig. 23 containing only the main formant areas will be needed. The ordinate (down) is hearing loss in dB for pure tones of the frequencies indicated on the abscissa. This diagram printed on audiograms has come to use at hearing clinics and schools for the deaf, e.g., for the investigations performed by WEDENBERG (1951, 1953) concerning speech communication with severely hard-of-hearing children.

Supplementary spectrum and wave shape data

Long-time-average speech spectrum

Long-time-average speech spectra for a male and for a female subject each reading a 70 seconds long text are shown in Fig. 24. These curves were derived from planimetric integration of sound energy from band-pass pre-filtered, square-law rectified, and smoothed time-functions recorded on the galvanometer oscillograph. It can be seen that the curves compare quite well with the long-time-average curve given by FRENCH and STEINBERG (1947) for American English. The fourth formant of the male subject and the third formant of the female subject are reflected by peaks at 3,500 c/s and 3,000 c/s respectively. Statistical analysis of the average speech spectrum performed by TARNÓCZY (1957) on Hungarian speech also compares well with the American data. These agreements indicate that the general properties of speech more than the characteristics of a specific language influence the long-time-average statistics. In this connection it should be observed that it is the higher vowel formants rather than the main formants of the unvoiced stops and fricatives that determine the spectral energy level in the 3,000—5,000 c/s band.

The effects of voice level on speech spectra

The average spectrum is not much dependent on the particular text unless this is very short and contains a very restricted choice of vowels. The voice effort of the speaker is an important factor to take into account as shown by Fig. 25 pertaining to the sequence: "Ett, två, tre, fyra, fem". (Swedish for "One, two, three, four, five".) The speaker first read this sentence at a normal voice level, and the average reading of a monitoring instrument was noted. Next the subject read the same passage with a lower voice effort providing a mean

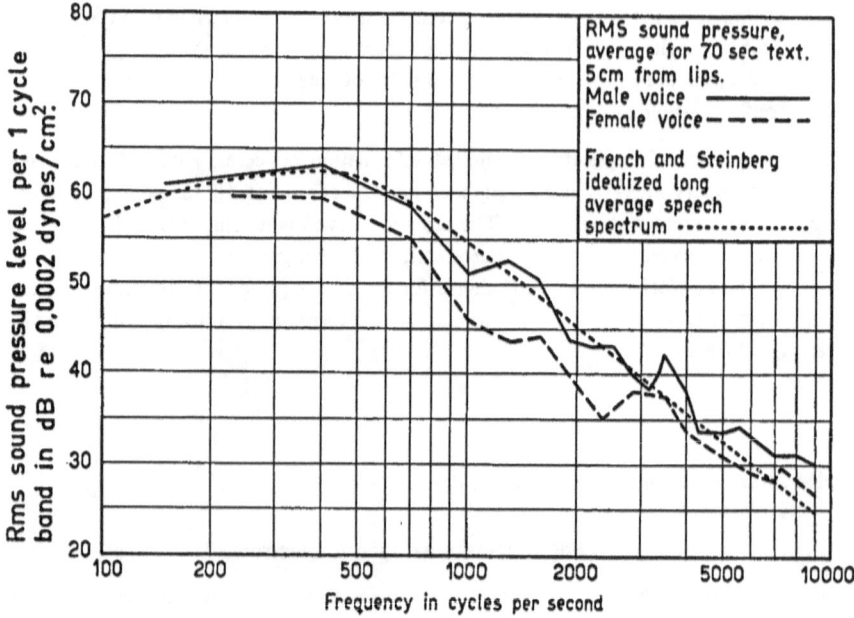

Fig. 24. Long-time-average speech spectra.

reading on the monitoring meter of —10 dB relative to the normal level and then at a higher voice level of +10 dB relative to this reference.

All three spectrum curves show a marked peak at 2,000 c/s representing the second formant of the *e-* and *y-*sounds involved in the particular text. An apparent increase may be observed of the spectral level above 1,500 c/s in excess of the increase in average sound level. Conversely, the intensity level in the frequency range of the voice fundamental increases less than the increase in average level. These effects can be described as an expansion at high frequencies and a compression at low frequencies by a factor of the order of 1.5—2.0 of the dB scale.

The results from a similar investigation on a single vowel are shown in Fig. 26 pertaining to the vowel [ɑː] sustained at three different voice levels. The absolute calibration of sound pressure levels is retained within the three spectra. It can be seen that the spectrum representing +10 dB shows a voice fundamental of only 9 dB higher level than in the spectrum pertaining to the —10 dB overall level. Comparing these two extreme spectra there may further be observed a 23.5 dB difference in the level of the first formant, a 26 dB difference

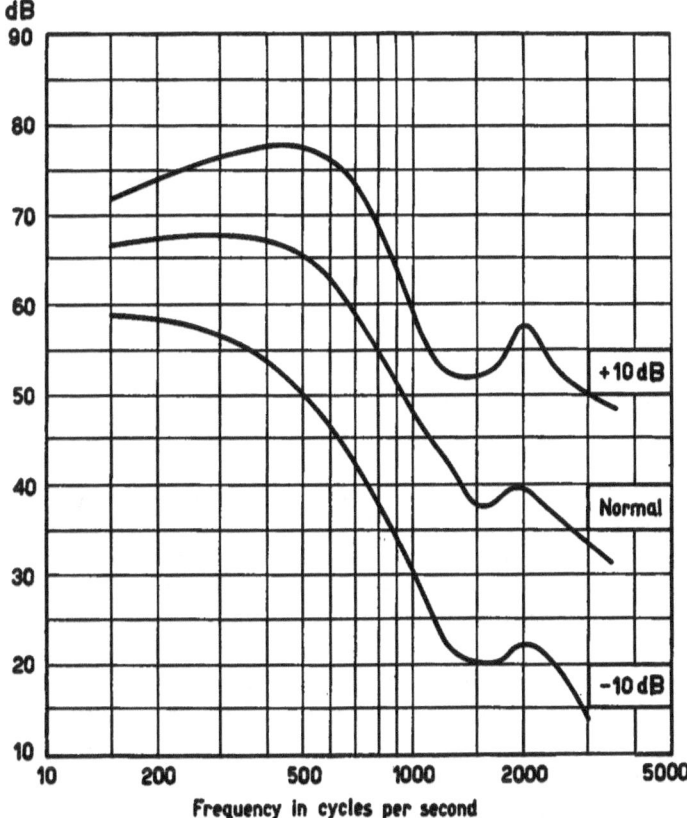

Fig. 25. Energy spectra of the spoken numbers "en, två, tre, fyra" at three different voice intensity levels.

in the second formant, a 24 dB difference in the third formant, and a 32 dB difference in the level of the fourth formant. A part of the increase in the first and second formant levels appears to be attributable to a decrease of formant bandwidth as observed from the tendency of a clearer peak structure at higher voice levels.

Similar investigations were carried out on the influence of voice effort on relative formant levels of other vowels. The following tabulation summarizes the results in the form of the sound pressure level increase in the voice fundamental and in the second, third, and fourth formants accompanying an increase of the level of the first formant from 10 dB below normal level to the normal level. The vowel transcription is made in terms of IPA and STA symbols; see further the second section of this chapter, "A study of Swedish vowels."

Vowel		L_0	L_1	L_2	L_3	L_4
STA	IPA	dB	dB	dB	dB	dB
$å_1$	[o:]	5	10	10	21	12
a_1	[ɑ:]	3	10	11	14	16
a_2	[a]	3	10	11	15	13
$ä_3$	[æ:]	4	10	13	14	16
u_1	[ʉ:]	4	10	14	15	13
e_1	[e:]	4	10	14	15	13
y_1	[y:]	5	10	19	17	15
i_1	[i:]	5	10	19	17	15
$ö_1$	[ø:]	5	10	14	16	17
Average		4	10	14	16	14

The most probable explanation of these systematic effects is that the increase of voice effort has resulted in a change in the spectral characteristics of the voice source, in particular a shift of the average slope of the spectrum envelope. As a rule of thumb these results may be interpreted as a + 3 dB/octave, high frequency emphasis up to a frequency of 3,000 c/s. This spectral change must by necessity correspond to a sharpening of the discontinuities of the pulsating air flow emitted past the vocal cords. The extent to which this sharpening affects the onset, peak, and/or decay of glottal air pulses is not quite clear from available evidence. The particular kind of voice and voice register must be taken into account.

In addition it appears probable that the relative pulse duration within a voice period is shortened; see further the discussion of data from the Bell Telephone Laboratories film of the vocal cords (FANT, 1958 a). The available data from this film and several other studies of the vocal cords indicate that there are not very great changes in the duration of glottal air pulses during speech and that the non-linear spectrum changes are mainly due to changes in rise time and degree of discontinuities. Minor irregularities, partially of cyclic recurrence within the spectrum, can be anticipated for very sharply bounded glottal pulses.

Providing the amplitude of the fundamental varies in proportion to the DC-component of the air flow, which is not an unreasonable assumption for low frequencies of the voice fundamental, it follows from the ratio of L_0 increase to L_1 increase of the order of 0.5 that the overall sound pressure amplitude (which is essentially conditioned by the first formant) varies approximately with the square of the DC-air flow amplitude. This relation, directly observed by VAN DEN BERG (1956) from synchronous measurements of air flow and sound pressure amplitude, may be regarded as an instance of increased efficiency of the voice source at higher voice levels and has probably very little to do with concomitant changes in

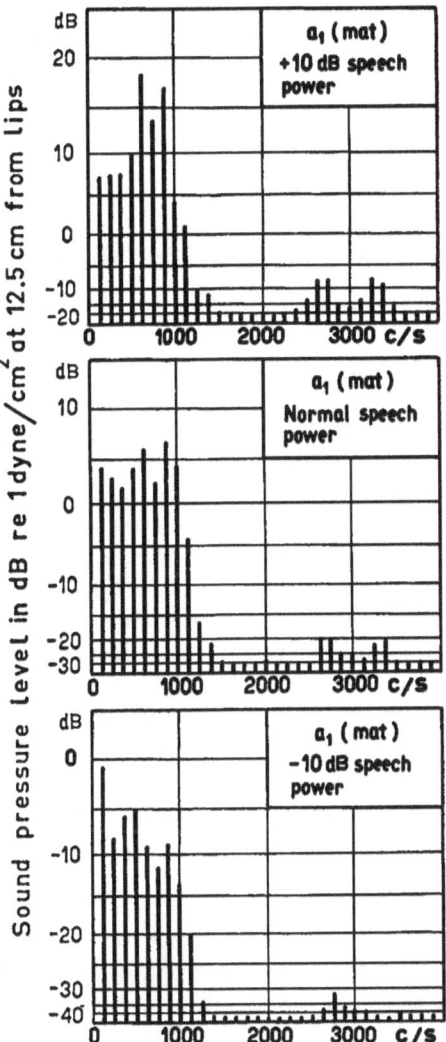

Fig. 26. Spectra of the vowel a_1 sustained at three different voice intensity levels.

the transmission properties of the vocal tract resonating system. Bandwidth changes affecting the Q-values of vocal resonances may contribute somewhat but changes in mouth-opening suggested by van den Berg to be of crucial importance appear to be of minor significance only.

Wave shape factors at varying voice level and fundamental frequency

The radical changes in overall spectrum envelope following changes in voice effort are also reflected in the peak factors and form factors as defined from ratios of peak to root mean square values and ratios of root mean square to the galvanometric mean value respectively. These wave shape factors are expressed in decibels and normalized to be zero for a sine wave. Figure 27 gives the results of some measurements on the vowel [ɑ:] in sustained form. At constant fundamental pitch there is an optimally high voice effort providing maximum peak factor and one for maximum form factor. At very low voice levels the voice fundamental dominates the spectrum and the wave shape factors are those of a sine wave. At very high voice levels the spectrum is dominated by the first formant and the number of simultaneously present harmonics of the same order of magnitude within the spectrum is then smaller than at the optimally high voice level where the voice fundamental and the first formant are of equal strength and the peak factor accordingly is larger.

The effect of a varying voice fundamental frequency at constant voice intensity (as controlled from a VU-meter) can similarly be discussed on the basis of the spectral composition. A decrease of the voice fundamental frequency will increase the number of harmonics within any formant area and thus cause an increase in the number of spectral components that add up to the peak value.

A mathematically simple example of superimposed oscillations is that of a spectrum dominated by two harmonic partials of equal amplitude. The root mean square value of the mixture is 3 dB above that of a single component, but the peak value of the two at those instances where the two partials happen to be in phase is 6 dB above that of one only. If this relation is extended to the doubling of the number of harmonics of equal amplitude there should follow an increase of the peak factor at a rate of 3 dB per halving of the voice fundamental frequency, and this is nearly the case as seen in the top diagram of the figure.

A similar reasoning can also be based on the time-function, referring to the change in the number of vocal pulses of fairly constant shape emitted per second. The second set of calculated points in the top diagram pertains to the assumption that the effective part of the vocal pulses (not necessarily the whole pulse) is a triangular wave of constant form. This approach also gives a good fit.

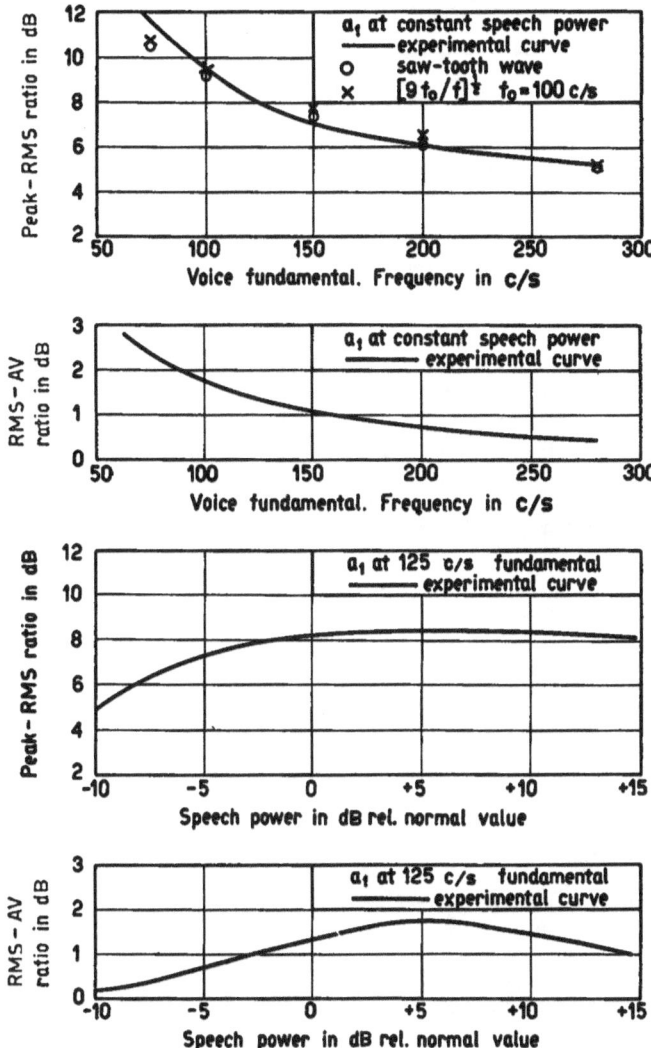

Fig. 27. Peak factor and form factor of the vowel a_1 as a function of voice fundamental frequency and voice intensity.

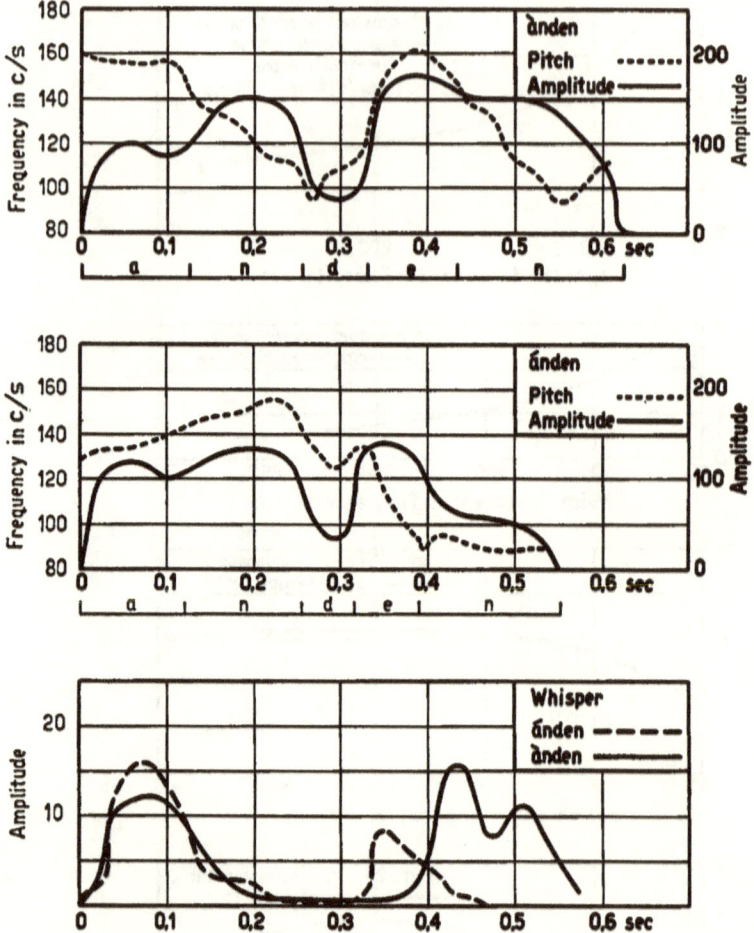

Fig. 28. Voice fundamental frequency and overall intensity of the words *ànden* (the ghost) and *ánden* (the duck) illustrating typical features of the Swedish word accent.

The normalized shape factor of a mixture of two sine waves of equal amplitude but different frequency is 1 dB, which is the same as for random noise (BERANEK, 1949). An increase of the number of harmonics of equal amplitude will increase the form factor, but the latter is always smaller than the peak factor. The peak factor and form factor of the electrical counterpart of the acoustic speech wave will apparently be highly influenced by

Acoustic Description and Classification of Phonetic Units 79

the frequency response of the particular microphone and by the frequency dependent transmission properties of any other part of the system. Thus peak factors and form factors are generally higher in the speech wave current delivered by a carbon microphone than in the current delivered by a condensor microphone. The higher shape factors typical for low voice fundamental frequencies are also typical for male voices compared to female voices.

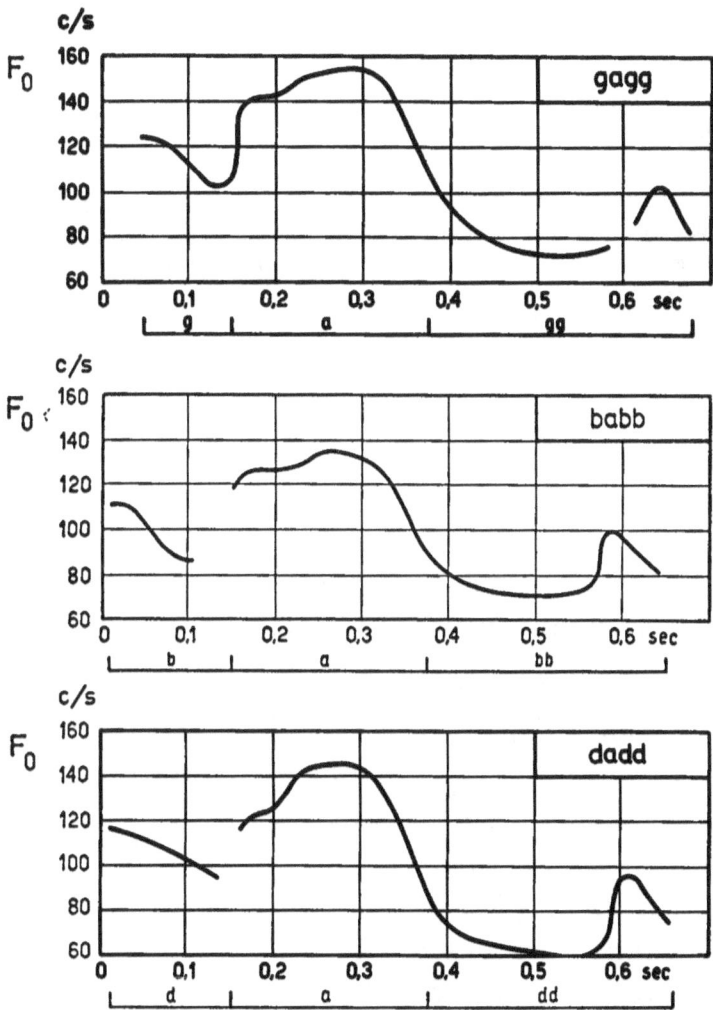

Fig. 29. Voice fundamental frequency variations in test words containing voiced stops (plosives).

Voice fundamental frequency variations in connected speech

Methods of automatic and continuous recording of voice fundamental frequency are described in an earlier report (FANT, 1957 b). Direct measurements from oscillograms will always be more accurate and are not very difficult to carry out. The examples of synchronous sound intensity and voice fundamental frequency, given in Fig. 28, pertain to the phonetically relevant distinction between the so-called one- and two-syllable word accents of Swedish, here represented by *ánden* and *ànden*, also called acute and grave word accents. These curves have been commented on earlier (FANT, 1954, 1957 b). The two-syllable accent of "riksspråk" (subject Gj-n) is characterized by the tendency of a double peaked intonation curve, a lower pitch level at the syllabic boundary, and a more pronounced second syllable, the latter characteristic retained in whispered speech. Referring to the first syllable only, the two-syllable accent is correlated with a more negative overall slope of the F_0-curve than for the one-syllable accent.

The voice fundamental frequency F_0 is essentially a free variable carrying the information on the speaker's intonation but is somewhat influenced by the articulation so that a tongue or lip movement causing a momentary closure or almost complete closure will react on the vocal cords, slowing down their speed of movement and thus increasing the period duration. This can be seen in the curves of Fig. 29 pertaining to the test words "gagg, babb, dadd". The low voice fundamental frequency during the occlusion period preceding the explosion is typical.

Bibliography

1. BACKHAUS,H: *Über die Bedeutung der Ausgleichvorgänge in der Akustik*. Z techn. Phys. *13*(1932): pp. 31—46.
2. BARCZINSKI, L, THIENHAUS, E: *Klangspektren und Lautstärke deutscher Sprachlaute*. Arch. Néer. Phon. exp. *11*(1935): pp. 47—68.
3. BERANEK, L L: *Acoustic Measurements*. New York 1949: 914 pp.
4. BERG, VAN DEN JW: *Direct and Indirect Determination of the Mean Subglottic Pressure*. Folia Phoniatrica *7*(1955): pp. 57—69.
5. BIDDULPH, R: *Short-Term Autocorrelation Analysis and Correlatograms of Spoken Digits*. J Acoust. Soc. Amer. *26*(1954): pp. 539—541.
6. BOERYD, A: *Undersökning av taleffekten (volymen) från en telefonapparat som funktion av telefonförbindelsens kvalitet*. Examensarbete i telegrafi och telefoni, KTH (Royal Institute of Technology), Stockholm 1957: 49 pp.
7. CHANG, S H, PIHL, C E, WIREN, J: *The Intervalgram as a Visual Representation of Speech Sounds*, J Acoust. Soc. Amer. *23*(1951): pp. 675—679.
8. CHIBA, T, KAJIYAMA, M: *The Vowel — its Nature and Structure*. Tokyo 1941: 235 pp.
9. DELATTRE, P, LIBERMAN, A M, COOPER, F S: *Voyelles synthétiques a deux formantes et voyelles cardinales*. Maître Phonétique *96*(1951): pp. 30—36.
10. DELATTRE, P, LIBERMAN, A M, COOPER, F S, GERSTMAN, L J: *An Experimental Study of the Acoustic Determinants of Vowel Color*. Word *8*(1952): pp. 195—210.

11. DUNN, H K: *The Calculation of Vowel Resonances and an Electrical Vocal Tract.* J Acoust. Soc. Amer. *22*(1950): pp. 740—743.

12. DUNN, H K, WHITE, S D: *Statistical Measurements on Conversational Speech.* J Acoust. Soc. Amer. *11*(1940): pp. 278—288.

13. ELERT, C C: *Svenska fonem och deras strukturella relationer.* Nordisk Sommaruniversitet 1954; Moderne videnskab, Orientering og debat *4*(1955): pp. 140—144.

14. ELERT, C C: *Bidrag till fonematisk beskrivning av svenska.* Ark. Nord. Filologi *72*(1957): pp. 35—60.

15. FANO, R M: *Short-Time Autocorrelation Functions and Power Spectra.* J Acoust. Soc. Amer. *22*(1950): pp. 546—550.

16. FANT, C G M: *Analys av de svenska vokalljuden.* L M Ericsson protokoll H/P 1035, 1948: 52 pp.

17. FANT, C G M: *Analys av de svenska konsonantljuden.* L M Ericsson protokoll H/P 1064, 1949: 139 pp.

18. FANT, C G M (1953 a): *Speech Communication Research.* IVA [Royal Swedish Academy of Engineering Sciences, Stockholm] *24*(1953): pp. 331—337.

19. FANT, C G M (1953 b): *Discussion of Paper Read by G E Peterson at the 1952 Symposium on the Applications of Communication Theory.* Publ. in Communication Theory, Ed. by W Jackson London 1953: pp. 421—424.

20. FANT, C G M: *Phonetic and Phonemic Basis for the Transcription of Swedish Word Material.* Acta Oto-Laryng., Suppl. *116*, 1954: pp. 24—29.

21. FANT, C G M: *On the Predictability of Formant Levels and Spectrum Envelopes from Formant Frequencies.* For Roman Jakobson, 's-Gravenhage 1956: pp. 109—120.

22. FANT, C G M (1957 a): *Den akustiska fonetikens grunder.* Royal Inst. Technol., Div. of Telegraphy-Telephony, Report No. 7 1957: 61 pp.

23. FANT, C G M (1957 b): *Modern Instruments and Methods for Acoustic Studies of Speech.* Royd Inst. Technol., Div. of Telegraphy-Telephony, Report No. 8 1957: 80 pp.; presented at the VIII Internat. Congr. of Linguists in Oslo 1957. (See also 1958 b).

24. FANT, C G M (1958 a): *Acoustic Theory of Speech Production.* Royal Inst. Technol., Div. of Telegraphy-Telephony, Report No. 10 1958; to be publ. by Mouton & Co., 's-Gravenhage.

25. FANT, C G M (1958 b): *Modern Instruments and Methods for Acoustic Studies of Speech.* Proc. of VIII Internat. Congr. of Linguists, Oslo 1958, and Acta polytechnica 246/1958: 84 pp.

26. FARNSWORTH, P R: *An Approach to the Study of Vocal Resonance.* J Acoust. Soc. Amer. *9*(1937): pp. 152—155.

27. FISCHER-JØRGENSEN, E: *Acoustic Analysis of Stop Consonants.* Miscellanea Phonetica *2*(1954): pp. 42—59.

28. FLANAGAN, J L: *A Speech Analyzer for a Formant-Coding Compression System.* MIT Acoust. Lab. Scientific Rep. No. 4 (AFCRC-TN-55-793), 1955: 114 pp.

29. FLANAGAN, J L (1957 a): *Estimates of the Maximum Precision Necessary in Quantizing Certain "Dimensions" of Vowel Sounds.* J Acoust. Soc. Amer. *29*(1957): pp. 533—534.

30. FLANAGAN, J L (1957 b): *Note on the Design of "Terminal-Analog" Speech Synthesizers.* J Acoust. Soc. Amer. *29*(1957): pp. 306—310.

31. FLETCHER, H: *Speech and Hearing.* New York 1929; 2nd Ed. 1953: 461 pp.

32. FRENCH, N R, STEINBERG, J C: *Factors Governing the Intelligibility of Speech Sounds.* J Acoust. Soc. Amer. *19*(1947): pp. 90—119.

33. FREYSTEDT, E: *Das Tonfrequenz-Spektrometer.* Z techn. Phys. *16*(1935): pp. 533—539.

34. GABOR, D: *Theory of Communication.* J Instn. Elect. Engrs *93*(1946): III, No. 93, pp. 429—457

35. GABOR, D: *A Summary of Communication Theory.* Proceedings of the 1952 Symposium on the Applications of Communication Theory. Publ. in Communication Theory, ed. by W Jackson, London 1953: pp. 1—24.

36. GJERDMAN, O: *Uttalsläran.* In Gjerdman—Henningsson: Svensk uttals- och vällasningslära, Stockholm 1950.

37. GJERDMAN, O: *Svensk fonetik.* Chapt. XVII in Nordisk Laerebog for Talepædagoger, Almindelig Del, Copenhagen 1954: pp. 372—394.
38. HALLE, M, HUGHES, G W, RADLEY, J P: *Acoustic Properties of Stop Consonants.* J Acoust. Soc. Amer. *29*(1957): pp. 107—116.
39. HUGGINS, W H: *A Phase Principle for Complex-Frequency Analysis and its Implications in Auditory Theory.* J Acoust. Soc. Amer. *24*(1952): pp. 582—589.
40. HUGHES, G W, HALLE, M: *Spectral Properties of Fricative Consonants.* J Acoust. Soc. Amer. *28*(1956): pp. 303—310.
41. JAKOBSON, R, FANT, C G M, HALLE, M: *Preliminaries to Speech Analysis.* MIT Acoust. Lab. Techn. Rep. No. 13 1952: 58 pp.
42. KOENIG, W: *A New Frequency Scale for Acoustic Measurements.* Bell Lab. Record *27*(1949): pp. 299—301.
43. KÜPFMÜLLER, K: *Die Systemtheorie der elektrischen Nachrichtenübertragung.* Zurich 1949: 386 pp.
44. KÅELL, Å: *Formanter för svenska språkets vokaler.* LM Ericsson protokoll H/P 885, 1943: 10 pp.
45. LAURENT, T: *Matematisk behandling av kontinuerligt inhomogena ledningar.* Tekn. Medd. K Telegrafstyrelsen 1940: pp. 113, 186.
46. LAURENT, T: *Zur Systemtheorie der Laufzeit und der Einschwingzeit in elektrischen Filtern mit Phasenverzerrung.* Arch. Elekt. Übertr. *6*(1952): pp. 91—98.
47. LAURENT, T: *Delay Time and Transient Time in Electrical Filters with Phase Distortion.* Proc. 1952 Symposium on the Applications of Communication Theory. Publ. in Communcation Theory, Ed. by W Jackson, London 1953: pp. 310—313.
48. LAURENT, T: *Telegraf- och telefonteknikens fundamentala principer.* Stockholm 1954: 194 pp.
49. LAURENT, T: *Vierpoltheorie und Frequenztransformation.* Berlin 1956: 299 pp.
50. LICKLIDER, J C R: *On the Process of Speech Perception.* J Acoust. Soc. Amer. *24*(1953): pp. 590—594.
51. MALMBERG, B: *Kort lärobok i fonetik.* Lund 1949: 188 pp.
52. MALMBERG, B: *Distinctive Features of Swedish Vowels, some Instrumental and Structural Data.* For Roman Jakobson, 's-Gravenhage 1956: pp. 316—321.
53. MALMBERG, B: *Nyare fonetiska rön och deras praktiska betydelse.* Nord. T. Döv. undervisn. 1957: pp. 53—93.
54. MEYER-EPPLER, W: *Die Schwingungsanalyse nach dem Suchton-Verfahren.* Arch. Elekt. Übertr. *4*(1950): pp. 331—338.
55. MEYER-EPPLER, W: *Übersicht über die Verfahren zur Charakterisierung aleatorischer Schallvorgänge und deren Anwendbarkeit auf die Geräuschlaute.* Z Phon. *6*(1952): pp. 269—284.
56. MILLER, R L: *Auditory Tests with Synthetic Vowels.* J Acoust. Soc. Amer. *25*(1953): pp. 114—121.
57. MOL, H, UHLENBECK, E M: *The Analysis of the Phonemes in Distinctive Features and the Process of Hearing.* Lingua *4*(1954): pp. 167—193.
58. MUNSON, W A, GARDNER, M B: *Loudness Patterns—a New Approach.* J Acoust. Soc. Amer. *22*(1950): pp. 177—190.
59. PETERSON, G E: *The Phonetic Value of Vowels.* Language *27*(1951): pp. 541—553.
60. PETERSON, G E: *The Information Bearing Elements of Speech.* J Acoust. Soc. Amer. *24*(1952): pp. 629—637.
61. PETERSON, G E, BARNEY, H L: *Control Methods Used in a Study of the Vowels.* J Acoust. Soc. Amer. *24*(1952): pp. 175—184.
62. PIPES, L A: *Applied Mathematics for Engineers and Physicists.* New York—London 1946: 731 pp.
63. POTTER, R K, KOPP, A G, GREEN, H C: *Visible Speech.* New York 1947: 441 pp.
64. POTTER, R K, STEINBERG, J C: *Toward the Specification of Speech.* J Acoust. Soc. Amer. *22*(1950) pp. 807—820.

65. POTTER, R K, et al.: *Technical Aspects of Visible Speech.* Bell Telephone System, Monograph B-1415, 1946; J Acoust. Soc. Amer. *17*(1946): 89 pp.
66. PRESTIGIACOMO, A J: *Plastic-Tape Sound Spectrograph.* Bell Telephone System, Monograph 2892, 1957; J Speech and Hearing Disorders *22*(1957): pp. 321—327.
67. ROSEN, G, STEVENS, K N, HEINZ, J M: *Dynamic Analog of the Vocal Tract.* J Acoust. Soc. Amer. *28*(1956): p. 767 (A).
68. SALINGER, H: *Zur Theorie der Frequenzanalyse mittels Suchtones.* ENT *6*(1929): pp. 293—302.
69. SOVIJÄRVI, A (1938 a): *Die gehaltenen, geflüsterten und gesungenen Vokale und Nasale der finnischen Sprache.* Helsinki 1938: 252 pp.
70. SOVIJÄRVI, A (1938 b): *Die wechselnden und festen Formanten der Vokale erklärt durch Spektrogramme und Röntgengramme der finnischen Vokale.* Proc. III Internat. Phonet. Conf. Ghent 1938, pp. 407—420.
71. STEVENS, K N: *Autocorrelation Analysis of Speech Sounds.* J Acoust. Soc. Amer. *22*(1950): pp. 769—771.
72. STEVENS, K N, KASOWSKI, S, FANT, C G M: *An electrical analog of the vocal tract.* J Acoust. Soc. Amer. *25*(1953): pp. 734—742.
73. SUND, H: *A Sound Spectrometer for Speech Analysis.* Trans. Royal Inst. Technol. 1957:112, 65 pp.
74. TARNÓCZY, T H: *The Speech Noise and its Spectrum.* Acta phys. Hungar. *7*(1957): pp. 87—106.
75. WEDENBERG, E: *Auditory Training of Deaf and Hard of Hearing Children.* Acta Oto-Laryng. Suppl. XCIV, 1951: 130 pp.
76. WEDENBERG, E: *Auditory Training of Severely Hard of Hearing Pre-School Children.* Acta Oto-Laryng. 1953: 79 pp.
77. WEIBEL, E S: *Vowel Synthesis by Means of Resonant Circuits.* J Acoust. Soc. Amer. *22*(1955): pp. 858—865.
78. VOSS, H H: *Realisierbare Tiefpässe und Bandpässe minimaler Phase mit geebneter Laufzeit und aperiodischem Einschwingverhalten.* Frequenz. *8*(1954): pp. 98—102.
79. ZINN, M K: *Network Representation of Transcendental Impedance Functions.* Bell Syst. Tech. J *31*(1952): pp. 378—404.

Chapter 4
A Note on Vocal Tract Size Factors and Nonuniform F-Pattern Scalings

Introduction

The common concept of physiologically induced differences in formant patterns when comparing males and females is that the average female formant frequencies are related to those of the male by a simple scale factor inversely proportional to the overall vocal tract length. Thus on the average the female F-pattern (F_1 F_2 F_3 etc.) is said to be scaled to about 20% higher frequencies than the average male F-pattern. Children have even higher formant frequencies than grown-up females and it is also well known that the individual size of the vocal cavities and thus of the F-pattern scale factor may vary appreciably within each age and sex category. Parallel reasoning is inherent in the common concept of perceptual invariance. Within certain limits, vowels retain their phonemic identity if formant frequency ratios are preserved. This can be judged by playing a tape or gramophone record at a somewhat higher or lower speed than normal.

The purpose of this report is to point out that the simple scale factor rule has important limitations. A range of typical and substantial deviations from this rule is concealed if the data are averaged over the whole vowel system of a language. Actually the female to male relations are typically different in the three groups of (1) rounded back vowels, (2) very open unrounded vowels, and (3) close front vowels. The main physiological determinants of the specific deviations from the average rule are that the ratio of pharynx length to mouth cavity length is greater for males than for females and that the laryngeal cavities are more developed in males.

Experimental data

In the years 1946–1947 I collected material on formant frequencies and formant amplitudes of sustained vowels uttered by 7 male and 7 female Swedish subjects of a fairly homogeneous dialectal background. These data were originally published in an internal report of the Ericsson Telephone Com-

This article originally appeared in Speech Transmission Laboratory Quarterly Progress and Status Report 4/66 (Stockholm, Sweden: Royal Institute of Technology, 1966).

Note on Vocal Tract Size Factors and Nonuniform F-Pattern Scalings

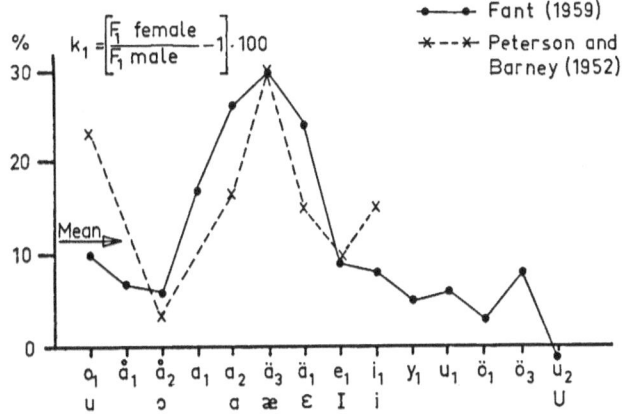
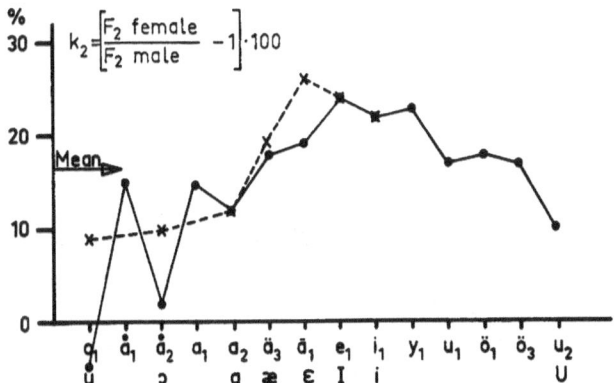
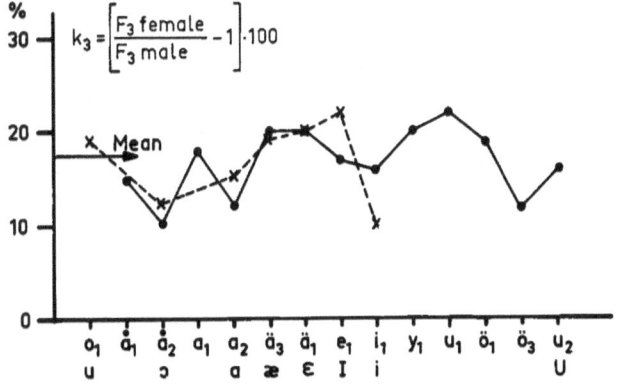

Figure 1. The average female/male formant ratio of F_1, F_2, and F_3. American English and Swedish data.

pany (Fant, 1948). A few years later the Peterson and Barney (1952) study of American English vowels was published. Their investigation at Bell Telephone Laboratories was concerned with formant data sampled within test words of an h+vowel+d structure. It is the most extensive collection of formant data ever published, based on 33 men, 28 women, and 15 children. This American English study and my Swedish study are the only reliable sources of data on both formant frequencies and amplitudes.

At an information theory symposium in London in 1952, I gave a brief review of the general conformity of the Peterson and Barney data with my own data (Fant, 1953), in particular with respect to the average female to male relations in various vowel categories. This correlation was also mentioned in my monograph on acoustic analysis and synthesis of speech (Fant, 1959) in connection with a review of the material on Swedish vowels and consonants.

Here follows a more detailed attempt at physiological-acoustic interpretation of how female F-patterns differ from those of men.

Figure 1 illustrates the relation of female to male formant frequencies of Swedish vowels and comparable American English vowels selected according to an approximate F-pattern match.

The basic data are included in Table 1.

The Swedish vowels are denoted by a technical alphabet with index 1 for long vowels and 2 for short vowels and 3 for long pre-r allophones. The American English vowels are denoted by their IPA symbols.

It can be seen that English and Swedish data correlate well. The first formant "sex factor" k_1 displays a pronounced maximum of 30% in the very open back and front vowels [a] and [æ] and a minimum of the order of 5% in the rounded, half-open back vowels [o] and [ɔ]. Close front vowels and especially close rounded front vowels also show a low k_1.

The second formant "sex factor" k_2 is significantly lower in back vowels than in front vowels. Some irregularity in the back vowel region can be ascribed to the inherent spread of the original data. The k_3-data does not show equally prominent vowel class dependency. An exception is the relatively low k_3 of [ɔ]. The k_n-average of the entire ensemble of Swedish vowels is 11.5% in F_1, 16.5% in F_2, and 17.5% in F_3.

Similar trends are found in a comparison of the American English male and children data, as can be seen from Figure 2. The children's formants are about 35%–40% higher than those of the male group. The extreme range within any of the formants and any of the vowels are the $k_1 = 20\%$ of [ɔ] and the $k_1 = 54\%$ of [æ]. The k_n-curves of the children are fairly parallel to those of the women and about 20% higher. It can accordingly be concluded

Note on Vocal Tract Size Factors and Nonuniform F-Pattern Scalings

Table 1.

(A)	(S)	F_1 (Hz)	k_1 (Hz)	F_2 (Hz)	k_2 (Hz)	F_3 (Hz)	k_3 (Hz)
	o_1	310	10	710	−5	2230	
u		300	23	870	9	2240	19
	å$_1$	402	7	708	5	2460	15
	å$_2$	487	6	825	2	2560	10
ɔ		570	3.5	840	9.5	2410	12
	a$_1$	582	17	940	15	2480	18
	a$_2$	680	26	1070	12	2520	12
a		730	16.5	1090	12	2440	15
	ä$_3$	606	30	1550	18	2450	20
æ		660	30	1720	19	2410	18.5
	ä$_1$	438	24	1795	19	2385	20
ɛ		530	15	1840	26.5	2480	20
	e$_1$	334	9	2050	24	2510	17
I		390	10	1990	24.5	2550	20
	i$_1$	256	8	2066	22	2960	16
i		270	15	2290	22	3010	10
	y$_1$	257	5	1928	24	2420	20
	ʉ$_1$	283	6	1633	17	2140	22
	ö$_1$	363	3	1690	18	2200	19
	u$_2$	416	−1	1070	10	2315	16
U		440	7	1020	14	2240	19.5
	ö$_3$	525	8	1103	17	2430	12
Λ		640	19	1190	17.5	2390	16.5
ɚ		490	2	1350	21.5	1690	16

American English (Peterson and Barney, 1952)   (A)
Swedish (Fant, 1959)   (S)

$$k_n = \left(\frac{F_n, \text{female}}{F_n, \text{male}} - 1\right) \cdot 100\%$$

that while children's F-patterns are scaled fairly proportionally relative to females, this is not the case when the females are compared with the men.

Physiological interpretation

The major anatomical constraints on vowel articulation that can be correlated with these findings are the relatively greater pharynx length and more pronounced laryngeal cavities of grown-up males compared with females and children (see Chiba and Kajiyama, 1941, pp. 188–193). These authors state that in a girl of eight years the length of the mouth cavity, between the incisor and the pharynx wall, is 30% shorter than that of a grown-up male while the length of the girl's pharynx is 56% shorter than that of the male. Chiba and Kajiyama (1941) also exemplify the overall vocal tract length in relative numbers as 1.0 for males, 0.87 for females, 0.80 for a boy of nine, and 0.70 for the girl of eight.

Now, in a first attempt to explain the systematic trends in Figure 1 it is first apparent that formants produced with a typical double Helmholtz resonator configuration as, for example, F_1 and F_2 of rounded back vowels, are less critically dependent on the overall vocal tract length than other formants. A shorter overall length could be compensated for by more narrow lip opening and a more narrow tongue hump passage. Thus there results the low k_1 and k_2 of these vowels as will be discussed in more detail at the end of this article.

In other vowels the vocal cavities behave more like standing wave resonators. If the tract approximated a uniform tube, as in the neutral vowel, a reduction in length by 18% would cause all formants to rise by the same amount. The American English [ʌ] conforms fairly well to this pattern in terms of the observed k_1, k_2, and k_3.

The extent to which a small reduction in length of any of the major vocal tract cavities or constrictions affects the F-pattern is known from my earlier work (Fant, 1960, 1965). The percentage of relative increase in formant frequencies associated with the removal of one-half centimeter of the pharynx of the vowel [i] is (see Fant, 1960, Table 2.33–4 on p. 120), 3.5% in F_1, 4.7% in F_2, and 0.5% in F_3. Similarly a removal of one-half centimeter section of the frontal mouth cavity of [i] results in a 1.3% increase in F_1, a 0.2% increase in F_2, and a 6.1% increase in F_3.

Inversely, the observed $k_2 = 22\%$ of [i] of the Swedish data above would correspond to a $22/2 \cdot 4.7 = 2.3$ cm shorter pharynx for the females compared to males. Similarly, noting the close association of F_3 with the mouth cavity and working from $k_3 = 16\%$ of [i] we arrive in a $16/2 \cdot 6.1 = 1.3$ cm shorter female mouth cavity. The extremely small contributions of mouth

Note on Vocal Tract Size Factors and Nonuniform F-Pattern Scalings 89

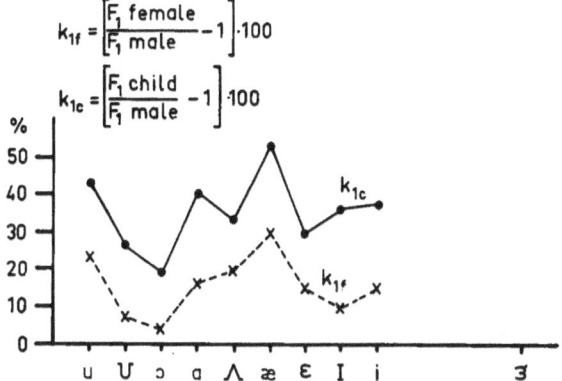
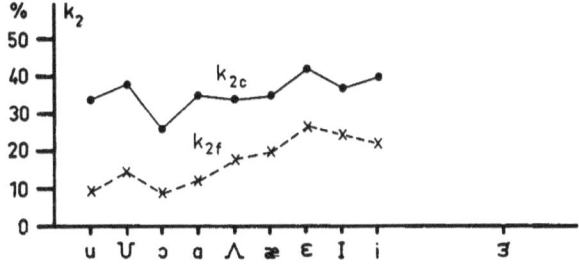
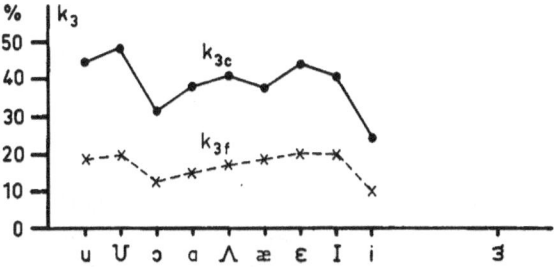

Figure 2. The average child/male formant ratio. American English data.

cavity length to F_2 and of pharynx cavity length to F_3 have been neglected in the calculations above.

In my earlier work I accordingly referred to F_2 of [i] as pharynx dependent and F_3 of [i] as mouth-cavity dependent. These "formant-cavity affiliations" are apparent in a two-tube simplified model of the vowel [i] comprising a wide back tube and a narrow and somewhat shorter front tube. F_2 is associated with a half wavelength resonance of the back tube and F_3 with a half wavelength resonance of the narrow front tube. The lengths of these tubes matching the average Swedish male [i] would be

$$l_b = \frac{c}{2F_2} = \frac{35,300}{2 \cdot 2070} = 8.5 \text{ cm back tube}$$

and

$$l_f = \frac{c}{2F_3} = \frac{35,300}{2 \cdot 2960} = 6 \text{ cm front tube.}$$

In the next degree of approximation the mouth is conceived of as a symmetrical double horn with the two connecting narrow throats in the center of the mouth. Here again F_3 is associated with the basic "one-quarter wavelength" resonance of the front horn which is the same as the half wavelength resonance of the entire mouth.

It should be stressed that the above estimates of a 2.3 cm shorter female pharynx and a 1.3 cm shorter mouth cavity are only approximate since the coefficients were derived from a Russian articulation and are valid for small perturbations only.

For the normal male the total mouth cavity length from the incisors to the back pharynx wall is of the order of 8 cm. This value is appropriately 2 cm greater than the front cavity length of the vowel [i] above. The total pharynx length from the soft palate to the level of the glottis is of the order of 8.5 cm. According to the calculations above, the corresponding female measures would be 8 cm − 1.3 cm = 6.7 cm and 8.5 cm − 2.3 cm = 6.2 cm.

How do these inferred data compare to actual physiological data? From material collected by the radiologist Paul Edholm of Karolinska Sjukhuset, Stockholm, the details of which have not been published, I have collected the following measurements. A male articulating the vowel [i] had a pharynx length from glottis to the soft palate of 9.1 cm, and a mouth length from the incisors to the back pharynx wall of 8.25 cm. The corresponding female values were 7.0 cm and 7.0 cm, respectively. Thus the female pharynx was 2.1 cm shorter than the male pharynx and the female mouth 1.25 cm shorter than

Table 2. Observed and calculated data for the vowel [i]

	F_1 (Hz)		F_2 (Hz)		F_3 (Hz)	
	obs.	calc.	obs.	calc.	obs.	calc.
male	225	156	2060	2060	2960	3290
female	240	247	2600	2650	3550	2900

the male mouth, which conforms well with the previously inferred values. Furthermore, a detailed mapping of the vocal tract area functions involved provided the basis for calculating the vocal resonances of the subject's [i] which are shown in Table 2. There is a specially good agreement in terms of F_2. The ratio of male to female pharynx lengths $9.1/7.0 = 1.30$ is close to the observed $2650/2060 = 1.26$ ratio and the calculated 1.28 ratio of female F_2 to male F_2. The observed female F_3 divided by the observed male F_3 is $3550/2960 = 1.20$ and the corresponding calculated ratio is $3290/2900 = 1.14$; these are to be compared with the ratio of male to female mouth lengths $8.25/7 = 1.18$. In terms of absolute measures projected on the simple closed tube model referred to above, a male pharynx length of 9.1 cm should provide an F_2 of $35,300/2 \cdot 9.1 = 1940$ Hz which is only 6% below the value of the complete calculation.

Chiba and Kajiyama (1941) do not provide directly comparable measures. However, their data on the mouth and pharynx length of a girl of eight compared with a grown-up male are expressed as a mouth cavity scale factor 0.77 and a pharynx scale factor 0.64 which reflect the same tendency.

Now returning to the average Swedish male and female data and given the particular $\Delta l_p = 2.3$ cm shorter female pharynx and $\Delta l_m = 1.3$ cm shorter female mouth, what is their differential effect on the formant patterns of vowels other than [i]? The tabulated data on p. 120 of Fant (1960) provides the necessary basis for such a check:

$$k_n = \left[\Delta l_m \left(\frac{dF_n}{dl_m} \right) + \Delta l_p \left(\frac{dF_n}{dl_p} \right) \right] \frac{1}{F_n}.$$

For the Russian vowel [e] corresponding to the Swedish [ä₁] we get

$k_1 = 20\%, k_2 = 20\%, k_3 = 19\%$

which is close to the observed

$k_1 = 24\%, k_2 = 19\%, k_3 = 20\%$.

Inserting the perturbation coefficients of Russian [a] for use with Swedish [a] we calculate

$k_1 = 28.5\%, k_2 = 23\%, k_3 = 9.5\%$

which is to be compared with the observed

$k_1 = 26\%, k_2 = 12\%, k_3 = 12\%.$

The relatively high k_1 is predicted as well as a low k_3 but the predicted k_2 is too high.

For the rounded back vowel [ɔ] the simple length perturbation leads to much higher k-values, 27%, 24%, and 19% compared with the observed 6%, 2%, and 10%, respectively. Also the k_1 of [i] comes out at 19.5% compared with the $k_1 = 8\%$ observed.

The vocal tract filtering may be approximated by a simple lumped element (Helmholtz) resonator for F_1 of [i] and double Helmholtz resonator for F_1 and F_2 of [u], [o], and [ɔ]. The general formula for such a resonator of volume V, orifice length l, and orifice area A is

$$F_r = \frac{c}{2\pi}\sqrt{\frac{A}{l \cdot V}}.$$

If all dimensions are linearly scaled by one and the same factor k, the resonance frequency is found to be F_r/k, which is the same effect as in standing wave resonances. If we assume that the length of the resonator neck (main tongue hump constriction and lip constriction) is the same for two speaker categories while all other dimensions (cavity length, cavity lateral width, and orifice effective diameter) are scaled by the same factor k we arrive at a resonance frequency of $F_r/k^{1/2}$. This scaling conforms with the observed k_1 of close front vowels and of rounded back vowels which are smaller than the average. The above physiological explanation is only one variant of many possible combinations. The low k_1 of the above discussed vowel category could also be the result of an attempt to tune F_1 closer to the male reference by decreasing the orifice areas A by more than k^2.

These results may be summarized as follows:

1. The scale factor relating average female formant frequencies to those of men is a function of the particular class of vowels. The American English vowel data display the same vowel category dependency of this factor as the Swedish data.

2. The female-to-male scale factor is of the order of 18% averaged over the whole vowel system. The typical deviations from this rule are:
(a) The first and second formants of rounded back vowels have relatively low scale factors;
(b) This is also the case with the first formant scale factor of any close or highly rounded vowel, i.e. high front vowels;
(c) Very open front or back vowels display a first formant "sex factor" k_1 which is substantially higher than the average.

3. These findings conform with anatomical constraints of the average female vocal tract. The particular scaling from male to female tract reduces the pharynx length more than the length of the mouth. Other differences may also contribute,* for example the relatively small female laryngeal cavities. More detailed anatomical studies and calculations are needed.

4. The scaling of children's data from female data comes closer to a simple factor independent of vowel class.

These female/male departures from a uniform scaling are of some interest when attempting to normalize formant data. It is not within the scope of the present article to discuss their perceptual implications. They may not have a very crucial importance for the phonemic identity of perceived vowels in connected speech but are undoubtedly of interest as speaker category determinants.

References

Chiba, T. and M. Kajiyama (1941). *The Vowel—Its Nature and Structure*, Tokyo.

Fant, G. (1948). "Analys av de svenska vokalljuden," L M Ericsson protokoll H/P 1035.

Fant, G. (1953). "Discussion of Paper Read by G. E. Peterson at the 1952 Symposium on the Applications of Communication Theory," *Communication Theory*, London, pp. 421–424.

Fant, G. (1959). "Acoustic Analysis and Synthesis of Speech with Applications to Swedish," *Ericsson Technics* 15, pp. 3–108. [Reprinted in part in chapter 3 of this volume.]

Fant, G. (1960). *Acoustic Theory of Speech Production*, 's-Gravenhage; second edition, 1970.

Fant, G. (1965). "Formants and Cavities," *Proceedings of the 5th International Congress on Phonetic Sciences, Münster 1964*, Basel, pp. 120–141.

Peterson, G. E. and H. L. Barney (1952). "Control Methods Used in a Study of the Vowels," *J. Acoust. Soc. Am.*, 24 pp. 175–184.

* It has been suggested by Sven Öhman that a proportionally larger female mouth opening is a factor to consider.

Chapter 5
Formant Frequencies of Swedish Vowels

Introduction

The purpose of our study has been to collect reference material on formant frequencies of Swedish vowels. Our previous reference, Fant (1959), pertains to a study at the Ericsson Telephone Company in 1946-1948. In that early study, vowels were sustained for a time of 4 seconds. This was necessary in order to perform a sweep frequency analysis. The obvious drawback was that the subjects could have difficulties in keeping a steady phonation and that the results might be more representative of singing than of speech. It is, accordingly, high time for the production of a more suitable reference. The present study is intended as a contribution to the collection of data for this purpose. Additional data on female and childrens' speech are needed. A limitation of the present study is that it includes long vowels only.

Data sampling

A group of 24 male students at the Royal Institute of Technology who took the course in Speech Communication in 1967 read a list of isolated long vowels in Swedish orthography noted as /o//å//a//ä//e//i//y//u//ö/ with about 1.5 second intervals between the sounds. The IPA correspondence of these alphabetic spelling forms are [u:][o:][ɑ:][æ:][e:][i:][y:][ʉ:][ø:]. Formant frequencies were measured from wide-filter spectrograms sampled at a time location of ¼ of the vowel length from the onset. An exception to this rule was made for the [u:] and [ʉ:] which were sampled at ¼ of the vowel length from the end of the vowel. The reason for making this exception was that the first part of a vowel [u:] may come very close to a vowel [o:] whereas the [u:] typically displays a downshift of both F_1 and F_2 or at least of F_1 during the course of the vowel as the result of a lip-closing gesture. The rela-

---

This article originally appeared in Speech Transmission Laboratory Quarterly Progress and Status Report 4/1969 (Stockholm, Sweden: Royal Institute of Technology, 1969).
   It was written with G. Henningsson and U. Stålhammar. Miss Henningsson was a part time employee in 1967-1968 and she carried out a main part of the data sampling. U. Stålhammar conducted the listening test for pronunciation control.

tion of the vowel [ʉ:] to [ø:] is similar. In the first part of the vowel they contrast less than at the end of the vowel where the lip-closing gesture of [ʉ:] accounts for a falling F_1 and F_2 transition. The vowels [i:] and [y:] have a tendency to be diphthongized with a closing gesture of the tongue toward the hard palate which causes a rise in F_3 at constant F_2. The contrast between [y:] and [ʉ:] would accordingly have been accentuated if we had sampled [y:] at the end just as [ʉ]. At the same time, however, the contrast between [y:] and [i:] would have become smaller.

This reasoning illustrates the dilemma encountered when choosing a sampling convention. An alternative would have been to sample at time locations where the pattern appears to be maximally close to that of an articulatory extreme which would imply the end part and not the beginning of [i:] and [y:].

Although [i:][y:][ʉ:] and [u:], that is, all the long Swedish vowels with extreme low F_1, generally are articulated with some degree of diphthongization as described above (see also Fant, 1968, 1969a), there exist considerable individual variations with respect to the extent and course of the gesture. Judging from the spectrograms, the typical pattern includes a terminating phase back to a less constricted articulation with a weak or breathy voice or merely an unvoiced friction. Some subjects have a more stationary pattern throughout the vowel. In these cases the observed patterns are fairly close to those considered to be typical for the particular vowels, according to the sampling conventions adopted here.

Results and discussion

Mean values of formant frequencies and durations are given in Table 1. The criteria for duration was the visible appearance of F_1 in the spectrogram. The general tendency of constant vowel duration noted in Fant (1969b) is apparent. Thus there is no significant tendency for open vowels to be longer than close vowels. On the contrary, there could be an opposite tendency. Thus the [y:] was on the average 3.5% longer than other vowels. The small differences observed could have been influenced by the sequential order in the reading which was not randomized. The general tendency, however, appears to be that isolated vowels are timed by a constant neural phonatory control pattern independent of articulation and possibly also independent of the relative degree of diphthongization of close vowels.*

* In a separate study U. Stålhammar and I. Karlsson (1972) have found a definite tendency of [a:] being shorter than [i:] in context-free articulations. These measurements pertain to boundaries not limited to the baseline voicing, i.e., at any formant carrying visible energy.

Table 1. Formant frequencies and durations

Vowel		Present study spoken vowels					Fant (1959) 4 sec duration			
IPA	STA	F_1 (Hz)	F_2 (Hz)	F_3 (Hz)	F_4 (Hz)	D (ms)	F_1 (Hz)	F_2 (Hz)	F_3 (Hz)	F_4 (Hz)
[u:]	o_1	290	595	2330	3260	390	310	730	2230	3300
[o:]	$å_1$	390	690	2415	3160	410	400	710	2460	3150
[a:]	a_1	600	925	2540	3320	410	580	940	2480	3290
[æ:]	$ä_3$	625	1720	2500	3440	410	610	1550	2450	3400
[ɛ:]	$ä_1$	505	1935	2540	3370		440	1795	2385	3415
[e:]	e_1	345	2250	2850	3540	400	335	2050	2510	3400
[i:]	i_1	255	2190	3150	3730	410	255	2065	2960	3400
[y:]	y_1	260	2060	2675	3310	425	260	1930	2420	3300
[ʉ:]	u_1	285	1640	2250	3250	410	285	1635	2140	3310
[ø:]	$ö_1$	380	1730	2290	3325	410	365	1690	2200	3390

Before the final averages of formant frequencies were calculated we discarded vowel samples which according to a control listening appeared to depart from a standard Swedish pronunciation. A comparison with earlier data from Fant (1959) included in Table 1 shows that the formant data of [u:][o:][a:] as well as [ø:] and [ʉ:] do not differ much. In the new data F_2 and F_3 of [i:][e:][æ:] and [y:] are 100–350 Hz higher than in the earlier data. Since overall vocal tract length provides the scale factor, we might be faced with a difference in the mean vocal tract size of the two groups. This explanation, however, is not very likely. A calculation of the individual scale factor for each speaker according to a formula* for an average F_3,

$$F_{3av} = \frac{F_{3ø} + F_{3e} + F_{3æ} + F_{3i} + F_{2i}}{5}, \tag{1}$$

gave a mean for all 24 speakers of $F_{3av} = 2590$ Hz compared with $F_{3av} = 2440$ Hz for the Fant (1959) data. The earlier study included seven male subjects. In the new study the standard deviation of F_{3av} among speakers was 5.2% or 135 Hz and only 30 Hz with respect to the mean of the group which accordingly should be rather representative.

A more probable explanation can be found by considering the sustained articulation in the early work as more typical of singing than of speaking.

* In this connection it was noted that a simple average of F_2 and F_3 of the vowel [e:] can serve as an approximate measure of F_{3av} which is 2% below the value calculated from Eq. (1), or close to 2550 Hz.

It is hard to sustain a vowel for 4 seconds without adopting a singing mode. Most of the subjects were, in fact, amateur singers. In the study by Sundberg (1968) the subjects tested in a singing mode showed 100–250 Hz lower F_2 and F_3 of [i:][e:][æ:] and [y:] than in speaking, which is of the same order of magnitude as the differences between the earlier and the new vowel data. These observations are strong evidence for the assumption that the observed differences are due to a speaking versus a singing mode rather than to differences in vocal tract average size. A lowering of the larynx is one means of increasing the overall length of the vocal tract which is a characteristic of the singing mode (Sundberg, 1968, 1969).

We shall next discuss the formant data as a basis of phonetic contrasts. Given the vowels as points in a multidimensional space we are concerned with the absolute location of these points and the multivalued vectors from each point to its neighbor's. With the physical dimensions limited to F_1 and F_2 a plotting of all the subjects displays an overlap of vowel regions which is much reduced if F_3 is included.

In our data we had a few cases of ambiguities such as that of one subject's [y:] having approximately the same F_1, F_2, and F_3, and even F_4 as a second speaker's [e:]. In these cases an inspection of the spectrograms most often revealed an erroneous formant measurement or a sampling at a less representative point within the vowel. Remaining ambiguities could always be removed by reference to the speaker's average F_3, that is, to his scale factor. Any subject thus preserves an invariance within his own vowel space. This implies that within his ensemble of vowels there is no confusion but that two vowels phonemically different and uttered by different subjects still could have been heard as phonetically the same when listened to out of context. This was not the case in our study but remains an interesting possibility to be investigated.

It is clear, however, that there is more information within an isolated vowel than merely the F-pattern, for example, F_0 and formant bandwidths. An important cue often present in the maximally close vowels [i:][y:][ʉ:] and [u:] is, as already noted, a diphthongization. The Swedish [e:] is rather close to [i:] and [y:] in terms of F_1 but there should always be a lower F_1 in the maximally close phase of [i:] and [y:] than in [e:]. It also seems possible that a correction for F_0 could remove an F_1 ambiguity in the sense of a positive correlation between F_0 and F_1 in a distribution with respect to speakers of different size factors (Fant, 1959). In the present data several exceptions were found from this average trend, that is, speakers with high F_0 and low F_{3av} or low F_0 and high F_{3av}.

To what extent are distances between formants more obvious cues than their absolute frequencies? According to Table 1 one apparent pattern aspect of the front vowels [e:][ɛ:][y:][ʉ:] and [ø:] is that $F_3 - F_2$ is close to 600 Hz but is almost 1000 Hz for [i:]. Also [i:] has a higher F_4 than any other vowel. This F_4 feature, however, was not observed in the earlier Fant (1959) data. The low F_3 of [ʉ:] and [ø:] close to F_2 is associated with a high $F_4 - F_3$ of the order of 1000 Hz for these vowels whereas F_4-F_3 of [y:] averages 650 Hz.

Thus, typically [e:] and [y:] are characterized by equidistant approximately 650 Hz spacings of F_2, F_3, and F_4 with higher bandwidths for [e:] than for [y:] and 200 Hz higher mean value of the F_2, F_3, F_4 group in [e:] than in [y:]. The vowel [i:] has the largest $F_4 - F_2$ span and the largest $F_3 - F_2$ of all vowels, and F_3 is typically closer to F_4 than to F_2. In [ɛ:] and [æ:] F_3 is somewhat closer to F_2 than to F_4 and in [ʉ:] and [ø:] F_3 is much closer to F_2 than to F_4.

The perceptual importance of these pattern aspects is not known. It appears that in female and children's voices the relative role of individual formants may differ while an overall pattern aspect, yet to be defined, could be similar. Within the group of male voices there also exist variations especially in the dynamic pattern of [y:]. Some speakers produced the [y:] without diphthongization and some among these had an F_3 closer to F_2 than to F_4. The transitional y-patterns all showed a rising F_3 while F_4 could be level or slightly falling contrary to the [i:] transitions where F_4 would be level or rising.

It is known that the phonetic interpretation of a vowel within certain limits is rather insensitive to variations in the amplitude of a single formant and to shifts in the spectrum level of F_2 and higher formants considered as a group. However, a shift up in frequency of F_4 may have the effect of concentrating the perceptual importance of the upper part of the spectrum to $F_?$ and F_2 providing F_4 does not have an excessively high amplitude. Similarly F_2 of [i:] appears to be of rather small perceptual importance.

In this connection one could reinterpret a finding of Fujimura (1967) as follows. In his 3-formant synthesis he found that an increase in the separation of F_3 and F_2 retaining their geometric mean would cause a shift of the response from [y:] to [ʉ:]. However, a small distance between F_3 and F_2 is more typical of [ʉ:] than of [y:] according to our data. It seems probable that F_3 of the Fujimura stimuli carried the role of F_4 in natural speech while his F_2 might substitute F_2 and F_3 of human speech.

There remains much to be learned concerning how various spectrum pattern aspects influence phonetic identification. One possible model of perception of F_2 and higher formants of front vowels would be to place the primary importance on some kind of mean frequency (Fant, 1969a). In the second approximation we would have to consider the frequency width of this higher group and perhaps also relative formant distances as that of F_3 with respect to F_2 and F_4. Two-formant synthesis now being carried out by Carlson and Granström may throw some light on these problems.

References

Fant, G. (1959). "Acoustic Analysis and Synthesis of Speech with Applications to Swedish," *Ericsson Technics* 15, pp. 3–108. [Reprinted in part in Chapter 3 of this volume.]

Fant, G. (1968). "Analysis and Synthesis of Speech Processes," in *Manual of Phonetics*, ed. by B. Malmberg, Amsterdam, pp. 173–277.

Fant, G. (1969a). "Distinctive Features and Phonetic Dimensions," STL-QPSR 2–3/1969, pp. 1–18. [Reprinted as Chapter 11 of this volume.]

Fant, G. (1969b). "Stops in CV-Syllables," STL-QPSR 4/1969, pp. 1–25. [Reprinted as Chapter 7 of this volume.]

Fujimura, O. (1967). "On the Second Spectral Peak of Front Vowels: A Perceptual Study of the Role of the Second and Third Formants," *Language and Speech* 10, pp. 181–193.

Stålhammar, U. and I. Karlsson (1972). "A Phonetic Approach to ASR," paper 10 in Conference Record of the 1972 Conference on Speech Communication and Processing, AFCRL, Bedford, Mass., IEEE Cat. No. 72 CHO 596-7 AE.

Sundberg, J. (1968). "Formant Frequencies of Bass Singers," STL-QPSR 1/1968, pp. 1–6.

Sundberg, J. (1969). "Articulatory Differences Between Spoken and Sung Vowels in Singers," STL-QPSR 1/1969, pp. 33–46.

Chapter 6
Consonant Confusions in English and Swedish

Introduction

Our study was initiated with three questions in mind.
What is the relative importance of various cues underlying a specific phonemic distinction?
What are the rough perceptual distances between a set of consonants?
Are English consonants more susceptible to distortion than Swedish consonants?
Confusion tests can provide some insight in all the three problems.

For evaluation of cues we need a set of varied and highly selective distortions. The perceptual distances should in general be defined for a situation without distortion but can also be defined with reference to some specific type of distortion. In the latter case it is of course necessary to state whether subjects have acquired learning under the specific conditions or not. The third question, whether any language is more difficult than others to perceive under specific conditions of distortion, has no simple answer either. In a rhyme test the contextual redundancy is minimal. This is a suitable starting point.

In order to gain some insight into this problem and some experience in methodology we designed a confusion test limited to one subject only who served both as speaker and listener. Our subject (HW), a teacher of English, is bilingual in the sense that he has, and has had, equal command of British English and Swedish since childhood. The purpose of this pilot study was to analyze the observed confusions in terms of the specific distortions involved and to interpret them in relation to spectrographic data.

Experiment

The experimental approach was that once introduced by Miller and Nicely (1955). We constructed nonsense syllable rhyme words of CV structure with $V = [a:]$. The set of words for the English test comprised all 22 possible

This article originally appeared in Speech Transmission Laboratory Quarterly Progress and Status Report 4/1969 (Stockholm, Sweden: Royal Institute of Technology, 1969).
It was written with B. Lindblom and A. de Serpa-Leitão.

consonant phonemes in initial position plus the voiced, flat, continuant fricative /ʒ/. The Miller and Nicely study was limited to 16 consonants. In the Swedish material we used all 17 possible initial single consonants.

For each language 10 randomized word lists were compiled. After recording in an anechoic chamber the entire speech material was submitted to the following processing:
1. No distortion.
2. Low-pass filtering at 2000 Hz with a high quality filter (60 dB per half octave).
3. White noise added to give a S/N of 13 dB. The speech materials were played over a high-quality loudspeaker to the subject now serving as a listener.

Hi-Fi condition

It is of interest to note that the performance under condition (1) was not 100%. The Swedish palatal continuant [ç] was once heard as the retroflex continuant [ʃ]. In the English material 3 out of 10 interdental unvoiced fricatives [θ] were heard as [f] and one such confusion occurred in the corresponding voiced pairs of [ð] and [v]. These distinctions are not very effectively maintained in speech.

LP filtering

Under condition (2) of low-pass filtering at 2000 Hz (see Figure 1), there is a clear tendency that dental stops and fricatives are almost never recognized as such. In the Swedish and the English material [t] is heard as [k] to almost 100%, as can be seen in the confusion matrices of Figures 1 and 2. In Swedish [d] is accordingly heard as [g] while the English [d] proves to be resistant. None of the Swedish [s] sounds nor the English [s] and [z] are heard as such, the Swedish [s] being confused with [ʃ], whereas in English [s] is mostly confused with [θ], and [z] with [ð]. The confusion of [ð] with [v] and [θ] with [f] is also typical.

The spectrograms of Figures 3, 4, and 5 provide a basis for discussion of confusion risks. Figure 3 illustrates the effect of filtering on the Swedish unvoiced stops. The removal of energy above 2000 Hz curtails the burst spectrum of [t] in [ta] so that it resembles that of the [k] in [ka] before filtering. The [k] loses very little of its energy by the filtering and the vowel [a] is also essentially intact since the loss of its third and higher formants has a very small perceptual effect. The F_2 transitional cues are almost identical for [ta] and [ka] and we infer that, normally, the burst provides a distinguishing cue.

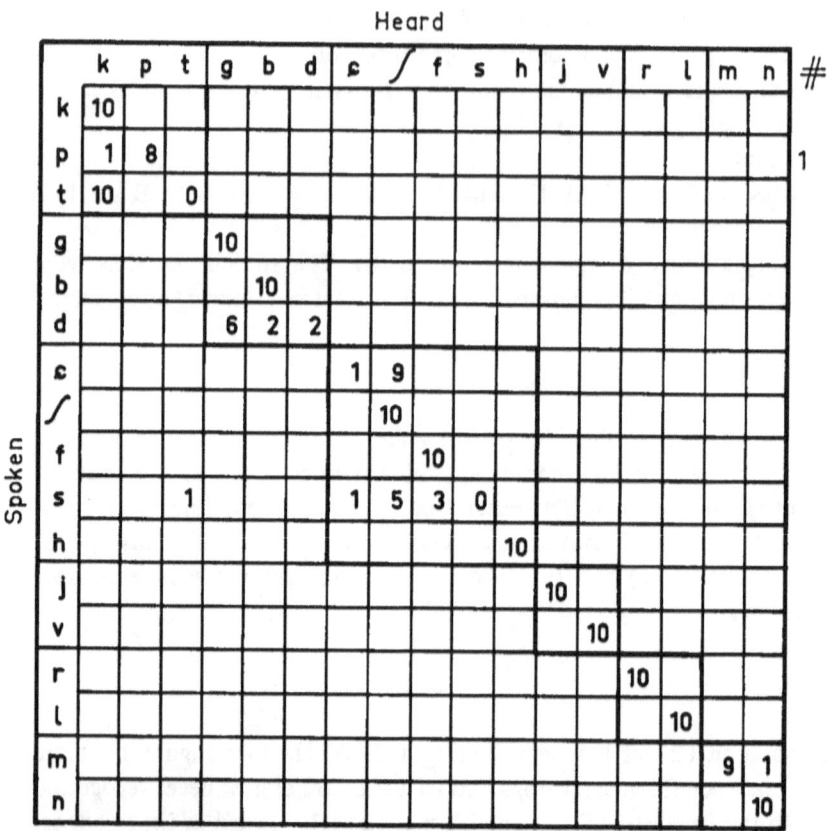

Figure 1. Confusion matrix of Swedish consonants in a Ca frame. One subject serving both as talker and listener. Low-pass filtering at 2000 Hz.

This is a methodological example of how filtering may be applied as a means of separating transitional and segmental cues.

However, the spectrograms indicate that there is some small difference in the [ka] and [ta] after low-pass filtering which may serve as a means of discrimination after sufficient learning.

A study of the unvoiced English fricatives in Figure 4 reveals an approximate similarity of [ʃa] and [sa] in terms of transitional cues as well as in terms of intensity of the noise segment. As is well known, they differ in the noise spectrum which has a lower boundary of 2000 Hz in [ʃa] and 4000 Hz in [sa]. The [fa] and the [θa] both have very weak noise segments, the [θa]

Subject H.W., English LP 2000

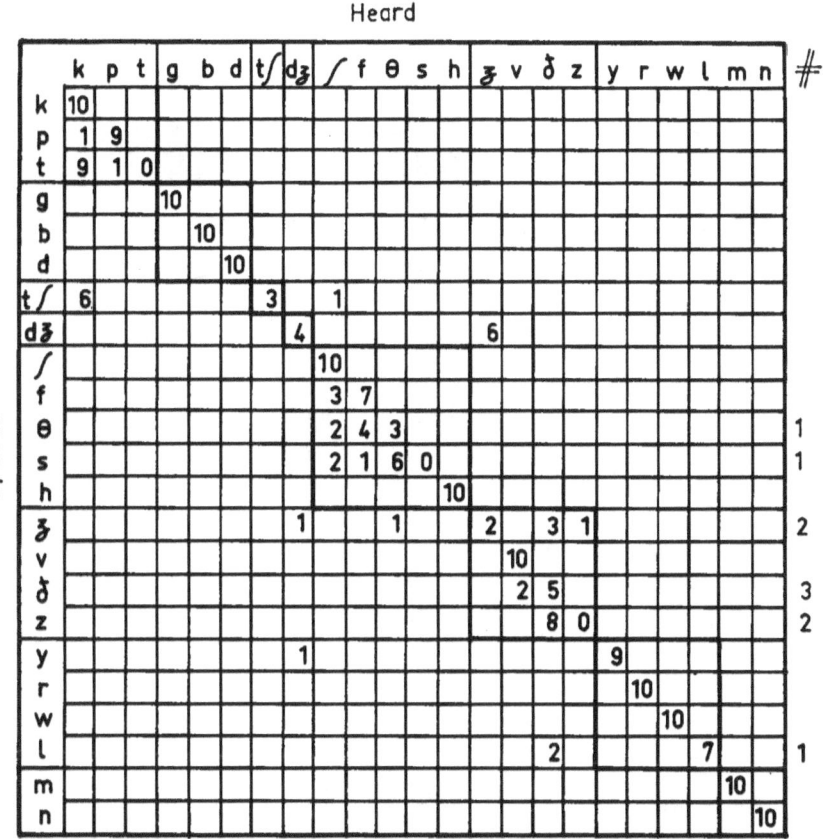

Figure 2. Confusion matrix of English consonants. Conditions same as those of Figure 1.

being characterized by a greater emphasis of the noise at higher frequencies and a higher F_2-locus. The F_2-locus of [θa] is quite similar to that of [sa] which in turn is slightly lower than the F_2-locus of [ʃa]. The [sa] after filtering at low-pass 2000 Hz loses most of its noise energy and the confusion with [θa] is therefore quite natural. The [sa] was also heard as [ʃa] once and as [fa] once, all of which is quite plausible in view of the spectrographic patterns.

The voiced fricatives of Figure 5 display the same relations. In addition the superimposed voicing striations may be seen in all fricative segments. A typical feature of voiced weak fricatives such as [v] and [ð] is that the noise

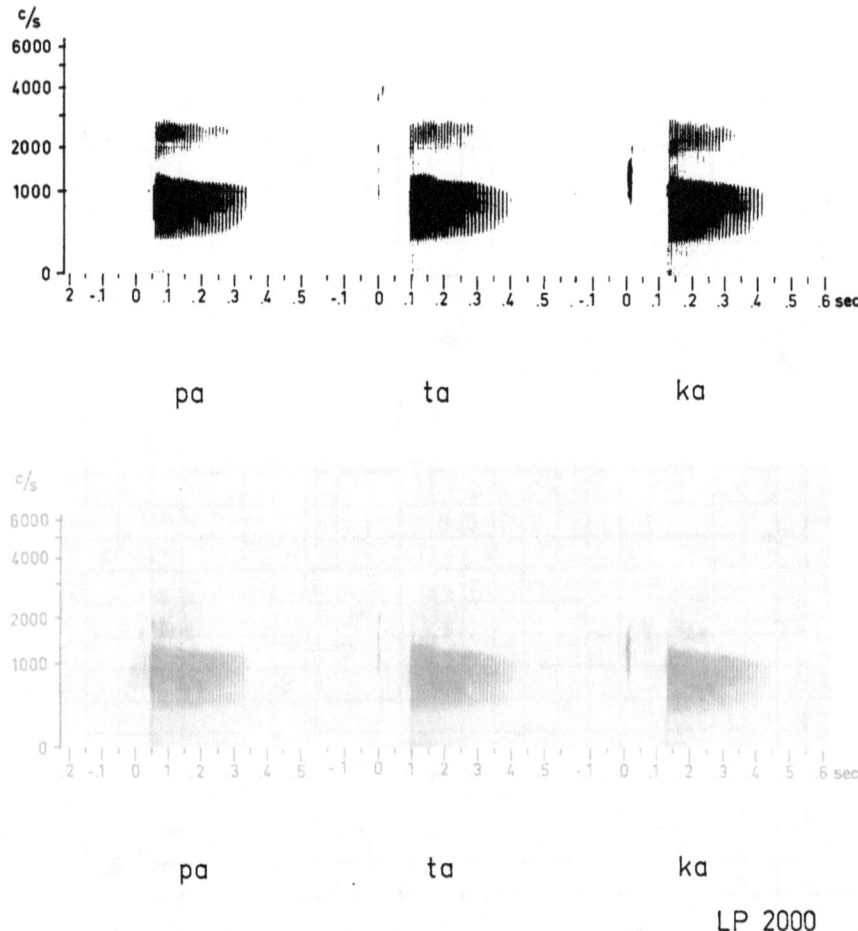

Figure 3. Spectrograms of Swedish stops before and after low-pass filtering at 2000 Hz. Observe the technical mel scale along the ordinate.

energy is even weaker than in corresponding unvoiced fricatives [f] and [θ] and therefore below the threshold of spectrographic marking. However, all the 10 [va] syllables were correctly identified, whereas 3 of the 9 [fa] were heard as [ʃa]. The higher resistance of [va] to degrading is probably due to the fact that the transitional cue extends further into the consonant segment than in [fa].

Of the affricates the unvoiced [tʃ] tended to be heard as [k] when low-pass filtered and the voiced [dӡ] was perceived as [ӡ]. The glides [y] and [w] and the [r] were all correctly identified after filtering whereas the English [l] was heard as [ð] twice.

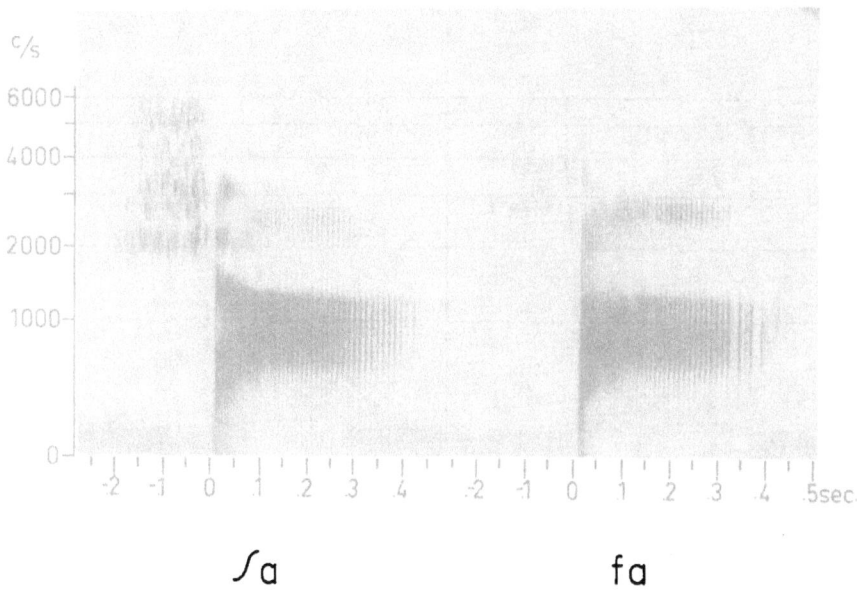
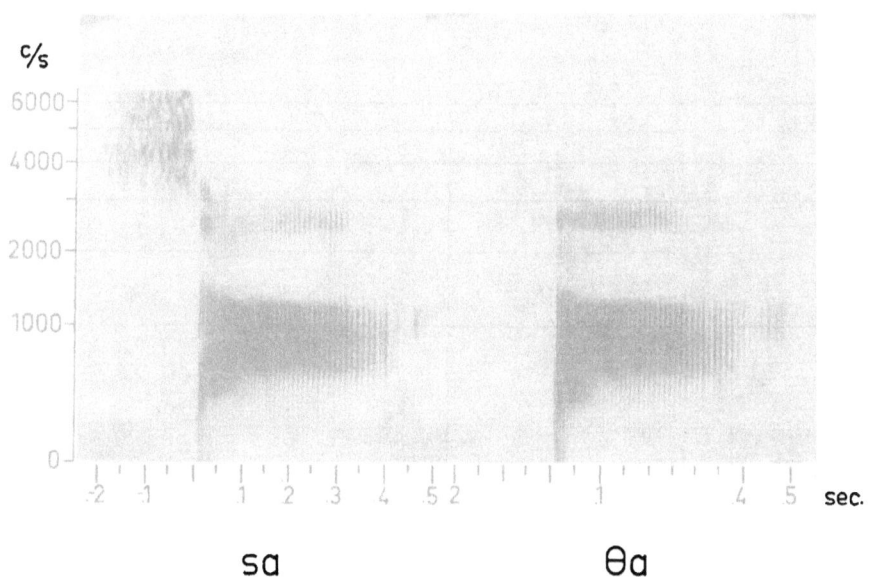

Figure 4. Spectrograms of English unvoiced fricatives.

106 Speech Analysis

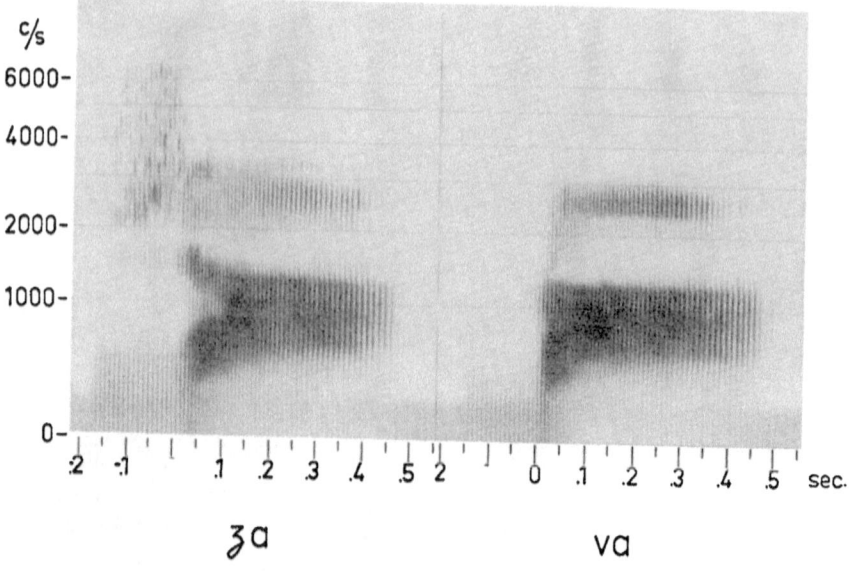

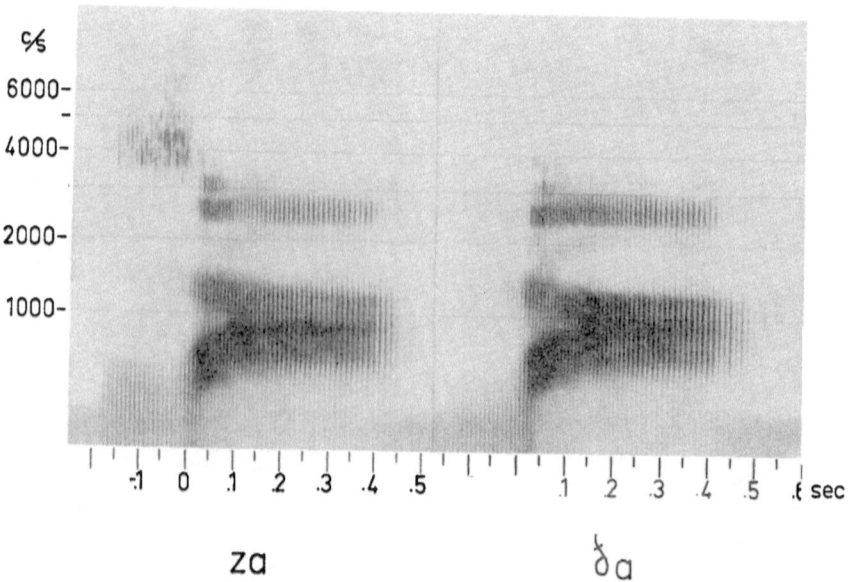

Figure 5. Spectrograms of English voiced fricatives.

Noise condition

The effect of the noise in experiment 3 was not as drastic as that of the filtering. The reason is the relatively low noise level, 13 dB below the average speech level. As can be seen in the confusion matrices of Figures 6 and 7 the noise affects the [p] which is heard as [h]. The interdental [θ] is heard as [f] and [ð] as [v] a few times.

Discussion

A few general statements remain to be made. The number of consonant con-

Subject H.W Swedish S/N = 13 dB

Heard

	k	p	t	g	b	d	θ	ð	f	s	h	j	v	r	l	m	n
k	10																
p		4							1		5						
t	1	1	7								1						
g				10													
b					9		1										
d					1	8			1								
θ							10										
ð							6	4									
f						1			9								
s										10							
h											10						
j												10					
v													10				
r														10			
l															10		
m																10	
n																	10

(Spoken, along vertical axis)

Figure 6. Confusion matrix of Swedish consonants. Noise of −13 dB relative signal level.

Subject H.W., English S/N = 13 dB

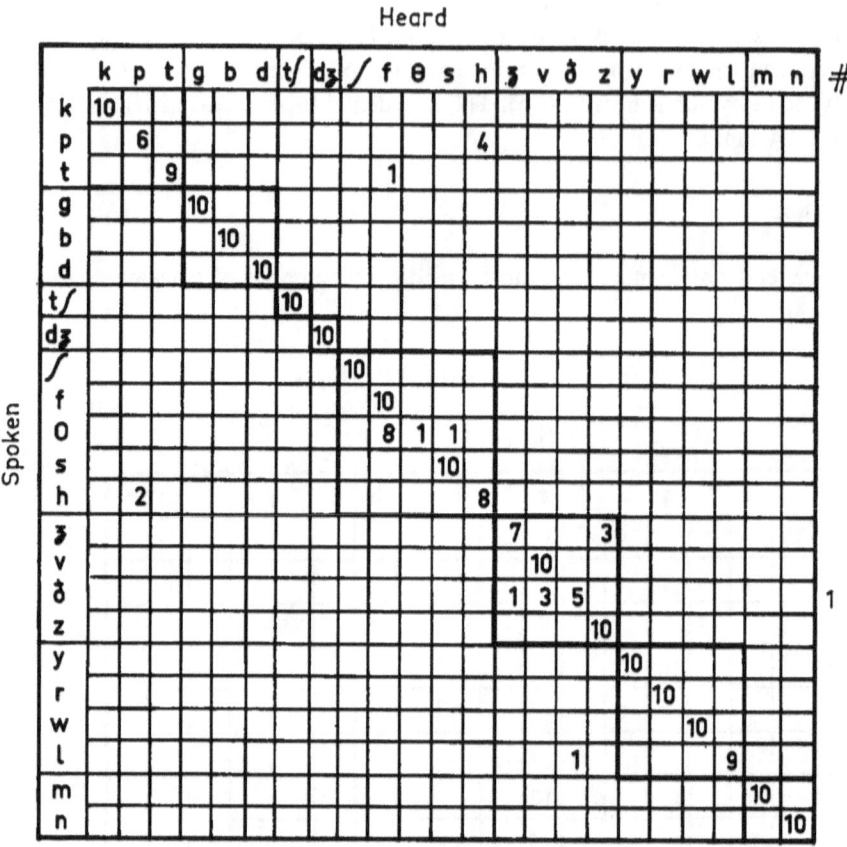

Figure 7. Confusion matrix of English consonants. Noise of —13 dB relative signal level.

fusions in the low-pass filter test was about twice as frequent in English as in Swedish. This is primarily the consequence of the larger ensemble of English consonants, 23 compared with 17 for Swedish. Within any subclass of consonants the number of confusions is about the same in Swedish and English. Consonants produced with different manner of production are more seldom confused. Nearly all the confusions are in terms of different places of articulation within a subclass of constant manner of articulation, as pointed out by Miller and Nicely (1955) and indicated by squares along the diagonals of our confusion matrices. The effect of noise differs from that of filtering by affecting the identification of manner of articulation just as much as the place of articulation.

Attention is drawn to the very extensive confusion tests in auditoria reported by Ormestad (1955). His work is concerned with 4 Norwegian dialects. The most frequent confusion he found was between [b] and [v]. Echo effects and reverberation tend to destroy some of the manner cues in speech whereas filtering typically affects the place cues.

Finally it should be pointed out that the very specific confusions we have noted with our subject (HW) to some extent reflect his specific speech habits rather than an average speaker listener behavior. Thus his Swedish [ç] and [ʃ] were less contrastive than is generally found.

A confusion test undoubtedly has a specific diagnostic value and should be used more extensively in studies of communication systems as well as of speech and hearing defects. It is certainly a valuable technique for evaluating the perceptional significance of spectrographic data.

References

Miller, G. A. and P. E. Nicely (1955). "An Analysis of Perceptual Confusions Among Some English Consonants," *J. Acoust. Soc. Am.* 27, pp. 338–352.

Ormestad, H. (1955). *Høreskarphet og taletydlighet og forståeligheten av norske språklyder,* Oslo: Akademisk Forlag.

Chapter 7
Stops in CV-Syllables

Introduction

The following study is an attempt to analyze a spectrographic material on stops in CV-syllables in terms of measurable pattern characteristics that can be given a phonetic interpretation. Several aspects are treated:
1. Segment durations.
2. Spectral patterns.
3. Coarticulation and syllable organization.
4. Discussion of data with respect to production theory.
5. Discussion of data with respect to perception and feature correlates.

Since the material is limited to one speaker this should be considered as a pilot study which exemplifies what problems can be treated and how they can be attacked. The results are discussed in relation to established theory and should have some significance for synthesis strategies as well as for general phonetic theory.

Material

The six Swedish stops [k][p][t][b][d][g] in syllable initial position were combined with each of the nine long vowels [u:][o:][a:][ɛ:][e:][i:][y:][ʉ:][ø:]. These CV-syllables were spoken in isolation by Björn Lindblom at regular intervals of about 2 seconds. The complete set of spectrograms was published by Fant, Lindblom, and Mártony (1963). Part of the spectrographic material has appeared in other publications, Fant (1957/68) and Fant (1968). The voiced and unvoiced stops before the vowels [a:][i:][ø:] and [u:] are illustrated here in Figures 1–4.

This article originally appeared in Speech Transmission Laboratory Quarterly Progress and Status Report 4/1969 (Stockholm, Sweden: Royal Institute of Technology, 1969).

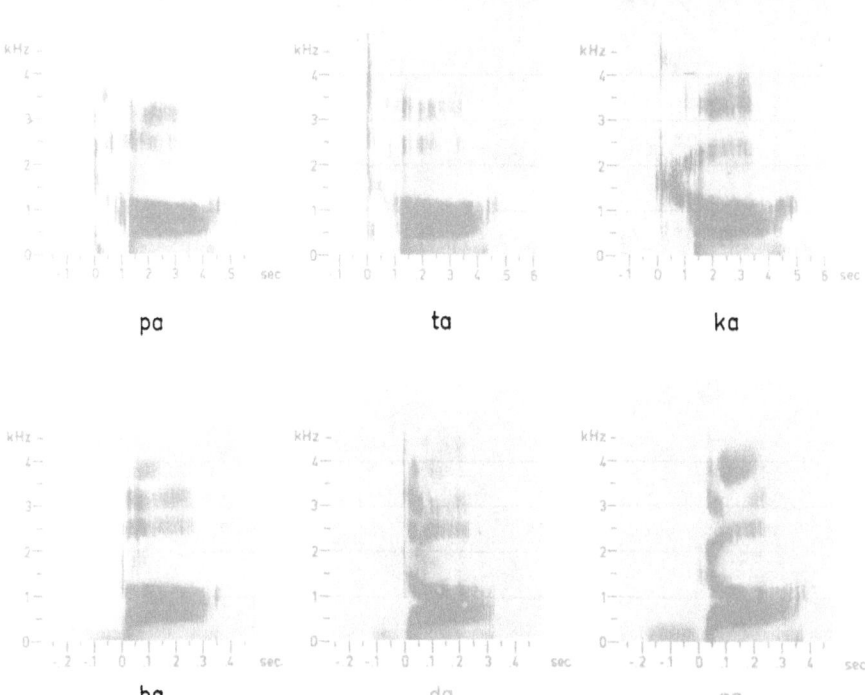

Figure 1. Spectrograms of [p][t][k][b][d][g] before the vowel [a:]. Subject B.L.

Some theory, data, and discussion on segment durations

A fully developed unvoiced stop in stressed, initial position can be decomposed in five successive segments, Fant (1968). These are:

1. Occlusion, voiced or silent.
2. Transient. This is the response of the vocal tract to the pressure release, exclusive of any turbulence effects. The duration of the transient phase is that of the time constants of vocal resonances. It is of the order of 2–30 ms and

112 Speech Analysis

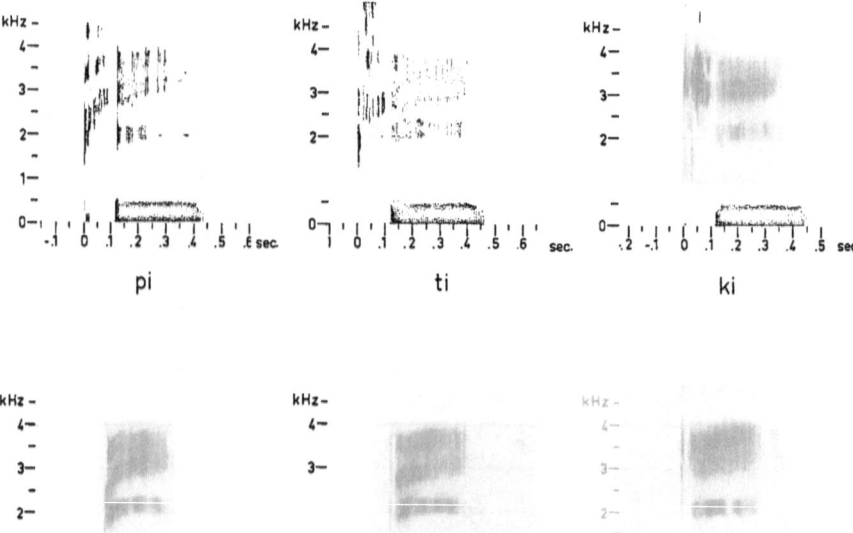

Figure 2. Spectrograms of [p][t][k][b][d][g] before the vowel [i:]. Subject B.L.

generally less than 10 ms. The formant structure of the transient phase is often obscured by highly time-varying effects and by the same zero function as fricative segments.

3. Fricative segment. This is characterized by noise produced at the consonantal constriction as in a homorganic fricative. Zeros interact so as to cancel "back cavity" formants, while "front cavity" formants prevail.

4. Aspirative segment. This is characterized by an "h-like" noise originating from a random source at the glottis or from a supraglottal source at a relatively wide constriction exciting all formants. The most typical constituents are

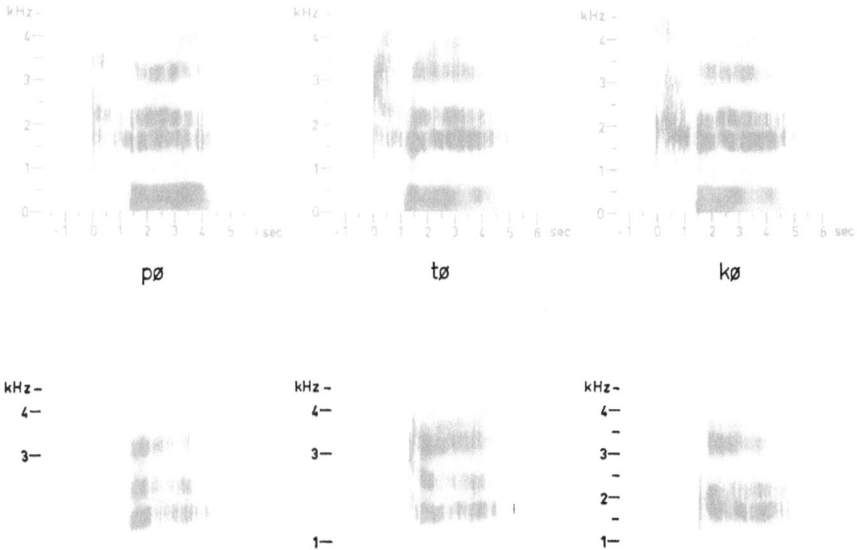

Figure 3. Spectrograms of [p][t][k][b][d][g] before the vowel [ø:]. Subject B.L.

F_2, F_3, and F_4. The aspirative segment can in part cooccur with the fricative segment but takes over as the degree of articulatory opening proceeds.

5. The initial part of a following voiced sound to the extent that it is influenced by coarticulation with the stop.

This complete sequence is typical of aspirated [t] and [k] whereas the frictional phase is rather weak or absent in [p] because of the low noise generating efficiency of the bilabial stricture and the rapid delabialization. In the terminology of the classical Haskins' synthesis the transient plus friction plus aspiration is treated as a single segment called the "burst."

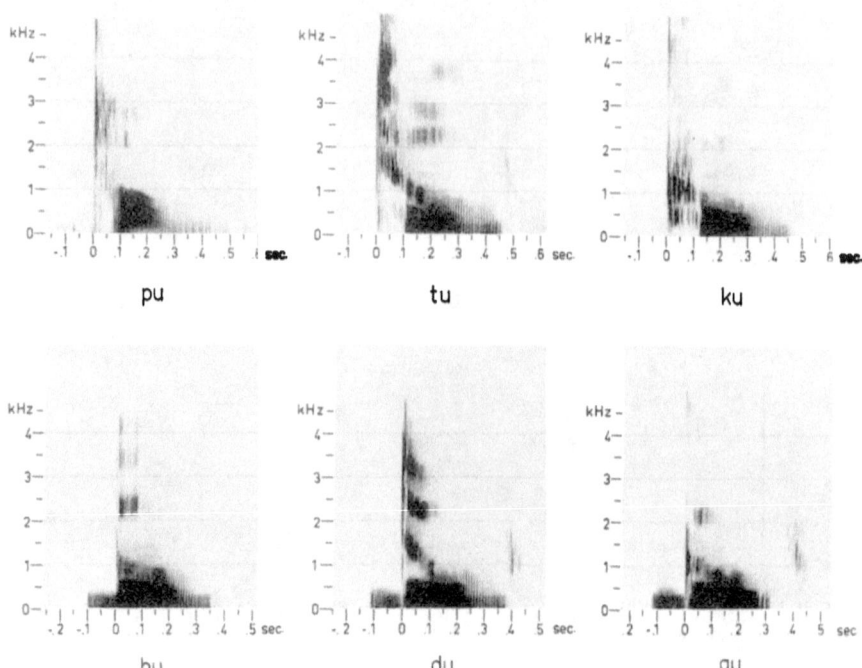

Figure 4. Spectrograms of [p][t][k][b][d][g] before the vowel [u:]. Subject B.L.

Voiced Swedish stops lack the aspiration phase. A short frictional segment can be seen in [d] and [g]. The [g] has the most apparent transient segment which can be ascribed to the high Q of the front cavity resonance and absence of dispersion effects of the main formant. Accordingly, the duration of the [g] and [k] transients is longer than in any other stops. Uninterrupted voicing can be superimposed during all phases of [b][d] and [g] in which case the transient appears as an extra spike in the background of voicing. It is more typical, however, that voicing is absent or very weak, some 50 ms before and 10–30 ms after the transient. The period of weak voicing after the release thus corresponds to the aspirative segment (4) in unvoiced stops and may coincide with a fricative segment in [d] and [g]. We shall return to the production theory in the later feature discussion.

A first inspection of the spectrograms (Figures 1–4) reveals some apparent aspects of the voiced-voiceless distinction. The unvoiced stops [k][p][t] have a "burst," that is, an unvoiced segment defined by the distance from release transient to the full voicing onset in the following vowel which is of the order of 125 ms compared with 10–25 ms for the corresponding segment in [b][d][g].

However, the duration of the voiced part of the vowel is approximately the same after all stops, voiced as well as unvoiced. Thus the temporal organization is not simply a matter of delay in voicing in [k][p][t] compared with [b][d][g] at the expense of the vowel length.

Table 1 provides quantitative data on these segmental aspects. The observed differences between vowel lengths in voiced and unvoiced contexts and with respect to the labial dental or velar place of stop articulation are rather small and need to be checked by studies on more extensive material involving several speakers. Our data indicate that open vowels are somewhat shorter than close

Table 1. Vowel durations in CV (C = stop) syllables

Mean values all contexts	ms
[i]	350
[e]	345
[ɛ]	335
[ʉ]	370
[y]	360
[ø]	325
[u]	340
[o]	330
[a]	320
average	345
After voiced stop	350
After unvoiced stop	340
After labial stops	340
After dental stops	350
After velar and palatal stops	345

Table 2. Voicing onset delay in ms after release in CV-syllables

	i	e	ɛ	ʉ	y	ø	u	o	a	mean
p	100	130	120	100	95	130	100	130	125	115
t	120	125	125	125	120	105	100	125	120	120
k	120	130	150	125	130	150	115	130	140	130
mean	115	130	130	115	115	130	105	130	130	120
db	<10	<10	<10	<10	10	15	0	0	15	<10
gd	10	15	30	40	25	40	10	10	15	20
g	25	25	20	15	35	15	15	20	35	25

vowels in this context, contrary to established rules of vowel length increasing with degree of opening (Elert, 1964; and Lindblom, 1968).

One factor that seems to add to the observed durations of close Swedish vowels is that they tend to be diphthongized with a homorganic fricative. Since my criterion for the termination of the vowel segment was the disappearance of F_1 in the spectrogram the vowel accordingly incorporates any frictional termination which is voiced. As shown in Table 2 the duration of the burst is somewhat shorter before [u] and [i] than before other vowels thus tending to reduce differences in the overall duration of syllables comprising various vowels after unvoiced stops.

The main finding above that the duration of the voiced part of a vowel is not substantially influenced by the nature of the preceding consonant conforms with the observations of Peterson and Lehiste (1960), as illustrated by their Figure 4 exemplifying spectrograms of "tug" and "dug," "tuck" and "duck." However, their average findings indicate that the vowel after a voiced stop exceeds the length of the voiced part of a vowel after an unvoiced stop by approximately one-half of the burst duration or 30 ms. Their vowel lengths are about 20% shorter than those reported here while the absolute value of their burst durations were of the order of 60% of ours indicating a heavier aspiration of the Swedish stops.*

These differences are probably related more to the complexity of the test words, CVC versus CV, than to language specific pronunciation, judging from other speech material at our disposal. Tempo and level of stress should also be considered. These conditional factors as well as the effect of location within a complex string of syllables need to be investigated further. As seen in Figure 5 aspiration is not lost in sentence initial unstressed syllables.

* This difference is mainly ascribable to our particular subject whose pronunciation of unvoiced stops was more "aspirated" than average for Swedish speakers.

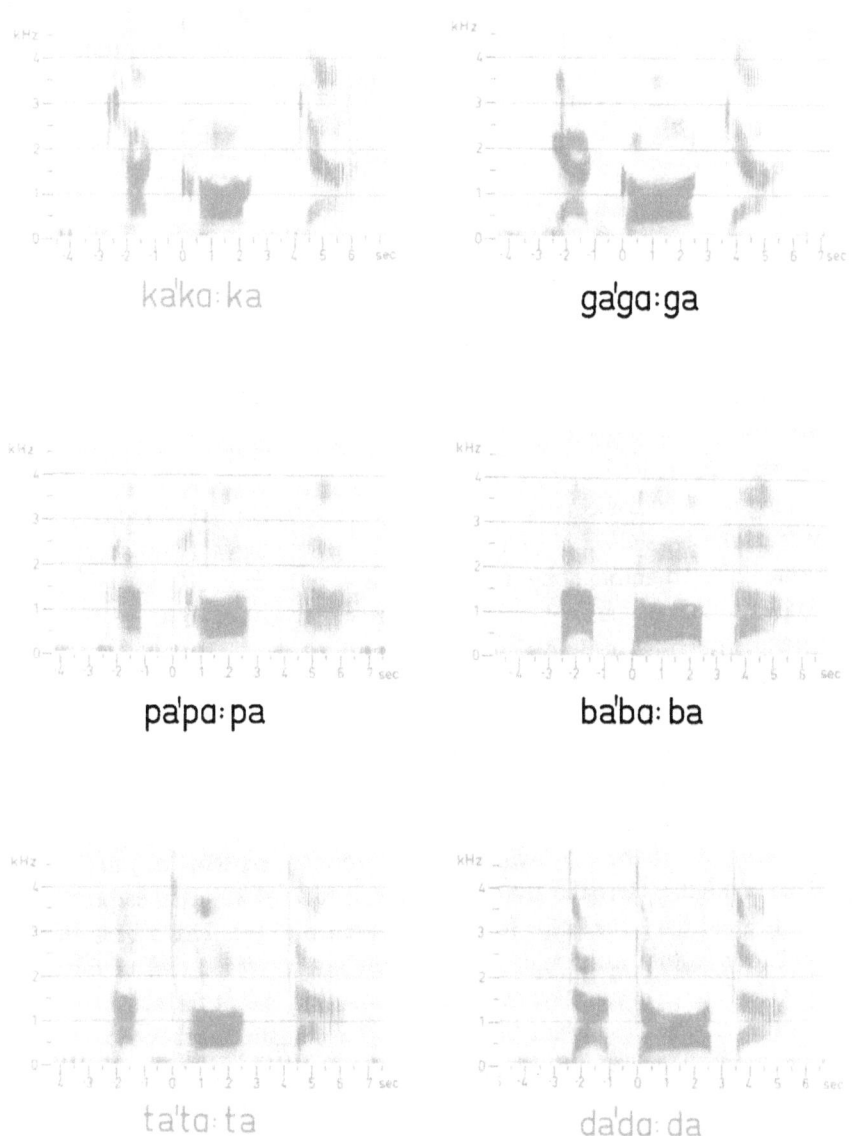

Figure 5. Ca'Ca:Ca with C = [k][g][p][b][t][d]. Same subject as in Figs. 1–4.

118 Speech Analysis

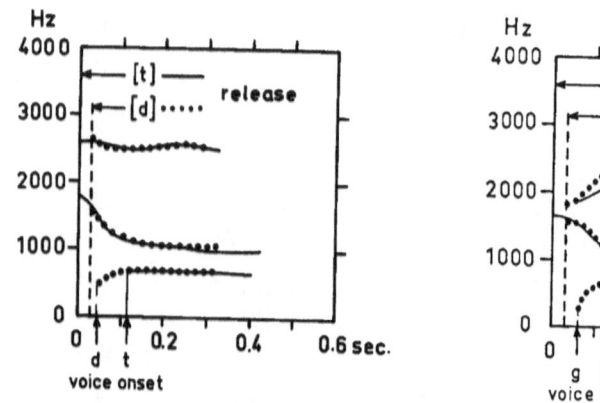
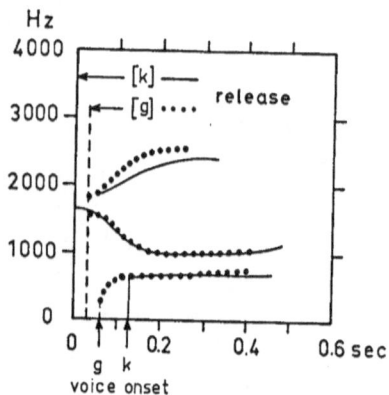

Figure 6. F-patterns of voiced and unvoiced stops matched for articulatory synchrony.

In these CVCV:CV words spoken by the same subject, B.L., the duration of the burst is of the order of 50–90 ms in stressed positions and 50–70 ms in unstressed sentence initial position.

Interesting material for comparison is offered by Öhman (1965). He used test words of the type CVCen (with C=g and k, V=long [a:] and short [a] with accent 2 word intonation) inserted in a carrier sentence (säga . . . igen). The durations of his [k]-bursts were more or less constant 80 ms. When two utterances differing in the voiced/voiceless distinction of the first C were compared and synchronized with respect to overall intonation pattern he found that the instant of stop release occurred 40 ms earlier in [k] than in [g].

Öhman also claims that the same relative timing pattern occurs if the articulation of the following vowel and not the intonation is taken as a basis of comparison. This rule also appears to hold in the present CV material as shown by Figure 6 exemplifying the overlaying of traced formant patterns of [ta:] and [da:], [ka:] and [ga:]. Here the release of the [t] is located 30 ms ahead of the release of [d] and the same holds for [k] compared with [g]. This means that the articulatory gesture after release is different in the voiced and unvoiced plosives. This difference can have two dimensions. One is that the articulatory pattern is different at the instant of release and eventually reaches the same dynamic pattern, though at different times for the two stops, or that the initial articulatory pattern is more or less the same, except for the larger glottal opening at the release of the unvoiced stop, while the offset gesture proceeds at a slower rate in the first 40 ms after release of the unvoiced stop.* The latter appears to be the case with palatal stops and possibly also for most dental stops.

*Articulatory data on English stop+vowel dynamics published by Houde (1967) are of some interest in this connection.

The terminal F-patterns are not so different when comparing [g] and [k] or [d] and [t] as when comparing [p] and [b] in a position before a back vowel where unvoiced stops have a much higher terminal F_2 than voiced stops. This holds for Swedish as well as for English as will be shown in a later part of this article.

Returning to matters of segment durations it appears first of all that available data on the differences in voiced vowel length with respect to the influence of the voiced/voiceless distinction of the preceding stop are less variant on an absolute than on a relative time scale. Thus the Peterson-Lehiste (1960) data can be expressed as an average of 30 ms longer vowel after voiced than after unvoiced stop and the Öhman data are close to the 40 ms difference which holds in short as well as in long vowels. The latter observation is remarkable in view of the fact that the long vowels are about 60% longer than the short ones. If the present material of CV syllables is to be analyzed in exactly the same way as that of the other two studies mentioned we must add to the length of the vowel, after a voiced stop, the duration of the voiceless or weakly voiced interval between release transient and visible onset of the following vowel. In all we would then have a 20 ms vowel length difference in the g-k comparison, a 25 ms in the d-t contexts, and a 25 ms in the b-p contexts.

A simple numerical rule for relating these facts would be that the vowels after voiced stops are prolonged by the same amount as the latency of the instant of voiced stop release compared with the unvoiced stop release. In Öhman's material this leads to absolute synchrony of the instant of vowel termination before the stop gap of the following consonants. Approximately the same could be true of the Peterson-Lehiste data since the difference in vowel lengths is of the order of one-half of the burst length. In our CV-material, however, the excessive length of the burst, average 125 ms, accounts for a relative prolongation of the instant of voice offset of the vowel preceded by an unvoiced stop. This prolongation assuming maximum vowel synchrony is apparently equal to the burst length minus the voiced stop release lag minus the difference in voiced vowel length.

This discussion is perhaps carried further than is motivated by our meager data. However, the purpose is to stimulate further work on the formulation of rules for segmental programming. It is possible that in the specific mode of reading isolated CV-syllables the segmental programming is governed mainly by a rhythmical demand of producing equally spaced, equally loud vowel nuclei. Tests on the timing of syllable production in synchrony with a periodically repeated auditory signal performed by Lindblom and Sundberg* indicate that the instant of major intensity increase in the syllable, a special case of which is the instant of switching from voiceless to voiced segment, governs the

* Unpublished data.

timing. These data support the syllabic timing rules proposed by Kozhevnikov and Chistovich (1965).

One typical example of the role of voicing boundary as a determinant of segmental organization can be studied in the [CaCà:Ca] (C = k, p, t, g, b, d) spectrograms of Figure 5. The time interval between onset of voicing in the first and the second vowel and between the second and final vowel is shown in Table 3 together with data on the duration of the three vowels.

The stability of these temporal reference points of vowel onsets holds for variations in place of articulation within 10 ms and within 30 ms for the voicing distinction. The increase in consonant length with unvoicing is somewhat larger than for reduction of the vowel length. Thus the V+C intervals of Table 3 are about 15 ms longer when C is unvoiced than when C is voiced. The initial vowel is close to 40 ms longer when the consonant is voiced in agreement with previous findings. The second and fully stressed vowel is 60 ms longer in a voiced context whereas the final vowel which is unstressed does not vary much in length depending on the voicing of the consonant. The latter observation conforms with the reduction of the acoustic distinction between voiced and unvoiced stops in noninitial unstressed position. The relatively large effects on the second vowel could be ascribed to the added influence from both preceding and following consonants. A further discussion of the k/g, p/b, and t/d distinctions follows in a later part of this article.

Before leaving the topic of segmental structure, a word should be said about the terminal boundary of a vowel followed by a stop. If voicing is continued straight through the occlusion the boundary is set by the articulatory closure as seen by the termination of the F_1 transition towards base-line position. Vowels followed by unvoiced stops are terminated by an active devoicing gesture of the vocal cords which is synchronized to turn off voicing at or just before the articulatory closure. The articulatory closing gesture may well contribute to the final interruption of the voice source but this is not a necessary requirement. In heavily stressed positions the voicing has died out well before the articulatory closure. Vowel duration is influenced more by the following

Table 3. CaCà:Ca segmental analysis, time in ms.

C =	k	g	p	b	t	d
Onset V_2 − onset V_1	260	250	270	250	270	240
Onset V_3 − onset V_2	370	360	365	360	370	350
Duration V_1	85	125	75	110	85	120
Duration V_2	180	240	180	240	190	250
Duration V_3	170	180	170	160	170	170

consonant than by a preceding consonant (see Peterson and Lehiste, 1960; Elert, 1964; and Karlsson and Nord, 1970).

Transitional patterns

The purpose of the following section is to discuss the material on formant patterns and transitions in the CV-material in relation to earlier studies, notably those of Lehiste and Peterson (1961), Öhman (1966), and Fant (1959).

The term "formant transitions" is to be understood as the dynamic variation of the F-pattern, that is, F_1, F_2, F_3, F_4 as a function of time. The extent to which the F-pattern dynamics signals the place of articulation is one problem of general interest. Another is the possibility of inferring coarticulation features from F-pattern analysis. We shall attempt to compare voiceless and voiced stops in Swedish and English accordingly. As a control on some of the measurements using a vocal tract model we shall simulate transitions that are difficult to follow in spectrograms. Finally we shall discuss data, vocal tract theory, and proposed models of perception in relation to feature theory of stop sounds.

First, a few words about transitions and sampling techniques. The main object of our measurements has been to sample the F-pattern extrapolated to the instant of the beginning of the transient release of the stop closure. This is not an unambiguous process. The first part of the transition after release may be very rapid and difficult to follow. A fact which often is overlooked is that a CV-transition is often complex, comprising first a rapidly progressing part related to the release of the consonantal obstruction plus an overlayed transition of longer time constant related to the main tongue body movement. This is typically the case with labials but also with alveolars and dentals.

It may be difficult to follow a formant transition in unvoiced segments, but the reverse can also be true. An intense aspiration may provide more favorable conditions for F-pattern tracking than a very low-pitched voiced segment. It was considered of interest to sample the F-pattern of unvoiced stops not only at release but also at the initiation of voicing after aspiration.

The collected F-pattern data on F_2, F_3, and F_4 are documented in Tables 4 and 5. No F_1 data are included. The extreme value of F_1 in the occlusion is of the order of magnitude of 200 Hz for all voiced stops. On the other hand F_1 at onset of voicing after unvoiced stop is generally close to the target value of F_1 except in occasional instances of unvoiced stop plus [a:]. Other aspects of articulatory movements such as tongue body place shifts, or a labial or palatal closing gesture may continue during the vowel. Obviously, a simple time con-

122 Speech Analysis

Table 4. F_2, F_3, F_4 at instant of release

	i	e	ε	ʉ	y	ø	u	o	a	formant	range min–max
p	1800 2250 3200	1800 2200 ?	1700 2200 ?	1750 2300 3200	1800 2200 3300	1700 2100 3300	1600 2100 ?	1400 ? ?	1750 2250 3400	F_2 F_3 F_4	1400–1800 2100–2300 3200–3400
b	1700 2300 3200	1800 2300 3300	1600 2250 3200	1600 2300 3200	1600 2150 3200	1400 2150 3050	900 2200 3200	900 2200 3400	1000 2400 3050	F_2 F_3 F_4	900–1800 2150–2400 3050–3300
t	1800 2600 3600	1850 2700 ?	1800 2700 ?	1800 2650 3300	1850 2600 3250	1850 2700 3300	1700 2400 3200	1600 2700 3500	1700 2700 3500	F_2 F_3 F_4	1600–1850 2400–2700 3200–3600
d	1850 2600 3400	1850 2500 3300	1650 2600 3300	1700 2500 3400	1750 2500 3200	1800 2650 3200	1600 2400 3200	1400 2400 3200	1400 2600 3300	F_2 F_3 F_4	1400–1850 2400–2650 3200–3400
k	2100 3100 3500	2200 3200 3800?	2200 2950 3600	1900 2400 3400	2000 2600 3300	1900 2200 3000	1200 2000 ?	1200 2000? ?	1600 1900 ?	F_2 F_3 F_4	1200–2200 1900–3200 3000–3800?
g	2000 3100 3600	2100 3000 3500	2000 2900 3350	1800 2300 3400	2000 2600 3400	1700 2100 3300	1100 2300 ?	1000 2000 2800	1600 1900 3100	F_2 F_3 F_4	1000–2100 1900–3100 2800–3600

Table 5. F_2, F_3, F_4 at instant of voice onset after unvoiced stops

	i	e	ɛ	ʉ	y	ø	u	o	a
p	1900	1950	1950	1750	1750	1600	800	700	1000
	2750	2650	2500	2200	2200	2100	2200	2400	2500
	3500	3200		3200	3250	3200			3250
t	2000	2100	1900	1750	1950	1650	1000	900	1050
	2750	2700	2600	2350	2500	2250	2200	2500	2500
	3550	3600	3550	3350	3400	3300	2900	3200	3300
k	2100	2200	2000	2000	2000	1750	850	750	1100
	3050	3050	2800	2250	2500	2200	2100	2200	2150
	3600	3600	3500	3400	3400	3300			3250

stant one for each formant independent of consonant and its vocalic context is not sufficient for CV-synthesis.

The first object of the analysis was to explore how much the initial F_2 and F_3 values of a stop vary with respect to the associated vowel. It can be seen from Table 4 that the extreme low $F_{2i}=1400$ Hz of [p] occurs with the vowel [o:] and the maximally high $F_{2i}=1800$ Hz with the vowels [i:], [e:], and [y:]. The voiced cognate [b] has the same maximum F_{2i} value and a minimum $F_{2i}=900$ Hz. Such data on extreme ranges of second and third formant terminal frequencies are summarized in Figure 7.

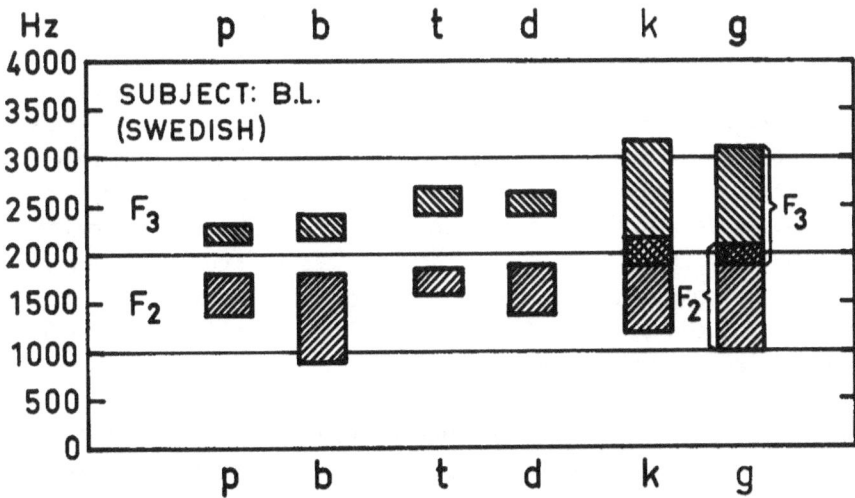

Figure 7. Range of initial F_2 and F_3 of Swedish stops in combinations with all possible long vowels.

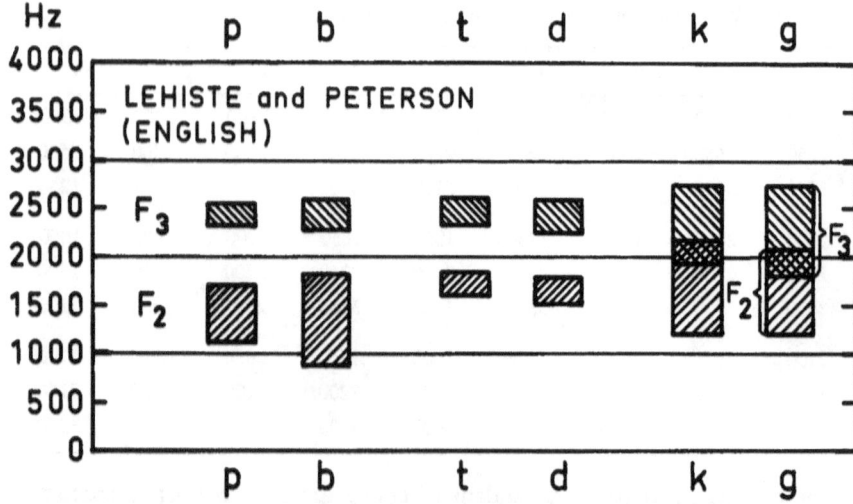

Figure 8. Lehiste-Peterson data on range of initial F_2 and F_3 of stops.

Figure 8 shows a set of corresponding data extracted from an article by Lehiste and Peterson (1961). A first glance at the two figures reveals basic similarities; the small range of variation for dentals, the large range for velars, and palatals as a single group with the overlap of F_{2i} and F_{3i} ranges. The greater range for voiced than for unvoiced labials, already mentioned above, is found in the Swedish as well as in the English data. A more detailed analysis reveals that the extended initial F-pattern range of voiced labial stops can be ascribed to a closer coarticulation with back vowels [u:][o:] and [a:] whereas unvoiced labial stops start from a more neutral tongue position at the instant of release.* A similar trend appears with Swedish dentals. The lower bound of the F_{2i} domain for Swedish [g] is also somewhat lower than that of [k]. Following the coarticulation model developed by Öhman (1967) these effects could at least in part be ascribable to the relative timing of articulatory programming. As discussed previously in connection with Figure 6, the voiced stop tongue movement is equal to that of the unvoiced one released 30 ms earlier. If we hypothesize the same semineutral tongue body target of voiced as well as unvoiced stops, the mere translation of the vowel influence curve to the "right" in time for the unvoiced stop would reduce the effect of vowel coarticulation on the terminal values of formant frequencies.

The range of terminal F-pattern variations would be even greater if we inserted different vowels before the consonants, that is, if both the following

---

* See first footnote on page 126. Cineradiographic control is badly needed.

and the preceding vowels were varied independently as in the study of Öhman (1966). Our study above can be regarded as a special case where the consonant is preceded by a neutral vowel. Öhman has shown that in V_1CV_2 syllables with C=voiced stop [g][b] or [d] and V_1 and V_2 equally stressed vowels [u:] [a:][ø:] or [i:] varied independently the transitional pattern in any part of the test words is influenced by both vowels and the consonant. Thus the initial F-pattern after release as well as the following transition of the CV_2 part depend on the particular V_1 and conversely the V_1C offglide transition is influenced by V_2.

One pattern aspect studied by Öhman was the consonant "locus" in the specific Haskins Laboratories' sense. Their "locus" is defined as a common point on the frequency scale about 50 ms ahead of the release which is regarded as the virtual starting point of F_2 transitions from one and the same consonant to all possible vowels that can follow. Delattre, Liberman, and Cooper (1955) claimed from synthesis experiments that [d] has a locus of 1800 Hz, [b] a locus of 720 Hz, and [g], if produced with nonback vowels, 3000 Hz. The articulatory significance of the loci are claimed to be invariant vocal tract configurations. This is an oversimplification and the significance of the "locus" is primarily limited to two-formant synthesis rules. Öhman states that given a specific V_1 and C the four possible V_2's of this test provide transitions that can be extrapolated back to a common "locus" providing C is either [d] or [b] and with the locus being a function of the F_2 of V_1. However, a closer view of Öhman's data shows that the invariance of [b] loci with respect to V_2 is not very good. A brief study of the spectrograms of our CV material supports the notion that [b] does not have a unique locus. That [g] has a variable locus was evident already in the early Haskins Laboratories' work although they choose to speak of two [g] loci, one for front vowels and one for back vowels.

Transitions studied by analog simulation

Before entering a discussion on the relative importance of various acoustic cues for stop consonant identifications it is worthwhile to consult production theory for the support of some of the more uncertain measurements and to provide some general basis for feature analysis.

The transitions of labial stops to a following vowel are not always easy to follow in the spectrogram. The major part of the labial opening phase is often completed in less than 20 ms. Production theory (Fant, 1960) states that an increase in lip-section area, everything else being equal, cannot result in a downward shift of any formant located at a frequency lower than $c/4l_0$, where

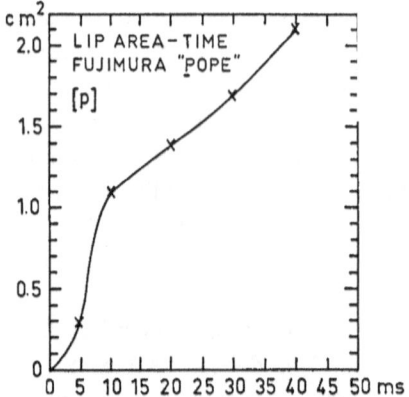

Figure 9. Fujimura (1961) data on lip opening as a function of time for the test word "pope."

l_0 is the length of the lip passage which in practice applies to all observable formants of the F-pattern. However, the extent of the upward shift of formant frequencies varies with the particular formant and the vocal tract configuration. As has been pointed out earlier, a superimposed tongue body movement may produce a transition of opposite sign to that induced by the lip passage opening, and it generally extends over a longer period of time. A relative prominent falling transition may result, see [pɑ:] in Figure 1 and [pu:] in Figure 4.* The same feature is found in Danish [pʰo] (Fischer-Jørgensen, 1954).

An obscure detail in the [bɑ:] spectrum is the vertical spectral line from 1000 to 2000 Hz in the released transient. It was observed already in my spectrographic work at the Ericsson Telephone Co. in 1946–1949 (Fant, 1959, Figure 42). One object of the analog calculations would be to find out if it had anything to do with F_2 and F_3 transitions. Another object was the study of formant transitions from [b] to a front vowel [i]. For this purpose I adopted for a simulation study with our line analog LEA the lip-opening cross-sectional area as a function of time (see Figure 9, experimentally determined by Fujimura, 1961). The area function of the rest of the vocal tract was kept constant. One set of measurements† was made with a vocal tract area function appropriate for the Russian vowel [ɑ:], one for [i:], and one pertaining to the palatized [pʲ] (see Fant, 1960).

At the interval of complete lip closure F_1 should not drop to zero but to a value limit of about 150 Hz determined by the enclosed air volume extreme

* The high F_{2p} of [pɑ:] could reflect subglottal coupling rather than a fronted tongue position at the instant of release (see Fant et al., "Subglottal Formants," STL-QPRS 1/1972).
† I am indebted to Doc. J. Sundberg for carrying out this work.

and the mass distribution at the vocal walls. Accordingly (see Fant, 1960), all F_1 values were corrected by a root square summation,

$$F_{1e} = (F_1^2 + 150^2)^{1/2}.$$

The results of the calculations are shown in Figure 10 and Table 6. According to Figure 9 the lip opening has reached 50% of the final value at 10 ms and then proceeds at a slower rate. A major part of the F_1 and F_2 transitions are also completed at 10 ms after release. All transitions are positive as expected. The F_2 and F_3 transitions of [ba:] are small and it can accordingly be concluded that the release transient above F_2 should be disregarded in transition studies.

In [bi:] F_{2i} jumps up 500 Hz in the first 5 ms. The terminal value 1200 Hz is lower than the $F_{2i}=1700$ Hz measured from spectrograms. This difference could be explained by limited means of following such a rapid transition in the spectrogram. Another source of deviation of the model from the spoken data could be that the tongue body configuration at the instant of release in [bi:] is not that of a pure [i:] but is perturbed in the direction of a neutral position as in the palatalized [b,] of Figure 10, where the terminal value of F_{2i} is closer to

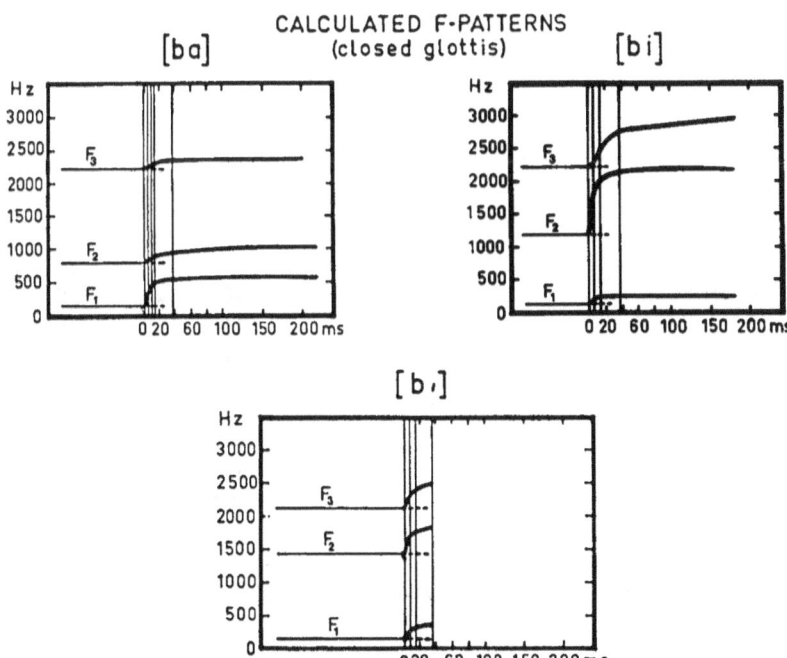

Figure 10. Calculated dynamic F-patterns of voiced labial stops.

Table 6. Calculated F-pattern variations after release of hypothetical labial stops constructed from area functions of Russian vowels [a:] and [i:] and the soft labial stop [p,], from Fant (1960). Lip-opening data, Fujimura (1961).

	time (ms)	LEA no.	Area (cm²)	F_1	$(F_1^2 + 150^2)^{1/2} = F_1^1$ F_{1a}	F_2	F_3	F_4
[pa:]	0	∞	0	150	150	800	2230	3220
	3.5	16	0.16	251	293	813	2250	3225
	5.2	15	0.32	325	380	827	2260	3235
	7	14	0.65	412	439	853	2280	3235
	9	13	1.0	464	486	876	2290	3240
	15	12	1.3	495	516	898	2305	3250
	27.5	11	1.6					
	37.5	10	2.0	538	558	939	2325	3260
	final value		6	595	614	1039	2375	3280
[pi:]	0	∞	0	150	150	1200	2225	3520
	3.5	16	0.16	169	226	1625	2245	3530
	5.2	15	0.32	193	245	1860	2275	3530
	7	14	0.65	205	254	2010	2335	3535
	9	13	1.0					
	13			218	265	2120	2510	3555
	15	12	1.3					
	27.5	11	1.6					
	37.5	10	2.0	225	270	2155	2725	3570
	final value			230	275	2170	2930	3595
[p,]	0	∞		150	150	1440	2106	3420
	4.4	16/15		206	255	1600	2200	3436
	5.2	15		230	275	1640	2240	3440
	7	14		263	303	1710	2320	3450
	9	13		277	317	1740	2465	3460
	15	12		288	326	1760	2410	3470
	27.5	11		298	334	1780	2450	3470
	37.5	10		307	342	1790	2490	3470

F_1 = uncorrected; F_1^1 = corrected with respect to cavity wall vibration.

1500 Hz and the extent of the F_2 transition is smaller. In view of the wide range of coarticulation induced by a previous vowel in CVC-contexts and possible fluctuations in initial tongue configuration in production of CV-syllables it is, in any case, apparent that variations in F_{2i} of [bi:] can be expected.

On the whole, however, disregarding the lack of information in the first 5 ms, the calculated dynamical F-pattern of [bi:] in Figure 10 agrees well with measured data. One pattern aspect well known from spectrograms is that the F_3 transition goes on for a longer time than the F_2 transition and, with disregard to the first 5 ms, covers a greater frequency span than F_2.

As seen in Figure 2 the transitional pattern of the [pi:] aspiration is not less apparent than that of [bi:]. The main part of the F_3 transition is completed in 40 ms according to the simulation in Figure 10. In this time F_3 has moved from the 2200 Hz terminal value to 2750 Hz. This compares very well with measurements from the spectrogram in Figure 2. The F_3 transition in the following and later part of the spectrogram reaches a higher target value than in the simulated syllable which can be ascribed to the tongue body movement up to a higher degree of closure typical for the diphthongization of Swedish [i:]. However, apart from this added F_3 movement the longer duration of the F_3 transition compared with the F_2 transition is related to a higher, differential influence of the lip parameter on F_3 than on F_2 at relatively large degrees of lip opening. In terms of resonator theory this is explained by the fact that F_2 is a standing wave resonance of the pharynx and once the lip opening has reached a value high enough so as not to compete with the palatal stricture the F_2 influence will be minimal. Also, since F_3 of [i:] is a mouth cavity resonance it will be highly susceptible to variation in the lip area.

Experimental check of occlusion F-pattern

Vocal tract simulation is an indirect means of studying the F-pattern in articulatory closed parts of the utterance. It would be convenient if a continuous tracking of the F-pattern were possible in all parts of real speech. If we limit our object to voiced stops there exist some limited possibilities of studying F_1, F_2, and F_3 during occlusion providing a high frequency emphasis and extra gain is utilized in the spectrographic analysis. A limited pilot study* has provided us with data that support the findings above concerning [ba:] and [bi:]. It was thus found that F_{2i} of [ba:] was 1000 Hz and of [bi:] 1700 Hz as measured from a separate recording of the same subject. During [bi:] and [ga:] there were prominent transitions within the occlusion.

---

* This pilot study was carried out by S. Pauli utilizing both the Voiceprint Spectrograph and the 51-channel analyzer. A separate report on these studies is planned.

One technical difficulty in the analysis was the need for high input levels to the spectrograph and thereby the risk of overloading with intermodulation formants appearing. Another difficulty is the low level of the voice source immediately before release.

Identification of spectral components

Ambiguity often arises as to the identification of the true release transient of palatal and velar stops. As pointed out already by Fischer-Jørgensen (1954) there often occur double or triple spikes indicating a sequence of interrupted air injections through the articulatory stricture (see Figure 1).* These multiple spikes could reflect a suction reaction at the articulatory stricture by the Bernoulli pressure just as in the normal voice source. In voiced velar stops they may occur superimposed on the regular voice source operating in a breathy mode so as to damp out F_1. This reduction occurs both before and after the release and is thus not in itself indicative of the instant of release. The double spikes of the [k] burst could also originate from a reaction on the glottis at the release resulting in a momentary flow reduction. Further investigations are needed to reach a better understanding of these phenomena. Another problem of interest is the F_1 locus of unvoiced stops. The subglottal impedance shunting the supraglottal impedance in a circuit theory model would account for a substantial increase in F_1 and could also introduce traces of subglottal resonances. Because of the low energy level of F_1 in the aspiration it is hard to get reliable measures of an initial F_1 just before release. Just after release one observes values of the order of 300–600 Hz depending on the particular vowel (see Figures 1–4). However, F_1 of the aspiration is not very important for either perception or for synthesis and recognition work.

Acoustic characteristics and synthesis rules

When discussing the stops as a specific ensemble we need not worry about distinctive features in a general sense. We can proceed to discuss the relation of the subset [k][p][t] to that of [g][b][d] and further on investigate the triangular place relations within each subset, for example, what pattern aspects or cues are typical for each of the members within the subset in relation to each of the other members. We do, of course, find the expected similarities k/g = p/d = t/d etc. underlying the four natural categories which are traditionally referred to as (1) unvoiced/voiced, (2) velars and palatals, (3) labials, and (4) dentals. In this limited material composed of stressed and isolated CV-syllables

---

* See also illustrations of several speakers' [ka] and [ga] in Fant (1957/68).

the distinction between voiced and unvoiced stops is very clear, as has been discussed in the previous sections.

A synthesis of CV-stop plus long vowel syllables of the type studied here could proceed as follows:

1. Determine first, if needed with respect to the phrase prosody, a point on the time scale where the vowel shall start. If preceded by a voiced stop this is the instant of the stop release transient. If preceded by an unvoiced stop this is the instant of voicing onset after aspiration.

2. Choose the vowel length after more or less detailed rules starting from a mean value of 250–350 ms for long vowels according to tempo and degree of emphasis required. Add 30 ms to the vowel if preceded by a voiced stop. The instant of release transient of an unvoiced stop is placed 80–120 ms ahead of the voicing onset.

3. An appropriate F-pattern for the whole voiced stop plus vowel sequence is generated. This can be used as an approximation also for the corresponding unvoiced stop if synchronized to have its release transient coincide with a point 30 ms after the release of the unvoiced stop. The F-pattern for the initial 30 ms of the burst is traced by rules for linear extrapolation back in time. Labials before back vowels require separate F-patterns for voiced and unvoiced stops. These can, however, probably be derived from coarticulation rules. A minor correction for the effect of glottal opening on the F-pattern should be added. An open glottis increases F_2 and F_3 by about 50–100 Hz.

4. Make the F_0 contour synchronous with respect to the F-pattern. For unvoiced stops add an F_0 increment in the first 50 ms after voicing onset.

5. Choose an appropriate dynamic pattern of intensity and spectral distribution of the voice source. Our speaker consistently shifted his voiced source spectral balance to a more high-frequency deemphasized shape in the later half or third of the vowel. An aspirative final termination of voicing is frequent in the vowel [a:]. Although some of these characteristics vary with speaker, the trend of decreasing vocal effort with time is typical of the sentence final position.

6. Apply rules for spectrum and time shaping of release transients and fricative segments. These rules have yet to be worked out on the basis of production theory (Fant, 1960) and more quantitatively aimed pattern matchings, as will be discussed later. In general (see Fant and Mártony, 1962), the release transient should be synthesized with a DC-stop source and a friction segment with an appropriately shaped noise source. The release transient and the friction are both synthesized with the "K-filter," whereas the following aspiration is shaped with the "F-filter."

The initial F-pattern as a place correlate

We shall now return to a study of the data on F-patterns and transitions in order to evaluate how distinctive they are in identifying "place" of articulation of the consonant and what additional cues should be taken into consideration.

It is well known and rather obvious that the transitional patterns in the voiced part of a vowel after a heavily aspirated stop pertain to instances in time where the articulators have moved so far away from the consonant that their movements do not retain much distinctiveness. In Table 7 [p][t] and [k] are compared in terms of F_2 and F_3 at the voicing boundary. The reduction is especially apparent comparing [t] and [p] before the vowel [aː] and unrounded front vowels. The loss of transitional information within the stop burst is specified by Table 8. The amount by which voiced and unvoiced stops differ in F_2 and F_3 at the instant of the release transient is shown in Table 8. The earlier discussed differences in articulation of voiced and unvoiced labials before back vowels are apparent. In other combinations the differences are not larger than 300 Hz and generally smaller than 200 Hz.

The discriminative power of the second and third formant frequencies F_{21}

Table 7. F_2 and F_3 differences at instant of voice onset as place correlates within unvoiced stops

	i	e	ɛ	ʉ	y	ø	u	o	a
$F_{2t} - F_{2p}$	100	150	−50	0	200	50	200	200	50
$F_{3t} - F_{3p}$	0	50	100	150	300	150	0	100	0
$F_{2k} - F_{2t}$	100	100	100	250	50	100	−150	−150	50
$F_{3k} - F_{3t}$	300	350	200	−100	0	−50	−100	−300	−350

Table 8. Extent of F_2 and F_3 transitions within unvoiced segments (from release to voice onset)

	i	e	ɛ	ʉ	y	ø	u	o	a
ΔF_{2p}	−100	−150	−250	0	50	100	800	700	750
ΔF_{3p}	−500	−450	−300	100	0	0	−110	?	−250
ΔF_{2t}	−200	−250	−100	100	−100	200	700	700	650
ΔF_{3t}	−150	0	100	300	100	450	200	200	200
ΔF_{2k}	0	0	200	−100	0	150	350	450	500
ΔF_{3k}	50	150	150	150	100	0	−100?	−200?	−250

and F_{3i} is illustrated in Figures 11 and 12. The following general conclusions can be drawn. The main characteristic of dentals compared with labials is the 350–500 Hz higher F_{3i}. Dentals may have higher F_{2i} than labials if compared in context with the same vowel. The palatal [k] and [g] before the unrounded front vowels [i:][e:] and [ε:] comprise a peripherally located subset of higher F_{3i} and also somewhat higher F_{2i} than any dental. The [k] and [g] before rounded front vowels [y:][ʉ:] and [ø:] differ from labials and dentals by a somewhat higher F_{2i} only. The velar [k] and [g] before the back vowel [a:] has a lower F_{3i} than any labial plus vowel.

It is interesting to note that the initial F_2,F_3 pattern differentiates unvoiced stops somewhat better than voiced stops, which is fully in line with the previously inferred finding that at the instance of release the unvoiced stops appear to be less coarticulated with the following vowel than the corresponding voiced stops. This is also apparent by the smaller spread of the unvoiced data with respect to vowel context as already pointed out in connection with Figure 7. The detailed data on the unvoiced-voiced differences in F_{2i} and F_{3i} are given in Table 9. The negative values of $F_{3p} - F_{3b}$ are ascribable to the difference in coarticulation, as is typically $F_{2p} - F_{2b}$ of [u:][o:] and [a:]. It should be kept

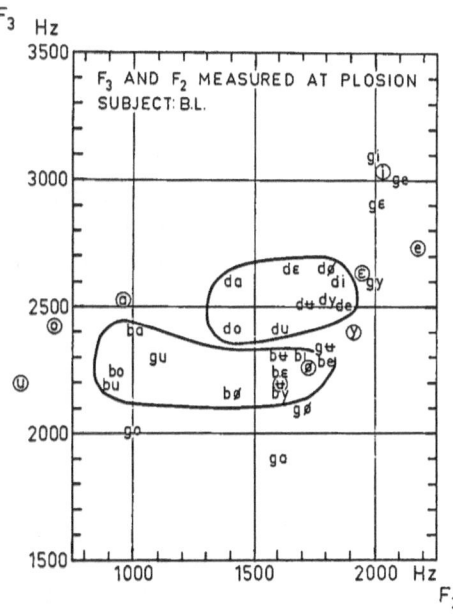

Figure 11. Initial F_2 and F_3 of voiced Swedish stops, subject B.L. The vowel targets are indicated in the figure.

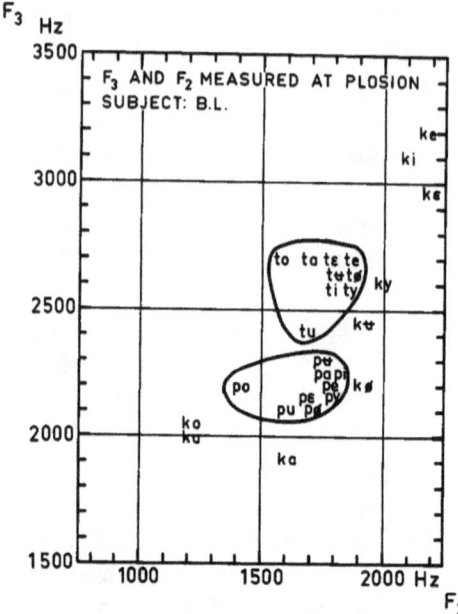

Figure 12. Initial F_2 and F_3 of unvoiced Swedish stops, subject B.L. The vowel targets are indicated in the figure.

in mind that the glottal shunt contributes to the trend of positive signs of the data with an average amount being of the order of $+100$ Hz.

Thus, with the exception of the infiltration of [gu:] and [gʉ:] in the labial area in Figure 10, all dentals are confined to one area, all labials are confined to a separate area, and the velar-palatals to a large range of peripheral locations outside these areas. For the corresponding unvoiced stops (Figure 11), there is no overlapping. The vowel targets are included in Figure 10 so as to allow a derivation of the direction of CV-transitions.

Table 9. Unvoiced and voiced stops compared with respect to F_2 and F_3 at instant of release

	i	e	ε	ʉ	y	ø	u	o	a
$F_{2p} - F_{2b}$	100	0	100	150	200	300	700	500	750
$F_{3p} - F_{3b}$	−50	−100	−50	0	50	−50	−100	?	−150
$F_{2t} - F_{2d}$	−50	−50	150	0	50	0	100	200	300
$F_{3t} - F_{3d}$	0	200	100	150	100	50	0	300	100
$F_{2k} - F_{2g}$	100	100	200	100	0	200	100	200	0
$F_{3k} - F_{3g}$	0	200	50	100	0	100	−300?	0?	0

Spectral energy cues. General feature discussion

An effective approach for testing the relevance of these transitional cues is to look up pairs of consonants in the same vowel context where the F-pattern data are the same or almost the same and then see what other cues there are to note. This technique was used by Öhman (1966) in his V_1CV_2 studies. He found that the CV_2 part of [ybo] was the same as that of [ygo] and concluded that V_1 and the V_1C transitional pattern carried the differentiating information. It would be interesting to check this experimentally by time segmentation of V_1C and CV_2 in the occlusion. I would rather guess that the CV_2 part carries the main differentiating information, although this is not immediately apparent from the spectrogram. Moreover, in Öhman's material the stylized F-pattern of [øgo] is almost exactly the same as that of [øbo]. It does not seem likely that some small differences in the traced F-patterns could be the main differentiating cue.

There exists an analogous situation in my CV-material. A vectorial distance in the F_{2i},F_{3i} plane of less than 250 Hz was found in the following minimal pairs: [ko]–[po], [go]–[bo], [kʉ]–[pʉ], [gʉ]–[bʉ], [kʉ]–[tʉ], [gu]–[bu], [ky]–[ty], [gy]–[dy]. A closer look at the [gu]–[bu] distinction from the spectrograms of Figure 4 verifies that the dynamic F-pattern is about the same. However, the [g] burst has a much more prominent F_2 component than that of [b]. Moreover, the [g] burst segment lacks energy in the F_1 range whereas F_1 is prominent in the corresponding part of the [b] spectrum. This is an instance of the general rules, discussed in earlier publications (Fant, 1958, 1960, 1968):

[k][g]
Spectral energy is concentrated, strong and continuously connected, without rapid initial transitions to the formant carrying the main pitch of the vowel (F_2 or F_3 and even F_4 in case of a prepalatal articulation).

[p][b]
Spectral energy is weak, more spread than in [k][g], and with an emphasis on lower frequency than [t][d]. Initial transitions are rapid and rising.

[t][d]
Spectral energy is spread, generally strong, with emphasis on higher frequencies than in [p] and [b] and extending higher than the main [k][g] formant.

An extension of the range of analysis to higher frequencies than 4000 Hz adds to the distinctiveness of these visually defined cues, mainly by displaying the high-frequency components of the [t] and [d] bursts.

The statements above concerning "spectral energy" refer to the first 10–30 ms after the release which appears to carry the main information on the place of articulation. Transient burst and the first part of a vowel when appearing within this segment should be regarded as a single stimulus rather than as a set of independent cues (Fant, 1960, p. 217; Stevens, 1967). When relating data from real speech to experiments with synthetic speech one should keep this in mind. As stated already by E. Fischer-Jørgensen (1954): "The listener does not compare explosion with explosion and transition with transition but compares artificial syllables comprising either explosion or transition with natural syllables that always contain both."

When discussing transitions it seems wise to distinguish two categories: (1) those related to the overall tongue body movement within the whole of a previous or a following vowel and (2) those related to the break of a consonantal obstruction or the movement toward closure. Those belonging to category 1 mainly reflect vowel coarticulation and are less distinctive than those of category 2. A typical example is the falling transition from labial stop to back vowel (see Figure 4), which reflects the tongue body movements whereas the labiality cues may be confined to the first 10 ms only and may not be visible in the spectrogram.

Production theory (Fant, 1960), provides a basis for an explanation of the origin of the general characteristic discussed above and is the starting point for derivation of synthesis strategies. Thus the main formant of the [k][g] sounds derives from the cavity in front of the tongue constriction and is represented by a free pole. The diffuse spectrum of [p] and [b] release originates from the lack of any front cavity. At release the dispersion effect is pronounced, pole frequencies rapidly moving in positive direction away from associated zeros which neutralize the poles before release.

The [k][g], on the other hand, have a free pole before release. In the critical segment after release this pole cannot display very rapid movements. The [t] and [d] have a small and narrow front channel behind the source which is associated with a high-pass sound filtering.

The mean frequency of the [k] and [g] bursts and their F-pattern associations in different vowel contexts have been measured and the data are presented in Table 10. The data vary over a 2500 Hz range, from 1000 Hz to 3500 Hz. The observed differences with respect to voicing are not very significant in view of the limited data.

Secondary correlates to the place of articulation for [k] and [g] are the approximately 30 ms delay from release transient to the appearance of the formant structure in the following vowel. The F_1 transitions after [b][d] and [g] are not much different except that the F_1 rise tends to be somewhat slower

Table 10. Burst formant areas of [k] and [g]

	i	e	ɛ	ʉ	y	ø	u	o	a
[k]	3200	3200	3100	2500	2600	2000	1300	1200	1750
[g]	3400	3500	3000	2200	2600	1950	1050	1000	1650
	F_3, F_4	F_3, F_4	F_3	F_3	F_3	F_2, F_3	F_2	F_2	F_2

Table 11. Target values of subject's formant frequencies toward the end of the vowel

	i	e	ɛ	ʉ	y	ø	u	o	a
F_1	225	300	370	250	200	375	250	350	650
F_2	2100	2200	2000	1600	1900	1700	550	600	950
F_3	3050	2700	2600	2100	2850	2300	2200	2500	2500
F_4	3600	3500	3500	3050	3200	3200	3000	2850	3050

after [g]. The differences in vowel targets conditioned by the particular place of articulation of the consonant could be measured but appear to be too small to be of any appreciable perceptual significance. The F_0 cues also contribute. Approximate vowel targets for the subject B.L. are shown in Table 11. They pertain to the final part of the vowel, in the case of close vowels (lowest level F_1) to the diphthongal termination. In [uː] and [ʉː] this is a lip closure which accounts for the falling F_2 and F_3. For [iː] and [yː] the diphthongal element is made with the tongue pressing harder against the palate. This accounts for the rise in F_3 at constant lip opening in [yː] and [iː]. A more detailed discussion of Swedish vowels was given by Fant (1969).

Intensity-frequency sections of the transient and burst spectra of Swedish stops have earlier been published by Fant (1959) and corresponding data on Russian stops by Fant (1960). These data support the conclusions above and support the feature frame of Jakobson, Fant, and Halle (1952/67) as to [k][g] being compact, [p][b] diffuse and grave, and [t][d] diffuse and acute (non-grave).

Although Chomsky and Halle (1968) improved the feature system by introducing tongue body features separate from the place of articulation features they have not been equally successful in defining "place" features that, irrespective of cooccurrence with other features, retain some perceptual invariance or at least similarity. Furthermore, they are highly disputable even on the level of production control (Fant, 1969). Although the feature "anterior" takes over the function of "diffuse" and thus could inherit the same correlates, there is real trouble with the "coronal" feature which loses its physiological basis when separating dentals from labials. The class of labial consonants is accordingly selected by reference to the negative of a feature referring to activities in muscles which have nothing to do with the lips.

From the perceptual point of view the feature [+coronal] separating dentals from labials when combined with the feature [+anterior] implies a high versus low frequency emphasis. When the coronal feature is used to differentiate [−anterior] fricatives, for example, Swedish [ṣ] and [ç], with respect to the tip of the tongue being up [+coronal] or down [−coronal] the acoustic effect appears to be the opposite, the [+coronal] (retroflexion) accounting for a lowering of the mean frequency of the spectrum. I cannot find any other spectral characteristics of the "coronal" feature that would be retained in combination with both + and − anterior. The "coronal" feature would not display this acoustical ambiguity if restricted to the class of [−anterior] consonants.

Stevens' (1967) theory of perceptual invariance conforms with the general statement on stop features above and has elements in common with that of Fant (1960, p. 217) and Jakobson, Fant, and Halle (1952/67). Thus, his treatment of velar sounds is almost the same as that of my earlier work. His floating reference of spectral energy with respect to the following vowel being low in labials is valid only for the short (=10 ms) delabialization segment and requires that the aspiration be identified with the vowel. I have a feeling that the reference to the vowel is not needed for discriminating [p] and [t]. Stevens' treatment of [g] as acoustically of lower pitch than a retroflex [ḍ] is valid for velar [g] only. In my view it is more natural to oppose velar [g] to palatal [g] pitch-wise, whereas the relation of [ḍ] to [g] is basically a matter of spread versus concentrated energy. The [ḍ] should rightly be opposed to [d], the [ḍ] being more "flat" and also less spread than [d]. The role of the feature "distributed" in this connection is not clear.

References

Chomsky, N. and M. Halle (1968). *Sound Pattern of English,* New York.

Delattre, P., A. M. Liberman, and F. S. Cooper (1955). "Acoustic Loci and Transitional Cues for Consonants," *J. Acoust. Soc. Am.* 27, pp. 769–773.

Elert, C-C. (1964). *Phonological Studies of Quantity in Swedish,* thesis, Uppsala.

Fant, G. (1957/68). "Den akustiska fonetikens grunder," Report No. 7, KTH, Speech Transmission Laboratory (Stockholm), new edition.

Fant, G. (1959). "Acoustic Analysis and Synthesis of Speech with Applications to Swedish," *Ericsson Technics* 15, pp. 3–108. [Reprinted in part in Chapter 3 of this volume.]

Fant, G. (1960). *Acoustic Theory of Speech Production,* 's-Gravenhage; second edition, 1970.

Fant, G. (1968). "Analysis and Synthesis of Speech Processes" in *Manual of Phonetics*, ed. B. Malmberg, Amsterdam, pp. 173–277.

Fant, G. (1969). "Distinctive Features and Phonetic Dimensions," STL-QPSR 2-3/1969, pp. 1–18. [Reprinted as Chapter 11 of this volume.]

Fant, G. and J. Mártony (1962). "Speech Synthesis," STL-QPSR 2/1962, pp. 18–24.

Fant, G., B. Lindblom, and J. Mártony (1963). "Spectrograms of Swedish Stops," STL-QPSR 3/1963, p. 1.

Fischer-Jørgensen, E. (1954). "Acoustic Analysis of Stop Consonants," *Miscel. Phonetica* 2, pp. 42–59.

Fujimura, O. (1961). "Bilabial Stop and Nasal Consonants: A Motion Picture Study and Its Acoustical Implications," *J. Speech and Hearing Research* 4, pp. 233–247.

Houde, R. A. (1967). "A Study of Tongue Body Motion During Selected Speech Sounds," thesis, Univ. of Michigan, Ann Arbor.

Jakobson, R., G. Fant, and M. Halle (1952/67). "Preliminaries to Speech Analysis: The Distinctive Features and Their Correlates," MIT, Acoust. Lab., Techn. Rep. No. 13 (1952); 7th edition publ. by MIT Press, Cambridge, Mass.

Karlsson, I., and L. Nord (1970). "A New Method of Recording Occlusion Applied to the Study of Swedish Stops," STL-QPSR 2-3/1970, pp. 8–18.

Kozhevnikov, V. A. and L. A. Chistovich (1965). *Speech: Articulation and Perception* (transl. from Russian), US Dept. of Commerce, JPRS:30, 543, Washington.

Lehiste, I. and G. E. Peterson (1961). "Transitions, Glides, and Diphthongs," *J. Acoust. Soc. Am.* 33, pp. 268–277.

Lindblom, B. (1968). "On the Production and Recognition of Vowels," thesis, Stockholm.

Öhman, S. E. G. (1965). "On the Coordination of Articulatory and Phonatory Activity in the Production of Swedish Tonal Accents," STL-QPSR 2/1965, pp. 14–19.

Öhman, S. E. G. (1966). "Coarticulation in VCV Utterances: Spectrographic Measurements," *J. Acoust. Soc. Am.* 39, pp. 151–168.

Öhman, S. E. G. (1967). "Numerical Model of Coarticulation," *J. Acoust. Soc. Am.* 41, pp. 310–320.

Peterson, G. E. and I. Lehiste (1960). "Duration of Syllable Nuclei in English," *J. Acoust. Soc. Am.* 32, pp. 693–703.

Stevens, K. N. (1967). "Acoustic Correlates of Certain Consonantal Features," paper C6 presented at the 1967 Conf. on Speech Communication and Processing, Nov. 6–8, Cambridge, Mass., pp. 177–185.

Part II
Features: Theory and Systems

Chapter 8
Structural Classification
of Swedish Phonemes

The following tabulation of Swedish phonemes in a distinctive feature code (see Table 1) is in all essentials based on the system of Jakobson, Fant, and Halle (1952) but with the modifications owing to the general advance of the theory and the specific views held by the author. The particular solution for the vowel system is the same as that proposed in recent publications (Fant, 1958, 1959), but differs from that of an earlier study (Fant, 1954). The consonant system has not been published before.

The distinctive feature scheme primarily serves the purpose of linguistic theory but includes acoustic descriptions which theoretically could be regarded as an instruction for machine recognition of spoken text. In practice, the acoustic definition of the features often involves stipulations concerning the differences between alternative phonemes. These abstractions may not be translated into identification rules without taking into account the specific range of qualities utilized by the particular speaker in a specific context.

Most of the distinctive features or rather "phonemic distinctions" are identical with elementary phonetic categories which are well established in linguistic theory. Any scheme for machine recognition of spoken items will to some extent rely on a classification in terms of these categories. On the other hand, it is clear that an optimal recognition process will differ from the traditional distinctive feature system in terms of the particular choice and definitions of features and the sequence of operations. Vowels could thus be identified directly from properly normalized formant frequencies. Independent of the purpose of the identification scheme, whether this be linguistic theory or machine recognition of speech, it should be recognized that distinctive features or the several cues which may underlie a distinction are not always static constituents of a single sound segment* but quite often involve several adjacent

---

This article originally appeared in Speech Transmission Laboratory Quarterly Progress and Status Report 2/1960 (Stockholm, Sweden: Royal Institute of Technology, 1960).
* The difference between the prosodic and inherent features are thus to some extent eliminated since both involve temporal relations. The prosodic features, however, generally operate over speech-wave units of a greater length than the inherent features.

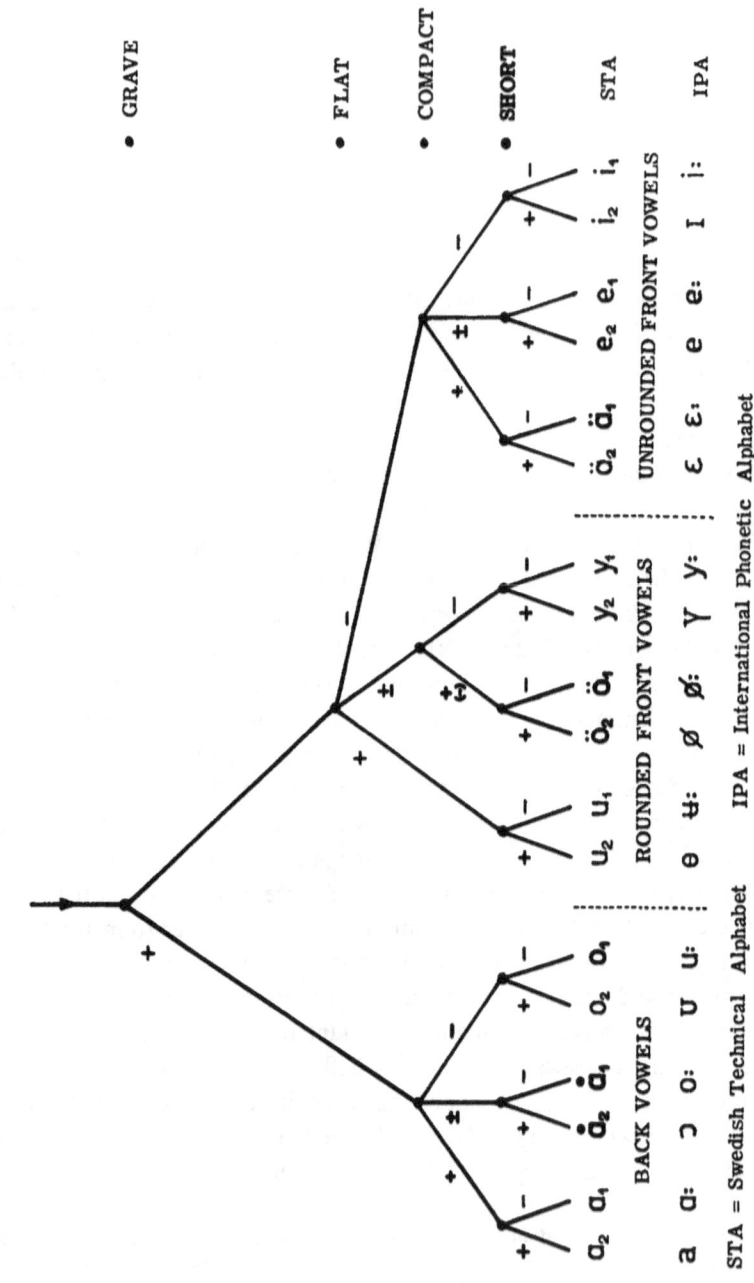

Figure 1. Distinctive feature coding of Swedish vowels. Back vowels separated in terms of compactness.

segments and dynamic relations within a sequence of segments. These are well-established facts.*

The Swedish vowel system comprises nine long vowel phonemes $/o_1//å_1/$ $/a_1//y_1//u_1//ö_1//i_1//e_1//ä_1/$ and nine short vowel phonemes $/o_2//å_2//a_2/$ $/y_2//u_2//ö_2//i_2//e_2//ä_2/$. These phonemic notations of the STA-alphabet conform to common Swedish orthography. Phonetic values of the basic allophones are indicated in Figures 1 and 2.

The relation of $/ä_1/$ to $/e_1/$ or of $/e_1/$ to $/i_1/$ specified by the compactness feature is that of an open versus a close vowel, referring to the mouth cavity. The relation of $/a_1/$ to $/å_1/$ or $/å_1/$ to $/o_1/$ may either be identified by the compactness feature as in Figure 1 or with the relation of unrounded to rounded (flat) vowels as in Figure 2. There are of course hybrid alternatives, such as the labeling of $/o_1/$ to $/å_1/$ as flat versus $/a_1/$ and opposing $/å_1/$ to $/o_1/$ in terms of compactness. This solution avoids the use of ± terms within the back vowels. The same relations hold for short vowels. The relations within the rounded front vowels $/y_1/$ $/u_1/$ $/ö_1/$ and $/y_2/$ $/u_2/$ $/ö_2/$ are more complex. The phoneme $/ö_1/$ is definitely compact compared with $/y_1/$ and $/ö_1/$ is compact compared with $/y_2/$ but the phonemes $/u_1/$ and $/u_2/$ cannot be consistently specified by this feature. Thus $/u_2/$ is generally a more compact vowel than $/ö_2/$ whereas $/u_1/$ is less compact than $/ö_1/$. In general, however, the relation of $/u_1/$ to $/ö_1/$ and $/y_1/$ or of $/u_2/$ to $/ö_2/$ and $/y_2/$ is the same as that of $/y_1/$ and $/ö_1/$ compared with $/i_1//e_1/$ and $/ä_1/$. This is the motivation for the classification of $/ö_1/$ and $/y_1/$ and similarly also $/ö_2/$ and $/y_2/$ as ± flat.

Within the consonant system (Figure 3), the alveolar phonemes $/rl//rn/$ $/rt//rd/$ are opposed to the pure dentals $/l//n//t/$ and $/d/$ in terms of the flatness feature. From a distributional point of view, however, the alveolars may be regarded as the realization of a phoneme $/r/$ plus a following dental phoneme. This is also the case for an $/rs/$ as opposed to $/s/$ with the complication that [rs] stands in complimentary distribution to a quite similar sound labeled [sj] which is not the result of a fusion between an [r] and a dental. Thus $/rs/$ is the same phoneme as $/sj/$. The phoneme $/sj/$ is acoustically flat (lower frequency of main formant) both in relation to the compact (palatal) $/tj/$ and the noncompact acute $/s/$.

The following is a condensed summary of acoustic correlates of phonemic distinctions with special reference to the Swedish phoneme system.†

---

* An attempt to construct a scheme of segment classification according to an inventory of narrow phonetic categories instead of phonemic distinctions has been undertaken in a recent article (Fant, 1960b).
† The articulatory correlates are well established except for some specific details of the Swedish vowel system. For a general discussion of articulatory correlates, see earlier publications, for example, G. Fant, *Acoustic Theory of Speech Production* (1960a).

146 Features: Theory and Systems

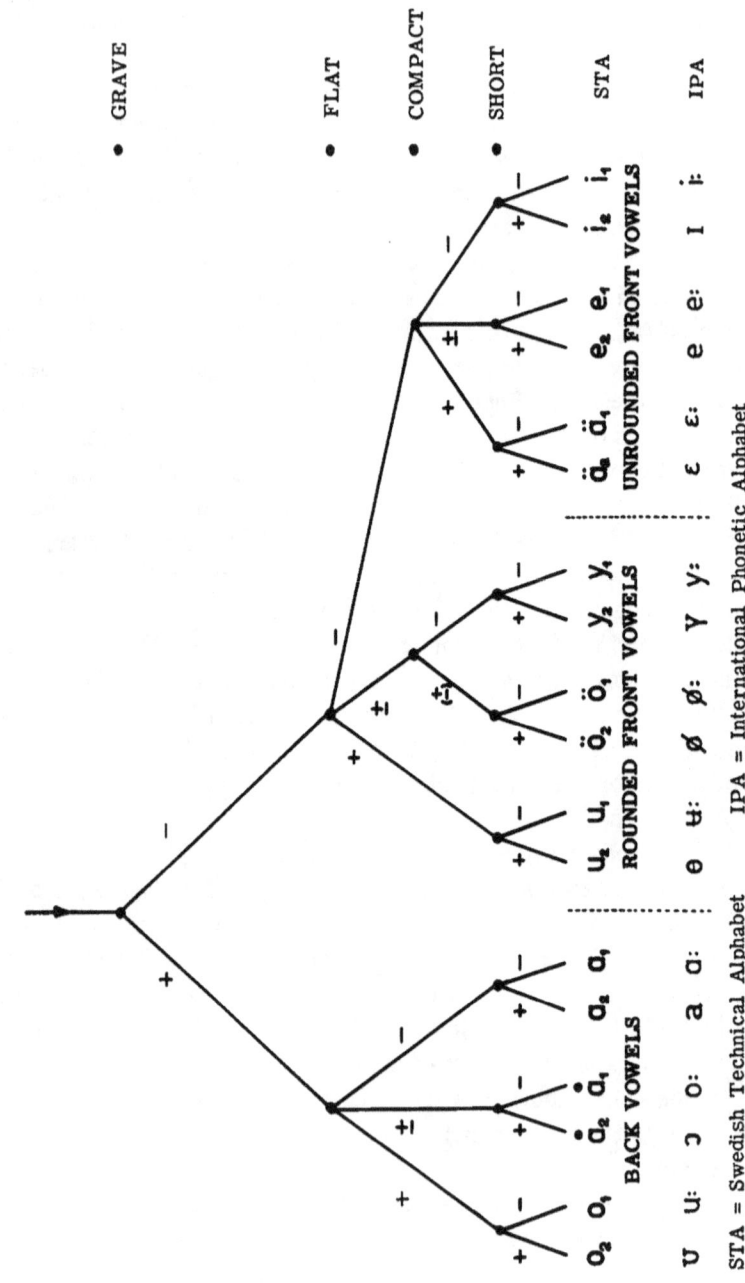

Figure 2. Distinctive feature coding of Swedish vowels. Back vowels separated in terms of flatness.

Structural Classification of Swedish Phonemes 147

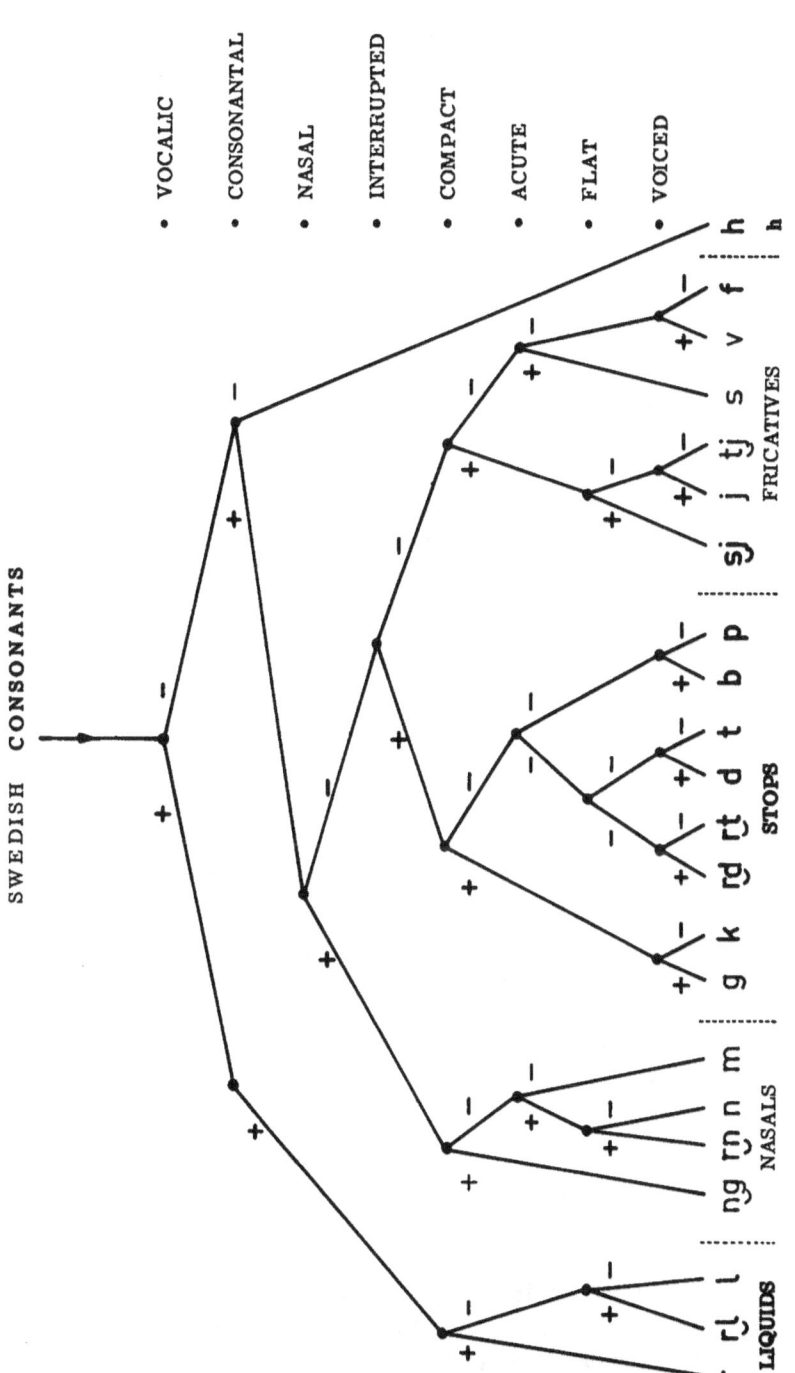

Figure 3. Distinctive feature coding of Swedish consonants.

Table 1.

		Swedish consonants																					
		r	ḍ	l	ng	ɱ	n	m	g	k	ɽɖ	ʈʈ	d	t	b	p	s͡j	rs	j	tj	s	v	f	h
I	Vocalic	+	+	+	−	−	−	−	−	−	−	−	−	−	−	−	−	−	−	−	−	−	−	−
II	Consonantal	+	+	+	+	+	+	+	+	+	+	+	+	+	+	+	+	+	+	+	+	+	−
III	Nasal				+	+	+	+	−	−	−	−	−	−	−	−	−	−	−	−	−	−	−
IV	Interrupted								+	+	+	+	+	+	+	+	−	−	−	−	−	−	−
V	Compact	+	−	−	+	−	−	−	+	+	−	−	−	−	−	−	+	+	−	−	−	−	
VI	Acute				+	+	−		+	+	+	+	−	−				+	−	−			
VII	Flat	+	−		+	−			+	+	−	−			+			−	−	−			
VIII	Voiced								+	−	+	−	+	−	+	−		+	−		+	−	

		Swedish vowels															
		a_2	a_1	$\mathring{a}_2$	$\mathring{a}_1$	o_2	o_1	$ä_2$	$ä_1$	e_2	e_1	i_2	i_1	$ö_2$	$ö_1$	y_2	y_1	u_2	u_1
1	Acute	−	−	−	−	−	−	+	+	+	+	+	+	+	+	+	+	+	+
2	Flat	(−)	(−)	(±)	(±)	(+)	(+)	−	−	−	−	−	−	±	±	±	±	+	+
3	Compact	+	+	±	±	−	−	+	+	±	±	−	−	+	+	−	−	−	−
4	Short	+	−	+	−	+	−	+	−	+	−	+	−	+	−	+	−	+	−

1. The vowel system
   (1) *Acute.* An acute vowel has a higher $F_2 - F_1$ than a corresponding non-acute (grave) vowel.
   (2) *Flat.* A flat vowel has a lower sum (with possible weighting) $F_1 + F_2 + F_3$ than corresponding nonflat (plain) vowels.
   (3) *Compact.* A compact vowel has a higher F_1 than a corresponding noncompact (diffuse) vowel.
   (4) *Short.* A short vowel within the Swedish vowel system has a shorter duration and generally a spectrum with a higher F_1 and a more neutral formant pattern than a corresponding long vowel of the same context.

The long vowel is combined with a short consonant and vice versa. The short/long distinction is in all essentials identical with the lax/tense distinction described by Jakobson, Fant, and Halle (1952).

2. The consonant system
   (1) *Vocalic.* The F-pattern formants (F_1, F_2, F_3) of frequencies F_1, F_2, F_3, respectively, are more apparent and the overall intensity is higher in a vocalic than in a nonvocalic phoneme.

(2) *Consonantal.* Consonantal phonemes are acoustically characterized by sound segments fulfilling one or both of the following conditions:
   a. The main energy is confined to other formants than F_1 and F_2.
   b. Low second formant intensity F_2 and generally a low first formant frequency position F_1 compared with adjacent sound segment.

These aspects of the consonantal feature appear as a temporal contrast effect either in the type of spectrum or in terms of a rapid transition of the formant frequencies and the sound intensity.

There is an appreciable overlap in the definition of the consonantal feature and the nonvocalic feature which parallels the classification of most consonants as being both consonantal and nonvocalic. The phoneme /h/ is classified nonconsonantal because of the lack of contrast in formant frequencies relative to an adjacent vowel but it is nonvocalic because of the lower intensity, especially in the first formant range. The liquids /l/ and /r/ have more vocalic formant patterns than other consonants and may thus be coded as +vocalic and +consonantal.

The nucleus of a common syllable is a single vowel or a diphthong, the speech-wave correlate of which is a vocalic nonconsonantal sound segment. An adjacent sound segment belonging to the same syllable is always consonantal and produces, together with the vowel, a temporal contrast owing to its lower intensity* or to its spectrum of a nonvocalic type. On account of the +vocalic feature liquids may be said to rank next after vowels in terms of "syllabicity." In a consonant cluster liquids always occur next to the vowel in conformity with the idea of a successive decay of syllabicity away from the syllable nucleus. A liquid /l/ or /r/ out of contact with a vowel would thus in itself constitute a syllabic nucleus. The /r/ possesses a greater syllabicity than /l/ on account of the greater compactness.

In unstressed syllables the vowel is of lower intensity, shorter duration, and possesses a formant pattern closer to that of a neutral vowel than in stressed syllables. The contrast between the vowel and adjacent consonants is reduced.

(3) *Nasal.* The formant structure of nasal sound segments has a reduced second formant intensity and possesses the typical qualities of the nasal murmur.

(4) *Interrupted.* Rapid onset or checking of the sound intensity combined with rapid formant transitions.

(5) *Compact.* The spectral energy of the sound segments of compact pho-

---

* It is probable that a proper frequency selective pre-emphasis in the intensity measuring procedure, favoring the frequency range below 3000 Hz, would invariably provide a larger intensity of a vowel than an adjacent consonant, for example, a fricative. Results from experiments on voicing detectors support this view.

nemes is concentrated to a more central location versus the main pitch of the immediately adjacent vocalic sound segments than non-compact (diffuse) phonemes.*

(6) *Acute.* Greater intensity of high-frequency formants than in non-acute (grave sounds).

(7) *Flat.* A shift down in the frequency location of formants retaining the general shape of the spectrum.

(8) *Voiced.* In Swedish consonants the voiced/voiceless opposition occurs in complimentary distribution with the lax/tense opposition. The common denominator is the relative lack or the shortness of duration of unvoiced segments of the speech wave. Examples are the burst and occlusion phases of voiced stops and the unvoiced segment of voiced (lax) continuants which are shorter in voiced than in unvoiced sounds.

References

Fant, G. (1954). "Phonetic and Phonemic Basis for the Transcription of Swedish Word Material," *Acta Oto-Laryngologica*, Suppl. 116, 83–93.

Fant, G. (1958). "Modern Instruments and Methods for Acoustic Studies of Speech," *Proc. of the VIII International Congress of Linguists*, Oslo University Press, Oslo, 1958, p. 282–358; also publ. in *Acta Polytechnica Scandinavica*, Ph 1 (246/1958).

Fant, G. (1959). "Acoustic Analysis and Synthesis of Speech with Applications to Swedish," *Ericsson Technics* 15, No. 1, pp. 3–108. [Reprinted in part as Chapter 3 of this volume.]

Fant, G. (1960a). *Acoustic Theory of Speech Production*, Mouton & Co., 's-Gravenhage; second edition, 1970.

Fant, G. (1960b). "Descriptive Analysis of the Acoustic Aspects of Speech," paper presented at the 1960 Summer Symposia at Burg Wartenstein, Austria, "Comparative Aspects of Human Communication," September 4–10, 1960. [Reprinted as Chapter 2 of this volume.]

Jakobson, R., C. G. M. Fant, and M. Halle (1952). *Preliminaries to Speech Analysis. The distinctive features and their correlates*, 7th ed., MIT Press, Cambridge, Mass., 1967.

---

* One suggested definition of main pitch is the second formant of a synthetic two-formant sound perceptually matching the quality of the sound segment. In first approximation this main pitch coincides with F_2 but is closer to F_3 or F_4 for high front vowels. In voiced stops and nasal consonants the front transitions carry a great part of the perceptually effective cues. The extent to which these cues may be included in the formulation above is not quite clear. In general the formant transitions and the consonantal sound segment constitute a compound stimulus.

Chapter 9
The Nature of Distinctive Features

INTRODUCTION

THE following essay is intended as a review of my own thinking on distinctive features. I have followed up only a part of all that has been written on this topic. I am more practically oriented than linguists and less bound to orthodox acceptance of working principles but I still find it a rather fascinating subject to sit down and work out alternative solutions, e.g., for ordering of Swedish vowels which was one of my early interests.

I certainly feel that a substantial revision of our old *Preliminaries* [15] has long been overdue. The major principles are still valid but I feel we need much more factual data before a substantial revision can be undertaken. Till then the following material may serve as an expression of my views on the subject.

Specialists in language and speech have displayed rather diverging reactions to the theory of distinctive features and misunderstandings have been frequent. Does it provide a condensed presentation of the most useful facts about speech or is it just an intellectual game, an end in itself for the structural linguist? High initial expectations of finding new and simple solutions to central problems of speech analysis, such as automatic speech recognition, have been followed by distrust. Now, the theory of distinctive features is not intended as a working recipe for technical application but it can provide some organizational principles and suggestions. The rather specific terminology does not stand for either radically new or very special features. The articulatory, acoustic, or perceptive correlates of distinctive features should comprise condensed transforms of the most relevant information from any of these stages within the complete speech communication system. A continued study of alternative solutions and descriptive forms is needed in the development of the distinctive feature theory as in speech analysis in general.

What is then really the concept of distinctive features? How are they defined, from the speech wave, from articulation, or from perception. Are they simply a part of the linguistic code for decomposition of phonemes in a bundle of smaller units?

This article originally appeared in *To Honor Roman Jakobson: Essays on the Occasion of his Seventieth Birthday* (The Hague: Mouton & Company, 1967). Reprinted with permission.

Reading the *Preliminaries* one finds that the distinctive features operate on all four levels but from which one do you start the analysis? Here as in phonemic analysis the set of distinctive features constitutes abstract units of the message code. The distinctive feature is a choice between one of two alternatives. In the *Preliminaries* distinctive features are referred to by terms as 'discriminations', 'choice', and 'selection' stressing the linguistic level. A distinctive feature generally recurs as a choice situation in several minimal distinction pairs within a language and it is of course required that the physical or physiological manifestations be consistent, i.e., one and the same feature shall have qualitatively the same articulatory, acoustic, and perceptive correlates independent of context of other features within the bundle. The modification 'qualitatively' here implies that the relation between the two opposites is the same in all contexts. Absolute values of descriptive parameters, however, generally vary with context. Failure to recognize the role of contextual bias is a frequent source of misunderstanding of the nature of distinctive features. A distinctive feature is by definition the same in all contexts. The underlying physical phenomena, on the other hand, referred to as 'correlates', 'cues', or 'parameters' need exhibit only relational invariance.

Distinctive features are really distinctive categories or classes within a linguistic system but just like in accepted phonemic analysis it is required that they are consistent with the phonetic facts and these phonetic facts on various levels have lent their name to the features. It is not within my competence to discuss the generality of distinctive features but it is apparent that they comprise, as they should, the essentials of the framework of classical phonetics and in addition some categorizations of a seemingly more novel appearance.

I shall now proceed to some specific points concerning distinctive features some of which are often brought up in discussions.

HOW IMPORTANT IS THE BINARY PRINCIPLE?

The binary principle obviously has its basis in the presence versus absence of an articulatory or phonatory event, e.g., presence versus absence of voicing, nasality, occlusion etc., or in a selection of one of two polar alternatives along a continuous parameter scale, e.g., more open as opposed to less open. In the analysis of vowels it can be motivated to recognize more than two significant levels of one and the same parameter, cif. the discussion on compactness in the *Preliminaries*, paragraph 2.414. As indicated in the analysis of the Swedish vowel system later in this paper one could conceive of instances, where up to four distinct levels of one and the same feature might be considered. In these instances a decomposition in terms of two binary categories is generally undertaken in order to allow a consistent use of the binary principle within the whole system.

The distinctive feature represents the linguist's condensed view of the minimal units for composing speech messages. If properly applied, categorization according to binary principles need not come in conflict with the physical reality. It is a matter of coding convenience only.

ECONOMY BUT AT WHAT PRICE?

If alternative solutions of distinctive features are possible it is established policy to adopt the one providing the best economy in terms of the smallest number of features or rather the least redundancy minimizing the number of alternatives that can be generated by the specific set of categories. However, this requirement can come in conflict with the principle of consistency, i.e., there is the risk that one or more minimal pairs in which a feature is supposed to operate do not conform sufficiently well with the rest of the system. Seemingly elegant solutions may thus have to be rejected because they do not apply in specific contexts. It is also apparent that the economy gained in treating consonants and vowels with the same features at times leads to somewhat remote analogies.

ARE DISTINCTIVE FEATURES ALWAYS ORTHOGONAL?

Distinctive features are handled as independent units on the linguistic level but their phonetic manifestations often lack orthogonality. The phonetic quality of a vowel may to a first approximation be specified by F1 and F2. In the F_1, F_2 plane, however, gravity, compactness, flatness, and tenseness all occupy specific vectors and interdependency is thus unavoidable. Even when such parameters as F_3, F_0, overall intensity, and duration are added in order to provide a better approximation it is not phonetically realistic to choose a consistenly orthogonal set of features.

HOW ARE DISTINCTIVE FEATURES DISTRIBUTED IN TIME?

People who lack training in experimental phonetics are generally rather surprised when they learn that the acoustic speech wave does not stand up very well to the ideal concept imposed by our intuitive phonemic view of speech as a sequence of discrete units with distinct boundaries. One major shortcoming of the *Preliminaries* is the lack of a realistic discussion of the time-varying aspects of speech patterns and the temporal distribution of the acoustic articulatory and perceptual characteristics underlying the distinctive features which might have saved phonetically inexperienced people from developing an oversimplified, often naive, view of the segment structure of speech.

It is said in paragraph 2.14 of the *Preliminaries* that "For practical purposes each phoneme can be represented by a quasi-stationary spectrum in which the transfer function is invariable with respect to time, except in the manner stated for transient effects." Phoneme boundaries are said to be related to rapid changes either in the source function or in the vocal transfer function. It is also said that inherent features in contrast to prosodic features are definable without a reference to the sequence. These rules are oversimplified and need to be reformulated and expanded.

The speech spectrogram displays a mixture of continuous and discontinuous elements. A succession of 'segments' is to be seen but what appears from the spectrogram appears to be a natural unit may constitute only a fraction of a phoneme, e.g., the aspiration segment or the occlusion segment of a noninitial unvoiced stop. In other instances a piece of speech that stands out from the rest of the sequence as a separate unit, e.g., in virtue of a continuity of voicing, may be associated with several successive phonemes.

No unique and simple rule exists for segmentation of speech on the basis of non-phonemic criteria. I would claim, however, that a non-phonemic segmentation [1, 2] could be of value as a rationale for articulatory or spectrographic systematizations per se and as an introductory form of transcription before imposing the linguistic message concepts on the signal data. The outcome of such confrontations of preconceived linguistic structure with the observed acoustic-phonetic structure is that the number of physical sound segments comes out to be larger than the number of phonemes. Because of coarticulation effects one sound segment generally carries information on two or more successive phonemes. Conversely, a single phoneme exerts an influence on several successive sound segments of the signal structure.

When it comes to discussing the distribution of distinctive features in time it must be made clear whether it is the abstract message structure or the physical manifestation of speech signals that is intended. In the former case distinctive features are bounded as the phonemes although there can be continuity of a feature from one phoneme to the next. It is thus said in paragraph 1.1 of the *Preliminaries* that "The difference between the distinctive features of continuous bundles permits the division of a sequence into phonemes. This difference may be either complete, as between the last two phonemes /i/ and /ŋ/ in the word wing (which has no distinctive features in common) or partial as between the last two phonemes of the word apt."

This statement is correct on the message level. Indeed, the phoneme /i/ is categorized as nonconsonantal, vocalic, nongrave, acute, and noncompact whereas the phoneme /ŋ/ is labelled consonantal, nonvocalic, nasal, compact. One would accordingly expect a maximum of acoustic contrast between the /i/ and the /ŋ/ of wing.

In a multidimensional articulatory or acoustic space, however, the contrast between the two corresponding segments is minimal only. The place of tongue articulation is identical or almost identical in American English, and both segments are produced with a lowered velum, the anticipatory nasalization being a normal feature generally affecting the entire segment assigned to the /i/. The raising of the tongue against the palate closing off the mouth cavity does not affect the sound much since a substantial part is directed through the nose already in the /i/ segment. In the case of a more reduced articulation the tongue never reaches the stages of full contact with the palate and the phoneme /ŋ/ is signalled merely as the nasalization of the sound segment. The perceptual importance of nasalization of a vowel as a cue for identification of an adjacent nasal phoneme is considerable [3].

The theory of segmentation of speech on various levels is a worthwhile object for further research and descriptive studies. The essential point to consider is that we can measure the duration of physical events such as sound segments in a spectrogram but there exists no unique method or convention of measuring the duration of a phoneme or of a distinctive feature.

SPECIFIC FEATURES. VOCALIC AND CONSONANTAL

One of the weaker parts of the distinctive feature theory is that of defining consonants and vowels. It is in my opinion quite motivated to categorize liquids as being both vocalic and consonantal but the classification of the consonant *h* (and glides) as being nonvocalic and nonconsonantal is a more arbitrary construction although arguments can be raised in favor of such a classification. The physical criteria for the vocalic and consonantal features have not been very rigid. A small damping of vowel formants has been one of the requirements in all versions of the system. The first edition of the *Preliminaries* stressed the voiced source of vocalic sounds but the Addenda and Corrigenda chapters of the later edition turned the emphasis on the formant pattern and formulated the consonantal feature as almost the negative of the vocalic feature in terms of formant reduction.

In *Fundamentals of Language* Jakobson and Halle [4] limits the consonantal feature to a low intensity alone. In a study of the classification of Swedish phonemes [5] I introduced a new formulation retaining the concept of formant reduction in defining the consonant feature but with intensity associated with the vocalic feature. One gain of this formulation is that the phoneme /h/ accordingly contrasts with vowels as being less intense. Also /h/ differs from other consonants in the lack of pattern contrast with adjacent vowels, motivating the minus consonantal feature.

The study of Fant (1960) [5] also includes comments on the theory of the syllable. The syllable nucleus must possess the vocalic feature and it displays a *temporal contrast* with respect to adjacent sounds in terms of either higher intensity or a more vowel like structure. Syllabicity should not be ascribed to intensity alone.

TENSE/LAX AND VOICED/VOICELESS

The subject of tense and lax vowels and consonants has been given a thorough treatment by Jakobson and Halle [6]. Their view on the subject does not depart substantially from that expressed in our earlier joint work. The tense versus lax opposition is intended to operate in vowels as well as in consonants. Tenseness is phonetically described by an "articulation with greater overpressure behind the place of the active source; in the case of vowels a higher subglottal pressure and in the case of stops and constrictives a higher pressure behind the place of articulation. Furthermore tenseness is associated with a more extreme articulation and with a greater time spent in an extreme articulatory position."

These last two characteristics were mentioned in our earlier work but I am somewhat sceptical about the higher overpressure. This factor when present indeed adds emphasis to tense consonants but in my opinion it has not been sufficiently well documented in experimental work. Recent studies of Malécot [17] suggest that the combined effect of pressure and duration expressed as a pulse integral could have a role in proprioceptive feedback. In my experience Swedish voiced and unvoiced stops are produced with the same subarticulatory pressure at the instance before release. This does not prove anything for English but it seems probable that the pressure factor, if present as a constituent in the opposition between American English unvoiced and voiced stops, is of relatively small significance and a secondary effect of glottal articulation. Several recent studies support the view of Lisker and Abramson [7] that it is the glottal articulation that is the basic factor.

The longer duration and higher intensity of the noise interval following at the release of an unvoiced stop is physiologically due to a delayed closing of the vocal cords compared with the voiced stops. The pulmonary pressure appears to be the same. Studies of subglottal pressure in Swedish speech does not reveal any difference in the pulmonary activity comparing voiced and unvoiced consonants or short and long vowels. I really doubt that subglottal pressure would have anything to do with the tense-lax opposition among English and French vowels.

On these grounds I hesitate to accept the use of the tense-lax opposition among American English consonants as well as vowels suggested by Halle [8]. In vowels it would be motivated if the pressure factor is forgotten. Within consonants it would be just as motivated to use the voiced-voiceless distinction as the tense-lax distinction. The economy gained by one and the same feature operating in vowels as well as in consonants is of course desirable but I find it more important that the match between phonetic facts and feature criteria is optimized. We need more experimental data to illuminate this very interesting problem.

DISTINCTIVE FEATURES AND PERCEPTION[1]

I do not hold the view that the decoding of speech in the brain up to the level of phonemic identification has to follow a functional scheme strictly conforming with a distinctive feature system of language analysis. This does not imply that I consider distinctive features unimportant in speech perception. Distinctive features as phonetic

[1] A more detailed treatment is contained in the QPSR article [16].

classes are a psychological reality as judged from confusion tests under varying types of distortion or mental disturbance. Even in rapid mimicking [9] the decoding proceeds along phonetic classes so that, e.g., place of articulation may be confused whilst the category of stop sound is correctly recognized.

When constructing models of speech perception we should not limit our choice to a representation in terms of either allophones or features. On the contrary it seems reasonable that a decoding in terms of phonetic classes (distinctive features) is paralleled by a direct attempt of allophone decoding. I am thus more in favor of a parallel analysis of features than of a serial analysis with a succession of decisions.

The question whether a translation to equivalent motor instructions precedes phonemic identification is not important. Of greater importance is to study what aspects of known features are of primary importance to perception [10]. It is observed that in some instances it is the TEMPORAL CONTRAST of two successive sound segments (e.g., stops, laterals, nasals) rather than the inherent quality of each of the segments that evokes the particular auditory sensation associated with the particular class (feature). The pertinent problem is to find what transforms we should apply to the speech wave data in order to extract the information bearing elements that operate in speech perception. Attempts to avoid the search for auditory relevant sound characteristics by an uncritical acceptance of the view that perception is merely a reconstruction of the production does not appear very fruitful.

Recent studies of Chistovich et al in Stockholm have revealed interesting results concerning vowel perception. These studies [11] support the view of a categorical perception of isolated vowels and the existence of an F_1 F_2 quantization in accordance with our working principles of acoustic phonetic analysis.

SWEDISH VOWELS.

The Swedish vowel system is generally presented in terms of nine long and nine short phonemes. Special pre-*r* variants of the open unrounded and rounded front vowels in Swedish orthography ä and ö stand out as well recognized allophones of an especially 'open' quality.

The following phonemic symbols referred to as the STA alphabet will be used for the nine vowels. Approximate IPA symbols are included as examples of phonetic values in contexts other than before [r].

GROUP	STA	IPA	STA	IPA
I. Back vowels	o_1	ʉ:	o_2	U
	$å_1$	o:	$å_2$	ɔ
	a_1	ɑ:	a_2	ɑ - a

158 Features: Theory and Systems

II.	Unrounded front vowels	i_1 e_1 $ä_1$	i: e: ɛ:	i_2 e_2 $ä_2$	I e - ɛ ɛ
III.	Rounded front vowels	y_1 $ʉ_1$ $ö_1$	y: $ʉ_1$: ø:	y_2 $ʉ_2$ $ö_2$	Y ɵ ø - œ

In my first attempt at ordering [12] I chose to oppose group I to group II and III in terms of the grave/acute distinction and group III was naturally opposed to group II in terms of the flat/plain feature. So far my views have not changed. However, a division within the three major groups in terms of articulatory opening, i.e., the compactness feature classifying not only /å₁/ and /e₁/ but also by an intermediate ± degree of compactness did not conform well with phonetic facts, the F_1 of /ʉ₁/ being the same as the F_1 of /y₁/. Also within the short vowels the F_1 of /ʉ₂/ was generally not significantly different from the F_1 of /ö₂/. I therefore chose in later works [5, 13, 14] to use three degrees of flatness assigning an intermediate value of flatness to the phonemes /y/ and /ö/ and to the phoneme /ʉ/ the maximal degree of flatness. This conforms well with the flatness criteria of low $F_1 + F_2 + F_3$ and the extreme degree of lip-rounding in the /ʉ/ and /o/ phonemes. In group I either flatness or compactness in three levels can be used for the further division.

An alternative solution which perhaps comes closer to the views of Roman Jakobson would be the following. In group I flatness is used to separate phonemes /o/ and /å/ from /a/, and /å/ is opposed to /o/ by the greater compactness. Now in group II and group III the opposition sharp/plain is introduced[2] to differentiate /i/ and /e/ from /ä/ and /y/ and /ö/ from /ʉ/. The criterion of sharpness is higher F_2 and F_3 everything else being equal. In this sense sharpness is given a function similar to that of diffuseness in Halle's vowel analyses [8]. By this arrangement one avoids introducing three degrees of flatness or compactness and four binary features specify the entire system as shown below.

FEATURE[3]	o	å	a	i	e	ä	y	u	ö
grave	+	+	+	−	−	−	−	−	−
flat	+	+	−	−	−	−	+	+	+
compact	−	+	+	−	+	+	−	−	+
sharp				+	+	−	+	−	+

In this solution /ʉ/ differs from /ö/ by two features. Within the system of short vowels /ö₂/ is opposed to /ʉ₂/ primarily by the sharpening (palatalization) whereas

[2] Suggested by S. Öhman.
[3] In terms of the compactness and sharpness features, the vowel [e] may be either + + or − −.

within the long vowels /ö₁/ differs from /ʉ/ primarily in terms of greater compactness. In terms of economy this new system is superior to my previous system. Four binary classes versus one binary and two ternary distinctions or 16 versus 18 as the maximal number of combinations of the code. However, the more redundant system may be phonetically simpler and more realistic. Further studies are needed to evaluate the various alternatives.

ROYAL INSTITUTE OF TECHNOLOGY (KTH)
STOCKHOLM

REFERENCES

[1] Fant, G., "Descriptive analysis of the acoustic aspects of speech", *Logos*, V (1962), 3-17.
[2] Fant, G., and Lindblom, B., "Studies of minimal speech sound units", STL-QPSR 2/1961, 1-11.
[3] Mártony, J., "The role of formant amplitudes in synthesis of nasal consonants", STL-QPSR 3/1964, 28-31.
[4] Jakobson, R., and Halle, M., *Fundamentals of Language* ('s-Gravenhage, 1956).
[5] Fant, G., "Structural classification of Swedish phonemes", STL-QPSR 2/1965, 10-15.
[6] Jakobson, R., and Halle, M., "Tenseness and laxness", in R. Jakobson, *Selected Writings*, I ('s-Gravenhage, 1962), 550-555.
[7] Lisker, L., and Abramson, A. S., "A cross-language study of voicing in initial stops: acoustical measurements", *Word*, XX (1964), 384-422.
[8] Halle, M., "Phonology in generative grammar", *Word*, XVIII (1962), 54-72.
[9] Kozhevnikov, V. A., and Chistovich, L. A., *Speech: Articulation and Perception* (English translation), US Dept. of Commerce, JPRS: 30, 543 (Washington, 1962).
[10] Fant, G., "Auditory patterns of speech", to be publ. in the *Proc. of the Symp. on Models for the Perception of Speech and Visual Form*, Boston, Mass., Nov. 11-14, 1964.
[11] Chistovich, L., et al., "Mimicking of synthetic vowels", STL-QPSR 2/1966, 1-18, and Chistovich, L., et al., "Mimicking and perception of synthetic vowels, Part II", STL-QPSR 3/1966, 1-3.
[12] Fant, G., "Phonetic and phonemic basis for the transcription of Swedish word material", *Acta Oto-Lar.*, Suppl. 116 (1954), 24-29.
[13] Fant, G., "Acoustic analysis and synthesis of speech with applications to Swedish", *Ericsson Technics*, XV (1959), 1-106.
[14] Fant, G., "Modern instruments and methods for acoustic studies of speech", *Acta Polytechnica Scandinavica*, CCXLVI (1958), 84 p.
[15] Jakobson, R., Fant, G., and Halle, M., "Preliminaries to speech analysis: The distinctive features and their correlates", Acoustics Laboratory, MIT, Techn. Rep. No. 13 (1952), 58 p.; 4th printing publ. by The MIT Press (Cambridge, Mass., 1963).
[16] Fant, G., "The nature of distinctive features", STL-QPSR 4/1966, 1-14 (the topics of speech perception and vowel classification are expanded in this edition).
[17] Malécot, A., "Mechanical pressure as an index of 'Force of Articulation'", *Phonetica*, 14 (1966), 169-180.

Chapter 10
Sound, Features, and Perception

THE SPEECH COMMUNICATION CHAIN

Speech communication may be considered as the transmission of information through a succession of stages within a speaker, a connecting medium, and a listener. Flow diagrams of this process can be elaborated in various forms depending on the detail of the analysis attempted and the aspects of the communication process on which the investigator focuses his descriptive efforts. The following tabulation of stages will be considered here.

A. Production
    (1) Intended meaning of message
    (2) Message sentence form
    (3) Neural production program
    (4) Myodynamic activity
    (5) Aerodynamic and acoustic processes

B. Technical medium
    (1) The acoustic speech wave emitted by the speaker
    (2) Speech signal representation in various parts of a technical communication system
    (3) The acoustic speech wave affecting the listener

C. Perception
    (1) Cochlear response
    (2) Primary neural analysis
    (3) Identification of phonetic elements
    (4) Identification of sentence structure
    (5) The message received

The terminal stages remain rather hypothetical in view of our limited insight in the organization of brain functions. Therefore, the formulation of the stages $A(1)$, $A(2)$ and $C(4)$, $C(5)$ above reflects our general concepts of successive levels of language structure rather than established neurological functions.

This article originally appeared in *Proceedings of the Sixth International Congress of Phonetic Sciences, Prague, 1967* (Prague, Czechoslovakia: Academia, 1970). It is a condensed version of a paper presented at the Sixth International Congress, Prague, Czechoslovakia, 1967. Detailed material including illustrations can be found in G. Fant, "Analysis and Synthesis of Speech Processes," in *Manual of Phonetics*, edited by B. Malmberg (Amsterdam: North-Holland, 1968).

Each stage is to be characterized by an inventory of specific signals specified by parameters which possess certain time and space characteristics that combine into patterns according to general rules and constraints. A major ambition is to derive rules for translating a representation on one stage to a corresponding representation on any other stage of the complete system. Stage $A(4)$ which comprises the dynamics of the speech organs may accordingly be described by a set of time varying articulatory parameters. One of the primary aims of general phonetics and speech research is to derive the rules for translating from this articulatory stage to that of the speech wave $B(1)$.

At the stage $A(5)$ comprising the acoustic production processes the signal structure can be divided into source and filter categories and each of these may be considered at two substages. Thus the filter-function is initially represented by the vocal tract "area-function", i.e. its resonator dimensions, from which their sound shaping properties may be derived by acoustic theory. Similarly, the source has a primary aspect of mean pressures and flows characterizing the aerodynamics of the exhaled air whilst the superimposed periodic or random disturbances constitute the raw material of voiced and unvoiced sounds.

This model of a successivity of encoding stages that the speech message has to pass from the transmitter to the receiver through the entire speech communication chain cannot be quantitatively studied with the same rigor as for instance a telegraph communication system. The main purpose of the model is to serve as a frame for formulating research objectives and discussing descriptive theory whilst the application of a quantitative signal and information analysis generally is beyond our capacity.

One sometimes encounters statements proposing that the information rate is very low at higher brain centers and increases towards the periphery with a maximum at the speech wave. This reasoning suffers from a confusion of the message and signal aspects of the communication. Ideally, the message is the same at all stages and the rate of information flow thus the same everywhere. It is more valid to speak of an ncreasing redundancy in the sense that the signal structure gets more complex and utilizes a larger number of parallel pathways whilst the information remains the same. Even this statement is rather loose in view of our limited insight in the neurological levels.

At present it is not possible to accomplish anything like a complete description of signal structure at any stage with the exception of the acoustic speech wave where all details of the waveform may be sampled and studied. However, even if we cared to carry out a maximally detailed sampling it would not be worth the labor. Also, there exists an infinite variety of transformations for expressing one and the same fact by different parameters, i.e. by different descriptive systems. Thus, in spite of apparent visual differences a narrow-band spectrum contains essentially the same information as a broad-band spectrum.[1]

---

[1] The signal data contained in a spectrogram are mathematically equivalent to that of an

We have to accept the limitation of any quantification being approximate only but we require that it shall preserve a maximum of message information with as simple a signal description as possible. The extent to which such "minimum redundancy" or "compact" descriptive systems can be worked out is first of all a matter of how well the investigator is acquainted with the stage and its constraints and how complex abstractions he is capable of introducing.

THE NATURE OF DISTINCTIVE FEATURES

Complete formant specifications of a piece of speech is of practical use for synthetic reproduction only and is too detailed for comparative phonetic studies. What we need is a phonetically oriented data sampling system that allows us to sample the speech wave less densely than at intervals of the inverse of the bandwidth. The segmentation theory outlined by Fant and Lindblom (1961) and Fant (1962A and B) is a starting point for developing such a system. Segmental boundaries are mainly derived from changes in the "manner of production" whilst the "place of production" determines a more continuously varying element of segment patterns, in the first place the F-pattern (F_1, F_2, F_3, F_4) reflecting the continuous movements of the speech articulators.

This system operates with a terminology of speech production categories that is in part identical to that of the distinctive feature system of Jakobson, Fant and Halle (1952). The main difference is that the distinctive feature system serves a phonemic minimal redundancy classification purpose whereas the segment classification of Fant and Lindblom accounts for any production category irrespective of its communicative significance and is thus more phonetically detailed.

It should be appreciated that distinctive features in the sense utilized by Jakobson, Fant and Halle (1952) primarily constitute a system for subdividing phonemes and other components of the message ensemble. A distinctive feature has certain correlates on each stage of the speech communication chain and these correlates are described in terms of various parameters and cues, e.g. formant locations. A distinctive feature is thus a unit of the message ensemble rather than a property of the signal ensemble. The term "distinction" or "minimal category" would have been more appropriate and might have led to less confusion concerning their nature and use.

---

oscillogram providing the phase information is retained in the spectral representation. Relative phases within the spectrum would mathematically account for one half of the information concerning the signal structure but they are of rather minor communicative importance. Spectrographs are not designed to preserve phase information which in effect reduces the "redundancy" of spectral specifications by a factor of two compared to oscillographic specifications.

A formant representation is more condensed than a harmonic representation since a small number of formants can have the same descriptive power as a large number of harmonics. This economy is generally gained at some reduction of the accuracy in signal analysis. However, the harmonic representation is more detailed only when the voice fundamental frequency is low. The information gained in a low F_0 harmonic spectrum concerns irregularities of the voice source rather than the more important properties of the vocal tract transfer function.

The distinctive features are not intended as absolute descriptors of spectrographic qualities. The production or speech wave correlate of any feature will differ somewhat with the particular context of simultaneous and subsequent features. The invariance is generally relative rather than absolute. For instance, an invariable cue of compactness is the higher F_1 of the compact phoneme compared to the non-compact phoneme in the same context irrespective of which minimal pairs are inspected.

The relation between phonemes or features on the message level to speech segments and parameters on the signal level is generally complex. One segment may contain information about several successive phonemes and a single phoneme is generally related to several successive segments of the speech signal. As a rule the number of segments determined according to the principle of Fant and Lindblom comes out to be larger than the number of phonemes in the utterance. However, this is not always the case since in less careful articulation one or several phonemes of the intended message turn out to be produced in an extremely reduced fashion or omitted altogether without affecting the intelligibility. In practice we do not measure the duration of phonemes in the speech spectrogram but we measure the duration of sound segments and other characteristics of the speech signal.

A feature classification system can thus retain more or less redundancy and it can be more or less representative of actual encoding dimensions of the speech signal. The system of Jakobson, Fant, and Halle is too condensed for practical purposes such as comparative phonetic studies and development of automatic speech recognition schemes. The strength and novelty of the system is that it attempts to break the barrier between phonology and phonetics, linking the theory of message signs with the theory of their physical realization through the concept of the speech signal as a multi-dimensional event.

However, the specific choice of units still remains a disputable compromise between the two aspects. The extreme minimum redundancy objectives inherent in phonemic analysis have been the guiding principle for the selection of features. Accordingly, these constitute a very condensed and handy set for transcription of speech messages. Most of the features represent conventional phonetic categories which undoubtedly have a physiological and psychological significance. In a more phonetically oriented solution, on the other hand, one should increase the number of features so as to avoid or at least reduce the number of features operating in both vowels and consonants. In search for independent units on the signal level as opposed to a linguistic message level one might have to include major allophones of a language. The underlying principle would be to search for an inventory of speech production categories at our disposal for programming the phonatory and articulatory events. EMG, cineradiography, and direct recordings of the dynamical patterning of speech articulation will be helpful tools for such studies.

The search for generative rules of speech production may be exemplified by the studies of some of my colleagues, Lindblom (1963), Öhman (1966, 1967), and Öhman and Lindqvist (1965), who have tackled the problems of formulating rules for predicting vowel reduction, coarticulation, and intonation contours. Given a phonemic or allophonic unit of the assumed production inventory the corresponding speech wave realization may be thought of as the output of "black box" labelled production mechanism the input of which is the selected unit plus a set of other discrete units representing the immediate context of other simultaneous, preceding and following units, prosody included. By a consistent analysis in terms of such models it should be possible to reach a more profound insight in the actual inventory of independent signal categories.

The model of Öhman operates with separate sets of control signals for vowels and consonants and this principle is also followed by Borovičková and Maláč (1966). The frequent use of one and the same feature in vowels as well as in consonants of the Jakobson feature system cannot be supposed to reflect an actual sameness of neurological encoding. Thus it would not be hypothesized that one and the same neural motor command labelled compactness is triggered off in the production of a consonant (k) and a vowel (a).

As a consequence of the high degree of economy aimed at in the Jakobson system and the unavoidable pay off for this economy in terms of a reduced phonetic similarity of a feature in widely different contexts it is not advisable to scale the phonetic distance between two speech sounds in terms of the number of distinctive features by which the corresponding phonemes differ. An extreme example that I have elaborated on earlier, Fant (1966A), is that the last two phonemes of the word "wing" the (i) and the (ng) do not have any distinctive features in common as pointed out by Jakobson whereas the temporal contrast between the sound segments related to [i] and [$ŋ$] is minimal only. The place of articulation being the same and the consonant anticipated already by the nasalization of the [i] the transition from [i] to [$ŋ$] merely involves a closing gesture of the tongue towards the palate.

One weakness of the phonological feature system leading to this paradox is that the palatal articulation goes with compactness in the consonantal system and with noncompact acute sounds in the vowel system. However, from an abstract acoustic feature point of view the ($u\,i\,a$) interrelation show some similarities with the ($p\,t\,k$) relations. The relation [p/t] is a good parallel to [u/i] acoustically and the analogous role of (k) and (a) can also be supported in spite of the articulatory sameness of (i) and (k). From a perception point of view this similarity is superficial. In my view vowels and consonants are perceived through separate "feature channels", if any.

SPEECH PERCEPTION

From the accumulated experience on speech perception and especially experiments with speech-like synthetic stimuli it is apparent that speech is perceived categorically, Liberman et al (1967). We respond phonemically and tend to identify phonemes and allophones in the first place even when we are asked to discriminate small variations in quality, Liberman et al (1957). According to Liberman et al (1963) this effect is pronounced with consonants, whereas vowels are not perceived categorically. Stevens (1966) reports on categorical effects in vowel perception providing the vowel is embedded in a syllabic frame. This effect is interpreted by Stevens as an instance of a principle that all factors that contribute to make the stimulus or the general conditions of the experiment representative of actual speech condition the listener to perform in a "speech mode" characterized by his making message identifications rather than quality gradations, Stevens (1966). This effect is a result of the listener's language experience rather than a unique property of the acoustic signal, Liberman et al (1967), Stevens and House (1966).

The significance of the concept of distinctive features is quite apparent from perception experiments. However, some investigators have interpreted the term distinctive feature at its face value only and accordingly identified it with the concept of a single important parameter or a cue. This has caused some confusions and distrust in the principle of distinctive features. As already stressed a feature is a recurrent phonemic distinction within a language and a major purpose of perception research is to evaluate the physical parameters and cues which signal the distinctions and phonemes of a language. The term cue is the same as an important physical parameter but can also be more complex in the sense that certain parameters combine to a characteristic pattern.

The Haskins Laboratories' systematic studies of the perception of simple stylized formant patterns have contributed greatly to our knowledge of the perceptual significance of formant data. However, the potential risk when working with simplified synthetic stimuli is that they may become insufficient carriers of phonemic cues and that the conclusions drawn from such experiments will be valid for the particular synthesizer only and not for human speech. This was the cause of the somewhat pessimistic conclusions Liberman et al (1957) made concerning the ambiguity of acoustic data as opposed to articulatory data in a study of F_2-locus as a cue for identifying (d) and (g). It can be shown that the syllables (da) and (ga) have approximately the same F_2-transition but this ambiguity is resolved by combining F_3, F_2 and the release burst into a single cue, Fant, Lindblom, and de Serpa-Leitão (1966), Fant (1968).

There remains much to be studied concerning the speech wave characteristics of phonemes and distinctions. A practical strategy is to start out with a detailed list of observable spectrographic pattern cues. In order to make a specification of contextual variants feasible it is advisable to present the data on each phoneme or feature in a few reference contents only and add contextual rules derived from studies of coarticulation, reduction, etc. After this preliminary analysis there follows an evaluation by synthesis. One should not start directly with synthesis experiments and an incomplete knowledge of the speech wave characteristics. It is helpful to construct alternative hypotheses concerning effective cues already in the analysis stage of the work.

A method of parameter evaluation which has been extensively used in perception research is to make systematic variations of the sound stimulus and determine the boundary where the response shifts from one phoneme to another. When this technique is applied to several minimally contrasting pairs of phonemes the data can be interpreted on a distinctive feature basis. The absolute values of the boundaries will vary with the particular context of simultaneous, preceding, and following features of the sound matter as well as with prosodic elements. This is the so-called "contextual bias". In an integrated view based on all parameters of importance for a distinction the distinctive feature or rather its speech wave correlate can be conceived of as a vector perpendicular to the hypersurface constituting the multidimensional boundary. A similar formulation was given by Chistovich (1967) in her paper at the Congress. The main direction of this vector is the sole remaining attribute of the feature if a common denominator of all possible contexts is to be expressed as was the ambition of Jakobson, Fant, and Halle (1952).

However, a knowledge of this mean direction of the feature vector is not a sufficient end result in speech research. For general descriptive phonetics as well as for automatic speech recognition we need the detailed information of how these boundaries shift with context in the general distributional sense adopted here. The search for formulas enabling us to calculate the contextual bias from the discrete inventory of conditioning factors has already been mentioned in the previous discussion on speech production.

The greater accessibility to the problem from a generative speech production point of view than from a perception point of view has had a certain inhibiting effect on the work at the perception end. We would all agree that the categorization inherent at the production end is quite similar to that at the perception end of the speech communication chain but only defenders of a motor theory of speech perception would argue that perception is nothing but the association of the incoming acoustic stimulus with production categories at the listener's disposal when acting as a speaker. If production and perception categories were identical there no longer remains any difference between a sensory theory and a motor theory but merely a concept of economy in our storage of phonetic categories in a place of the brain common for production and perception.

However, by introspection we can certainly study our own stored sound images of distinctive features and phonemes some of which we might not be able to produce correctly if they belong to a language we are not so well acquainted with. When we mimick speech rapidly the motor activity must be the automatic consequence of a phonetic identification in a previous stage. An identification through what is going on in the efferent motor pathways appears to be an unnecessary complication.

Speech perception is a process of successive and simultaneous identifications in a chain of successively higher levels of language structure. We cannot expect to find a specific brain center for each linguistic category: feature, phoneme, syllable, morpheme, word sentence, but at least a lower level $C(3)$ and a higher level $C(4)$ as proposed in the introductory section. To the inventory belong short term and long term memory functions as well as feedback mechanism which allow storage comparison and correction. Also it allows a generative prediction of what the speaker is going to say at least at the levels of syntax and semantics, $C(4)$ and $C(5)$. At a level corresponding to a complexity of the order of the syllable $C(2)$ I conceive of an analysis through a window of the width of a few phonemes through which the speech signal passes. I do not hypothesize a strict principle of all phonemes being first identified by their features. Some phonemes are probably identified directly and independent of context, e.g. the (s). Also the identification is probably not strictly sequential but of arbitrary order within the time span of the window.

This principle overcomes the difficulty of some of the features being specifically sensitive to context. Each identification is a decision based on the probabilities existing at the particular instance and each completed decision influences the distribution of probabilities for the previous and following elements within the window. The general sequential constraints imposed by the language structure and of the speech production mechanism effectively limits the number of alternatives in any decision. This model is also the best principle we can follow in attempts of automatic speech recognition.

The principle indicated above is close to the model of perception outlined by Chistovich in her paper and has an interesting parallel in her experiments on psychological scaling of perceived distances between each of two alternative phonemes and a synthetic sound, the composition of which is varied to produce variations around a perceptual boundarry. According to the experiments of Chistovich (1967), Chistovich, Fant, and de Serpa-Leitão (1966) there is some evidence of a gross quantization and scaling at a stage preceding the phonetic identification but this effect is not well established yet.

Vowels, glides, nasals, and laterals appear to offer greater descriptive problems than stops, affricates, and fricatives. One reason is the greater dynamic variability and affinity to coarticulation. The other lies in the variation of scale factors with different speakers. The first and second formant frequencies, F_1 and F_2, are known to be more important than other parameters, but they are not sufficiently descriptive. The third and higher formants are also of considerable importance in front vowels and serve to differentiate [i] [y] [ʉ] [e] and also [ɛ] and [ö]. F2 and higher formants of front vowels appear to constitute a single perceptual cue which plays a role similar to that of an F2 alone in mid and back vowels. This cue is probably not sufficiently specified by a center of gravity only, Fujimura (1967). Spectral width and relative intensity may also be of some importance.

NORMALIZATION OF ACOUSTIC DATA

The average female voice shows 20 per cent higher formant locations than an average male voice and the same average difference is also found between the spectrum patterns of the voices of children (age 8) and female voices, Peterson and Barney (1952). However, the scale factors vary not only with the speaker but also with the specific vowel and the formant under observation. Thus F_1 of [o] varies but little with the sex of the speaker whereas the scale factor for F_1 of open vowels such as [a] and [æ] are appreciably greater than the average. The origin of these nonuniform variations lies in the non-uniform scaling of the female vocal tract with respect to the male vocal tract, Fant (1966B).

Even if we include all formants in a specification we might find ambiguities such that a female [ö] might have almost the same formant frequencies F_1, F_2, und F_3 as a male [e]. Such ambiguities have not been studied in detail but they might be resolved in part by reference to the center of gravity, intensity, and width of the upper group of formants, to a small part by relative levels of peaks and valleys, and in part by a reference to the voice fundamental frequency. It is not known to what extent the normalization with respect to F_0 is a psychological effect, i.e. F_0 acting as a label for the specific female vowel category or whether F_0 enters already in a weighting of the effective timbre. In connected speech we can also expect a normalization with respect to both the immediate and remote context. A related phenomenon is that time variable formants affect the identification more than constant frequency formants. However, it should be appreciated that because of the general relations between formant frequencies on one hand and formant levels and spectral shape factors on the other hand, Fant (1960), a formant F4 is not audible in a vowel [u] but has a sensation level equal to that of F1 and F3 in the vowel [i].

The boundary shift techniques has been successfully adopted by Fujisaki and Kawashima (1967) for an evaluation of the trading relations between the various vowel parameters. We have used this technique for studying the effect on the source level in the region of F2 and F3 as a factor influencing the F_2—F_3-boundary between [ʉ] and [y]. A 20 dB reduction of F2 and F3 intensity level shifted the $(F_2, F_3)^{1/2}$ threshold by no more than 50 Hz, i.e. rather little. However, the probability of [ʉ] identifications rose significantly within the main [y] region.

The extent to which we can approximate a vowel specification by F_0, F_1, and a few measures related to an effective upper formant region is not yet determined but is one of the hypotheses that we can test with synthetic speech. For this purpose the upper formant should be generated in parallel with F1 and shaped with a filter of greater width and selectivity than a simple formant circuit.

CONCLUSIONS

The concepts of distinctive features and cues should be kept apart as belonging to the message inventory and the speech signal inventory, respectively. In search of the physical and psychological reality behind the categorical effects in speech production and perception we might find a system of features constituting a natural ensemble of minimal message units. Such an ensemble can only in part be expected to conform with the system of Jakobson, Fant, and Halle (1952) and I expect it to be more redundant. There remain many questions to be studied concerning the relations between speech parameters and members of a feature or phoneme inventory.

ACKNOWLEDGMENTS*

I am indebted to Björn Lindblom and Sven Öhman for many fruitful discussions on form and contents of this paper.

REFERENCES

(1966) Borovičková, B. and Maláč, V.: "Towards the Basic Units of Speech from the Perception Point of View", *Proc. of the Seminar on Speech Production and Perception, Leningrad 1966*, 83—88 (Z.f. Phonetik, Sprachwissenschaft und Kommunikationsforschung, 21, Heft 1/2, 1968).

(1967) Chistovich, L.: "Method of Studying the Decision Rules Applied in Speech Perception", to be publ. in *Proc. of the 6th International Congress of Phonetic Sciences, Prague 1967*

(1966) Chistovich, L., Fant, G. ,and de Serpa-Leitão A.: "Mimicking and Perception of Synthetic Vowels. Part II", *STL—QPSR*, No. 3, 1—3 (Stockholm 1966).

(1960) Fant, G.: *Acoustic Theory of Speech Production* (The Hague 1960).

(1962A) Fant, G.: "Descriptive Analysis of the Acoustic Aspects of Speech", *Logos*, 5, 3—17 (1962).

(1962B) Fant, G.: "Sound Spectrography", *Proc. IVth Int. Congr. of Phonetic Sciences, Helsinki*, 14—33 (The Hague 1962).

(1966A) Fant, G.: "The Nature of Distinctive Features", *STL-QPSR*, No. 4, 1—14 (Stockholm 1966).

(1966B) Fant, G.: "A Note on Vocal Tract Size Factors and Non Uniform F-Pattern Scalings", *STL-QPSR*, No. 4, 22—30 (Stockholm 1966).

(1968) Fant, G.: "Analysis and Synthesis of Speech Processes", a chapter in *Manual of Phonetics*, ed. B. Malmberg. (North-Holland Publ. Co., Amsterdam 1968).

(1961) Fant, G. and Lindblom, B.: "Studies of Minimal Speech Sound Units", *STL-QPSR*, No. 2, 1—11 (Stockholm 1961).

(1966) Fant, G., Lindblom, B., and de Serpa-Leitão, A.: "Consonant Confusions in English and Swedish—A Pilot Study", *STL-QPSR*, No. 4, 31—34 (Stockholm 1966).

(1967) Fujimura, O.: "The Spectral Shape in the F2-F3 Region", *Models for the Perception of Speech and Visual Form*, ed. by W. Wathen-Dunn, 251-256 (Cambridge, Mass. 1967).

(1967) Fujisaki, H. and Kawashima, T.: "Roles of Pitch and Higher Formants in Perception of Vowels", *Digest of the 7th International Conference on Medical and Biological Engineering* Aug. 14—19, 1967, Stockholm, Session 24-2.

(1952) Jakobson, R., Fant, G., and Halle, M.: "Preliminaries to Speech Analysis. The Distinctive Features and Their Correlates", *Acoust. Lab.*, *M.I.T. Techn. Rep.*, No. 13 (Cambridge, Mass. 1952); 4th printing publ. by The M.I.T. Press (Cambridge, Mass. 1963).

(1957) Liberman, A. M., Harris, K. S., Hoffman, H. S., and Griffith, B. C.: "The Discrimination of Speech Sounds Within and Across Phoneme Boundaries", *J. of Exp. Psychol.*, 54, 358—368 (1957).

(1963) Liberman, A. M., Cooper, F. S., Harris, K. S., and MacNeilage, P. F.: "A Motor Theory of Speech Perception", Paper D3 in *Proc. of the Speech Communication Seminar, Stockholm 1962*, Vol. II (Stockholm 1963).

(1967) Liberman, A. M., Cooper, F. S., Harris, K. S., MacNeilage, P. F., and Studdert-Kennedy.

---

*) This study has been supported in part by Swedish and US governmental funds, more recently by NIH Research Grants NB 04003—05 and HD 02111-02 and by US Air Force Grant AF EOAR 67-34.

M.: "Some Observations on a Model for Speech Perception", *Models for the Perception of Speech and Visual Form*, ed. by W. Wathen-Dunn, 68—87 (Cambridge, Mass. 1967).
(1963) Lindblom, B.: "Spectrographic Study of Vowel Reduction", *J. Acoust. Soc. Am.*, 35, 1773—1781 (1963).
(1966) Öhman, S. E. G.: "Coarticulation in VCV Utterances: Spectrographic Measurements". *J. Acoust. Soc. Am.*, 39, 151—168 (1966).
(1967) Öhman S. E. G.: "Numerical Model of Coarticulation", *J. Acoust. Soc. Am.*, 41, 310—320 (1967).
(1965) Öhman, S. E. G. and Lindqvist, J.: "Analysis-by-Synthesis of Prosodic Pitch Contours". *STL-QPSR*, No. 4, 1—6 (1965).
(1952) Peterson, G. E. and Barney, H. L.: "Control Methods Used in a Study of the Vowels", *J. Acoust. Soc. Am.*, 24, 175—184 (1952).
(1966) Stevens, K. N.: "On the Relations Between Speech Movements and Speech Perception". *Proc. of the Seminar on Speech Production and Perception, Leningrad 1966*, 102—106 (Z. f. Phonetik, Sprachwissenschaft und Kommunikationsforschung, 21, Heft 1/2, 1968).
(1966) Stevens, K. N. and House, A. S.: "Speech Perception", a chapter prepared for *Foundations of Modern Auditory Theory*.

Chapter 11
Distinctive Features and Phonetic Dimensions

The purpose of this paper is to make some comments on the recent developments of distinctive feature theory with specific reference to the work of Chomsky and Halle (1968). On the whole I consider their feature system to be an improvement over that of Jakobson, Fant, and Halle (1952), one of the main advantages being the introduction of a set of tongue body features in common for vowels and consonants but separate from the consonantal 'place of articulation' features. The basic philosophy of treating phonetics as an integral part of general linguistics demands that features in addition to their classificatory function shall have a definite phonetic function reflecting independently controllable aspects of the speech event or independent elements of perceptual representation. However, there is a danger that the impact of the theoretical frame with its apparent merits of operational efficiency will give some readers the impression that the set of features is once and for all established and that their phonetic basis has been thoroughly investigated. This is not so. Many of their propositions are interesting and stimulating starting points for further research whereas others I find in need of a revision.

As pointed out by Chomsky and Halle there are still serious shortcomings in our general knowledge of the speech event. Their feature system is almost entirely based on speech production categorizations. The exclusion of acoustical and perceptual correlates was a practical limitation in the scope of their work but also appears to note the importance laid on the production stage. It is far easier to construct hypothetical feature systems than to test them on any level of the speech communication chain. This is really our present dilemma. Until we have reached a more solid basis in general phonetics any feature theory will remain 'preliminary'.

Here follows my reaction to some of the basic issues in chapter 7 of *Sound Pattern of English*. My earlier comments on distinctive feature theory may be found in the list of references, Fant (1960*a*, *b*, 1966, 1967, 1968).

This article originally appeared in *Applications of Linguistics. Selected Papers of the Second International Congress of Applied Linguistics, Cambridge, 1969*, edited by G. E. Perren and J. L. M. Trim (London: Cambridge University Press, 1971). Reprinted with permission.

Will we ever have a language universal, finite, and unique set of distinctive features?

The universality aspects are attractive but I am somewhat pessimistic about the outlook. Features are as universal as the sound-producing constraints of the human speech-producing mechanism and a finite number should suffice for the classificatory function. However, I am rather sceptical concerning the uniqueness and thereby a definite number of features, since one and the same facts often can be described in alternative forms and the criteria for selecting an optimum system are not very rigid. Even if we had all the knowledge we needed the choice of features would be dependent on the particular weight given to phonetic and general linguistic considerations and the preferences of the investigator would also determine some of the selections. The problem is the following.

Are the demands on a feature system different on the classificatory level and the phonetic level?

There are two ways of arriving at features: (1) by selecting an inventory of classes suitable for encoding of language structures and then determine their phonetic correlates, or (2) to start with an exhaustive analysis of the modes and constraints of the speech-producing mechanisms and perception and determine their distinctive function in language. Feature theory has to develop along both lines and investigators differ only in the relative importance laid on one or the other. The main approach of Jakobson *et al.* (1952) was to start out with an ordering of phonemic oppositions and to identify minimal distinctions as the same if motivated by phonetic similarities. The demand for the smallest possible number of features and the fargoing identification of features within the vowel and consonant systems, e.g. that of identifying the relation between dentals and labials with that of front and back vowels, resulted in an unavoidable pay-off between encoding efficiency and phonetic reality and specifiability. Chomsky and Halle (1968) avoided some of these difficulties by introducing a greater number of features.

One of their basic issues is that a feature system in addition to the classificatory efficiency should conform with a natural phonetic systematization. How have they managed in this respect? In many instances such as dealing with the classes of fricatives, stops, nasals, laterals, etc., the solution is straightforward. On the other hand, I find the encoding of the class of labial consonants as [+anterior] and [−coronal] to constitute a clear case of departure from the unifying principles. One single phonetic dimension, 'labiality', which has a distinctive function has here lost its identity on the phonological level. It appears to a rather far-fetched hypothesis that the actual neural encoding of labial consonants at some stage should include a selection of a maximal anterior point of articulation in the vocal tract and a lack of tongue tip evaluation in order for a lower level to find out that this command has to be executed by the lips and not the tongue.

The major class features 'vocalic' and 'consonantal' introduced already in the work of Jakobson *et al.* and the features 'sonorant' and syllabic display a complicated system of interdependencies as will be described in later sections.

The starting point for the major class features appears to have been the need to encode certain pre-established phonetic classes, whereas the voiced–voiceless feature is a typical example of the opposite approach, i.e. to start out with a natural phonetic dimension and study its distinctive role in language. A natural linguistic class, i.e. all [r]-phonemes, may have rather complicated sets of phonetic correlates and a natural phonetic dimension such as voicing may have to be studied together with several other dimensions as tensening, durations, and coarticulation when it comes to the discussion of its distinctive role.

Before we can accomplish the happy marriage between phonology and phonetics we have to work out the rules for predicting the speech event given the output of the phonological component of grammar. To me this is the central, though much neglected, problem of phonetics and it is of the same magnitude as that of generative grammar in general and will require a similar set of transformational rules. The starting point is the feature matrix of a message as successive phonological segments, i.e. columns each with its specific bundle of features, i.e. rows. The particular choice of classificatory features at this stage is not very important providing the conventions relating phonemes to alternative features systems are known.

The derivation of the rules of this 'phonetic component' of language aims at describing the speech production, speech wave, or perception correlates of each feature given the 'context' in a very general sense of co-occurring features within the phonological segment as well as those of following and preceding segments. One set of sequential constraints is expressible as coarticulation rules which may be both universal and language specific.

In addition to these more or less inertia dependent laws of connecting vocal gestures there may exist rules of neural reorganization of control signals for modifying the physical manifestation of a feature in accordance with a principle of least effort articulation, or the contrary, a compensation for maintaining or sharpening of a phonetic distinction dependent on what features occur or follow in the time domain. In addition rules enter for modifications dependent on stress patterns, intonation, tempo, speaker, sex, type, and dialect, attitude etc. Rules for speech segment durations and sound shapes have to be expressed in terms of larger phonological segments, generally several syllables defining a natural rhythmical unit in terms of stress and intonation. Very little is known about these rules. There is some evidence that the phase of maximal intensity increase within a syllable is a reference point for ordering rules concerning segment durations (B. Lindblom, personal communication).

This 'phonetic component' of the speech event receives very little attention in the work of Chomsky and Halle who merely refer to the phonetic correlates of a feature as a scale with many steps instead of the binary scaling on the classificatory level. A knowledge of linguistic structuring is of great importance in practical communication engineering undertakings such as the administration of synthesis by rule or automatic identifications. However, without access to the rules of the 'phonetic component' the phonetic aspect of features becomes as imaginary and empty as the 'Emperor's New Clothes' in the story by H. C. Andersen. Observing the speech wave we are not faced with phonemes or features but sound segments and more or less continuous sound shapes with a reciprocal many-to-one relation between phonological and physical units. The same is true of speech production studied in relation to the phonological transcript. In both cases there is the need to define inventories of physical units, Fant (1968), which are not identical to the distinctive features but are used to define their phonetic correlates. It may be quite practical to refer to a specific sequence of segments as a stop followed by a fricative at the phonetic level while we may want to refer to the whole unit as an affricate on the phonological level.

Those who want to increase their perspectives on phonology in relation to phonetics should read Ladefoged's monograph 'Linguistic phonetics' (1967a). A pure phonetic system was outlined by G. E. Peterson (1968).

What is the psychological reality of features?

As demonstrated in the previous section features must, at least under prototype conditions, have physical correlates as observed by an external observer of the speech communication act and they should hopefully reflect categorical phenomena in the encoding and decoding mechanism. This is not the same as ascribing each feature to a specific brain allocation. We can be aware of a feature by introspection but otherwise it may lack immediate neurophysiological correlates. The important thing is that the actual processes are phenomena that have some abstract relation to our feature matrices.

Is the binary principle important?

Not necessarily, but it is convenient. Language regularities and language developments may in some instances be more easily described by scales of three or more levels, cf. Ladefoged (1967a). It is also questionable whether formulations in terms of feature matrices always reveal more fundamental rules than formulations in terms of phonemes.

Are features independent and orthogonal?

This question can pertain both to the classificatory, 'phonological level', and to the phonetic level discussing the production speech wave and perceptual correlates. Besides the apparent constraints on possible sequences of phonological segments there exist universal constraints on feature combinations within one and the same segment. As discussed by Chomsky and Halle [+high] would contradict [+low]. Also, some features or combinations of features imply specific signs of other feature in the same bundle, as exemplified by [+vocalic] implying [+sonorant]. A closer analysis of interdependencies within the major class features reveals that the class of [+sonorants] by definition also incorporates all [+syllabics] and all [−consonantal] segments. Such constraints will be discussed in greater detail in the section of major class features. The phonological dependencies within this set of features are paralleled by phonetic similarities. Thus the class of [−consonantal] incorporating vowels and glides must have much in common with the class of [+vocalic] incorporating vowels and liquids. In other words 'vocalic' is almost the negative of the 'consonantal' feature.

The phonetic interdependencies are apparent even when they are not paralleled by classificatory constraints. The situation would have been ideal in the vowel system if the perceptually relevant number of dimensions had been the same as the number of classificatory features. We would have had a perfect orthogonal system if limited to the [+low] or [−high] and the [−back] dimensions corresponding to the $+F_1$ and $+F_2$ dimensions, respectively. The feature 'rounding' is correlated with $-(F_1+F_2+F_3)$ and thus only partially independent of other features. The same is true of the feature 'tense' which is related to the formant pattern (direction towards an extreme target) and duration. Additional features and/or scale values are needed for the Swedish vowel system as will be discussed later.

We accordingly have to resort to the minimal claim of Chomsky and Halle that features should be at least partially independent. At the same time we have to be aware of considerable interdependencies. This applies to their classificatory function as well as to their phonetic correlates.

Are differences in feature contents of matrices a reliable measure of phonetic distance?

No, not always. On an average basis it might be permissible to express differences between languages or dialects by summing binary units in the classificatory domain and expect such differences to represent their phonetic differences, Ladefoged (1969). However, one cannot expect the phonetic difference between any two phonemes to be proportional to the number of features by which they differ. The situation was especially severe in the Jakobson, Fant, and Halle system. It was stated that the [ŋ] and the [i] of the word 'wing' do not have any features in common, the [i] being [+voc] [−cons] [−compact] [−grave], the [ŋ] being [−voc] [+cons] [+nasal] [+compact]. On the phonetic level, on the other hand, the difference between the [i] and the [n] is minimal since the entire [i] is nasalized and the transition from [i] to [n] merely involves a gesture of tongue closure which in dialectal variants is omitted. Within the Chomsky – Halle framework the situation is indeed improved since the tongue body features [−back] [−low] [+high] are in common for the two segments. The [+nasal] feature is not phonemically distinct for the vowel and the tongue gesture toward closure is paralleled by the [+consonantal] feature on the classificatory level. The [−vocalic] feature of the [n] becomes an automatic consequence of the [+nasal] [+consonantal] combination in both systems.

The moral is, eliminate inherent redundancies before counting the number of plus and minus features by which two segments differ.

Review of the major class features

The three major class features, *sonorant, vocalic* and *consonantal*, relate to various aspects of the open–close dimension. Judging from a footnote on p. 302 of *Sound Pattern of English*, Chomsky and Halle recommend the use of a new feature *syllabicity* instead of *vocalic*. Accordingly, my analysis will be based on this revision, whereas almost all constructions in *Sound Pattern* are based on the *vocalic* feature.

The nature of these features is best reviewed with reference to phonetic classes:

[−consonantal] = vowels and glides+h
[+vocalic]   = vowels and liquids
[+syllabic]   = vowels, syllabic liquids and syllabic nasals
[+sonorants]   = vowels, liquids, nasals, and glides+h
[+consonantal] = liquids, nasals, and obstruents (fricatives, affricates, and stops)
[−vocalic]   = glides+h, nasals and obstruents
[−syllabic]   = glides+h, non-syllabic liquids and lasals, obstruents
[−sonorant]   = obstruents

It is thus seen that all [−consonantal], all [+vocalic] and all [+syllabic] segments must by definition also be [+sonorant] and, conversely, if a segment is classified as [−sonorant] it must by definition also be [+consonantal], [−vocalic] and [−syllabic]. The crucial difference between the 'vocalic' and the 'syllabic' features is that non-syllabic liquids are plus in terms of the vocalic feature but minus in terms of the syllabic feature. This has important consequences in segment classifications.

Before further discussing the inherent redundancies of combinations of these features I shall briefly review their phonetic definitions and add some comments on their acoustic correlates as I see them.

Consonantal sounds are produced with a radical constriction in the midsagittal region of the vocal tract. This constriction limits the flow of air in the obstruents and in the closed phase of r-sounds whereas it is 'shunted', i.e. by-passed, in laterals and nasals. Because of the variety of sounds to be included by the feature a formulation of the acoustical correlates becomes rather complex, the common denominator being a deviation from the ideal 'vocalic' pattern by a reduction of the second and/or higher formants.

Vocalic sounds are produced with an oral opening that shall not exceed that of the high vowels [i] and [u] and which by definition shall be greater than that of glides. In addition the vocal cords shall be positioned to allow for spontaneous voicing. This requirement rules out unvoiced vowels as being nonvocalic. Oral opening here includes lateral opening and in case of sonorant [r]-sounds the more open intervals. The acoustic correlate is a higher F_1 and higher overall intensity than in nonvocalic sounds.

Syllabic sounds form a syllabic peak in the sequence of sound events. Obstruents are by definition excluded from the possibility of forming syllabic peaks, whereas syllabic nasals and liquids between obstruents are basically characterized by the same criterion as that of vowels between obstruents or glides. A weighted sum of second and first formant intensity relative to that of an adjacent phonetic segment would be the simplest acoustic correlate.

Sonorant sounds. The relative degree of sonority can be based on exactly the same criteria as for syllabicity except that the relative degree of sonority is related to alternative compositions of one and the same segment whereas syllabicity implies comparisons in the time domain. The production correlate of sonority is the sum of vocal tract openings including oral, nasal, and lateral passages which is larger than that found in obstruents. Thus [−sonorant] = obstruent. An interesting claim not yet verified is that nonsonorant sounds would not allow 'spontaneous voicing' and that a compensation of glottal adjustment to counteract the impaired flow would be necessary.

The interdependencies between basic class features are as apparent on the phonetic level as on the classificatory level. The situation is even more complicated by the fact that the continuant-noncontinuant (stop) feature is the same as the consonantal feature, except that the degree of primary stricture is total in stops and in the closed interval of affricates but not total in the [+consonantal] [+continuant] fricatives.

I fully agree with Chomsky and Halle on the need for replacing the 'vocalic' feature by the 'syllabic' feature. The syllabicity seems to be more easily *testable* than the vocalicity which employs a disputable threshold between liquids and glides which does not focus on the important differences. Furthermore, I suggest a further reduction of the number of features dealing with vocal tract opening by replacing the features 'consonantal' and 'continuant' by one single feature (medially) 'closed' which is identical to the 'consonantal' feature but for an extension to separate stops and affricates from fricatives. Before applying this feature we shall study how some of the main phonetic classes are encoded.

Features that by definition are implied by other features of the same phonological segment are marked with parentheses. Blank spaces represent other instances of 'unmarkedness', i.e. (a) not applicable because of physiological constraints, (b) irrelevant for the classificatory function, or (c) occurrence in rare cases only. In detailed feature-analysis it would be valuable to have separate notations for these four different aspects of unmarkedness and also for the fifth aspect, that related to sequential constraints as implied by all higher levels of analysis. According to Chomsky and Halle the [+nasal] feature when added to stops could stand for prenasalization, i.e. instance (c) above, whereas +nasal, when added to vowels or liquids, is a contextual variant due to adjacent nasal consonants and can thus be omitted from the matrix (case (b) above).

TABLE I

	Vowels	Nasals		Laterals		r-sounds	
Syllabic	+	−	+	−	+	−	+
Consonantal	−	(+)	+	(+)	+	(+)	+
Sonorant	(+)	+	(+)	+	(+)	+	(+)
Nasal	.	+	+	−	−	−	−
Lateral	.	(−)	(−)	+	+	−	−
Continuant	.	.	.	.	.	.	.
Instant release	.	.	.	.	.	.	.

	Glides+h	Stops	Affricates	Fricatives
Syllabic	−	(−)	(−)	(−)
Consonantal	−	(+)	(+)	(+)
Sonorant	(+)	−	−	−
Nasal	.	.	.	.
Lateral	.	.	.	.
Continuant	.	−	−	+
Instant release	.	+	−	.

It is interesting to note that if the feature matrix is to be used for description of actual phonetic states, it would not be possible to distinguish between proper nasal consonants and nasalized [r]-sounds. This is a consequence of liquids being opposed to nasal consonants in terms of [−nasal] feature alone instead of by a specific complex as the [+vocalic] [+consonantal] in the earlier conventions.

A similar case of defining a phonetic category by the negative of another not directly related category is the encoding of [r]-sounds as [−lateral]. It is questionable whether an inhibition of the lateral command in the production of an [l] automatically results in an [r]-sound. Additional adjustment may be necessary. These examples are analogous to the [−coronal, +anterior] encoding of labial consonants which I consider more objectional. All these instances of classification in terms of combinations and selections from a finite set are acceptable provided we give up the demand that each feature represent an independent and specific production category.

180 Features: Theory and Systems

A coding tree related to Table 1 is shown in Fig. 1. The syllabic feature presides at the top but this is not crucial. The same number of yes-no branching points would have been needed if we put the sonority feature on top. Now, coding trees are deceptive in a way since all sorts of variations and hierarchies are possible because of inherent redundancies. However, the manipulation of coding trees has the pedagogical merit of bringing out these redundancies.

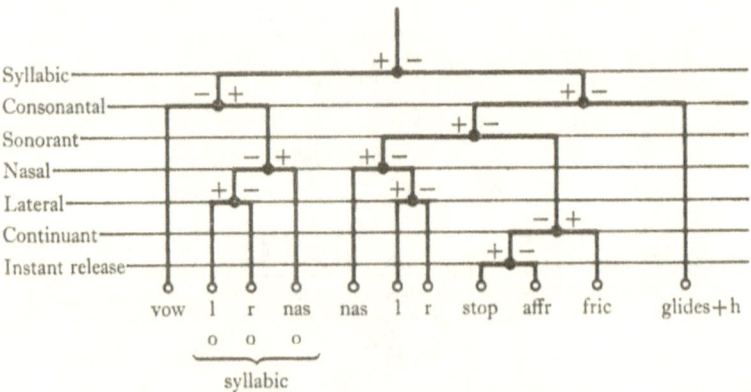

FIG. 1. Coding tree with the basic Chomsky–Halle features, 'syllabic' replacing 'vocalic'.

Examples of coding trees for the reduced set of features I have proposed are shown in Figs. 2 and 3. In one the syllabic feature is placed at the top, in the other it is given the lowest place and sonorant the top place. The economy in terms of branching points is the same in all three figures. Figs. 2 and 3 merely have the merit of a smaller number of features. It was actually during the construction of such trees that I observed the complementary distribution of [−continuant] and [+consonantal]. I prefer the tree of Fig. 2, which starts out with the sonorant feature related to vocal tract opening irrespective of where it occurs. It is logically followed by the feature of closure in the vocal tract midsagittal plane, then the manner of release of this closure which applies to [−sonorants] only. The medially closed sonorants are then separated into nasals, laterals, and r-sounds, as previously discussed, and glides are opposed to vowels as non-syllabic. The main acoustic correlate of voiced sonorants is their higher F_1 intensity, whereas the acoustic correlates of 'closure' is a reduction of formants higher than F_1. The specification of the nasal and the lateral correlates are not so simple. They will not be discussed here.

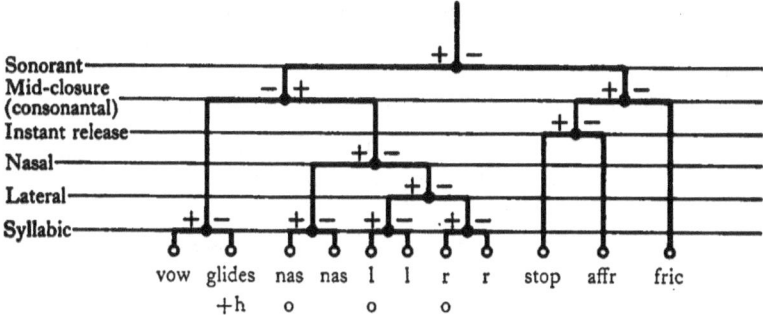

FIG. 2. Coding tree with the features consonantal and continuant replaced by a single feature 'mid-closure'. The feature 'sonorant' is given the top level.

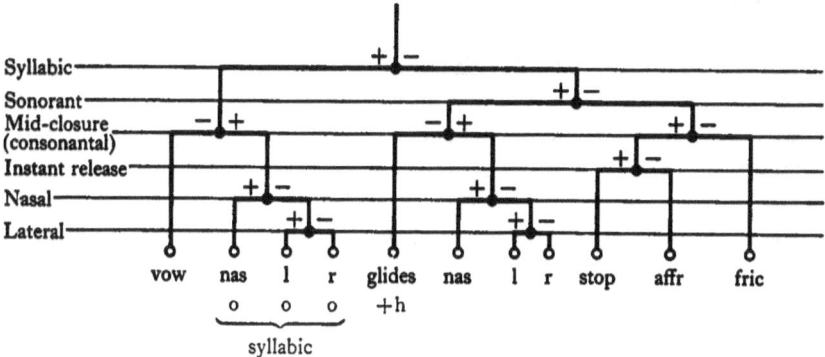

FIG. 3. Alternative coding tree with the same features as in Fig. 2 arranged in a different order, the feature 'syllabic' at the top. Note the relation to Fig. 1.

Some detailed comments

The class of *h-sounds* has always been a problem in feature analysis. I accept the classification of glides (semivowels) and h-sounds given by Chomsky and Halle as [+sonorant], [−consonantal][1] and [−syllabic] but I object to their contrasting of h-sounds to other glides as [+low]. This solution is an apparent mistake since h-sounds display perfect coarticulation with vowels whether [+low] or [−low]. The h-sounds, voiced or unvoiced, are produced with an active glottal readjustment.

The presence of the unvoiced h-sound in the class of sonorants weakens the simple acoustic correlate of intensity of this class since velar fricatives display similar acoustic patterns but with more noise in the region above F_2. The degree to which the intensity is associated with the vocalic formant

[1] Or [−mid-closure] instead of [−consonantal].

patterns is accordingly a necessary aspect to take into account. This fact also correlates with the affinity of sonorants to be found next to the syllabic nucleus.

Directly related to the classification of h-sounds is the treatment of *aspiration*. The statement of Chomsky and Halle that a feature of heightened subglottal pressures is a necessary requirement for aspiration is not tenable, see Fant, *Acoustic Theory of Speech Production*, pp. 277–9. Instead we need a new feature of 'glottal relaxation,' yet to be defined, that covers aspiration in general as well as the class of h-sounds.

On the whole, there is a need for further studies of the phonatory mechanism in various situations before we can single out the various phonetic components involved in the various manner of articulations of stop sounds. The difference between English or Swedish [p, t, k] and [b, d, g] involves both aspiration, tenseness and voicing as phonetic parameters. In initial stressed position the aspiration, i.e. glottal relaxation, is the obvious cause of the delay of voicing in [p, t, and k]. A higher intraoral stop pressure, when present, appears to reflect a larger glottal opening rather than a higher subglottal pressure. At the same time there appears to be a prolongation of the state of articulatory narrowing in [p, t, and k] which accounts for a high frequency 'fricative' noise superimposed on the first part of the aspiration.

There are also coarticulation differences. The range of F_2-locus at the instant of release is greater for the voiced than for the unvoiced stops, especially so with [b] compared with [p]. This can be seen in the data of Lehiste and Peterson (1961) and I have measured similar distributions for Swedish (forthcoming article). At the instant of release of [b] before a back vowel the tongue takes a position close to that of the following vowel while the instant of release of the [p] before the same vowel displays a much higher locus, typical of neutral tongue articulation. After about 40 msec from the release of the [p] the formant pattern follows essentially that observed immediately after the release of the [b]. These temporal relations should be studied more closely.

It could be, as stated by Chomsky and Halle, that the amount of vocal wall tensing could affect the possibility to maintain a prevoicing (before the release) but I consider the glottal adjustment to be primary and that it also is the primary cause of the small difference found in the time lag of voicing after release comparing the intervocalic [k, p, t] and [g, b, d] and associated with this time lag a difference in the F_1 contour (F_1 cut back).

The mere fact that there are certain 'tense–lax' elements associated with the distinction between the English or Swedish [k, p, t] versus [b, d, g] in addition to the obvious glottal adjustments is not sufficient basis for selecting the feature 'tense' rather than the feature 'voiced'. According to Chomsky and Halle the criterion for classifying [p, t, k] as [+tense] rather than [−voiced] would be that vocal vibrations are stopped because of articulatory interaction rather than by glottal relaxation. With this criterion I would place a greater importance on the voicing component than on the tenseness component. Further studies are needed.

The feature *distributed* which on the articulatory level is defined as a long versus short constriction in the direction of the air flow has not been analyzed very closely as to its acoustic correlates, and these are far from obvious. Differences in source location, size of front cavity, and the degree of coupling to the back cavities may be affected. A high frequency extension of the noise could be an acoustic correlate but I cannot really say anything definite before I have studied actual samples of spectrograms and cineradiograms. It appears to me that the main difference between labials and labiodentals is that of a less effective versus a more effective source and I am rather hesitant to equate it with differences in tongue articulations.

In Swedish there are both dental and alveolar apical stops, the latter being lexically induced by a previous /r/. The phonological component would have to work with classifications that differentiate these articulations. It is indeed questionable whether the phonetic difference is that of distributed–nondistributed.

Swedish vowels

The feature *covered* pertaining to narrowed, tensed pharynx wall and an elevated larynx is suggested to have some relevance for the difference between the Swedish vowels [y] and [ʉ]. There is no evidence to support this suggestion as far as I can see.

The Swedish vowel system is of considerable interest in view of the large number of sounds contained. I shall attempt here to construct a phonetic feature matrix of Swedish long vowel phonemes, [uː], [oː], [ɑː], [ɛː], [eː], [iː], [yː], [ʉː], [øː], and the pre-r allophones, [æː] and [œː] of [ɛː] and [øː], respectively. I shall first attempt to use the Chomsky–Halle tongue-body features back, low, high, and the rounding feature. In addition, I have defined two new features, which in the consistent articulatory terminology are named 'palatal' and 'labial'. These function as extreme degrees of tongue-height and lip-rounding, respectively. It has been long recognized that all Swedish long vowels of extreme low first formant frequency, [iː], [yː], [ʉː], and [uː] are pronounced as diphthongs towards a homorganic glide or fricative. However, what is not so obvious and often overlooked is that the vowel [yː] is made with a palatal closing gesture just as in [iː] but with added lip-rounding and that the front vowel [ʉː] is produced with a labial gesture towards closure just as in the back vowel [uː], Fant (1968). The historical origin of [ʉː] is a tongue fronting of [uː] which was replaced by an [oː] in a vowel shift. In the Swedish spoken in Finland [ʉː] and [uː] are not differentiated and are realized with a single sound shape. The tongue fronting of the 'long' [ʉː] has now progressed to an articulation close to that of [iː], [yː], [eː], and [øː], generally a little more open than [yː] and a little more close than [øː]. As far as I can judge the element of velarization has been completely lost.[1] The position of the mass of the tongue in the palatal-velar direction is not more 'velar' than that of the other front vowels, and the apex is often slightly raised thus tending to shift the location of the tongue-palate constriction somewhat anterior of [iː]. However, in the class of 'short', i.e. lax Swedish vowels, the tongue of [ʉ][2] is lower than that of [ø] but more velarized.

When sampling formant data on vowels the distinction between Swedish [oː] and [uː] and between [øː] and [ʉː] may be obscured if [uː] and [ʉː] are sampled at their onset and not at their target values where F_1 and F_2 are lower. Similarly, the contrast between [yː] and [ʉː] is increased if the sampling is performed at the later part of the vowel where F_2 of [ʉː] has been progressively lowered and F_3 of [yː] has been progressively increased. At the place of the vowel target the main constriction is at the lips for [uː] and [ʉː] but at the tongue-palate region for [yː] and [iː]. The progressively decreasing tongue-height in the series [uː], [oː], [ɑː] and in [iː], [eː], [ɛː], [æː] and in [ʉː], [øː], [œː] is paralleled by an increasing jaw opening, Lindblom (1967). It has been demonstrated by Lindblom and Sundberg (1969a and b) that with a minimum jaw opening but otherwise normal tongue movements the F_1 range is considerably reduced. The jaw opening thus adds not only to the tongue-palate distance but also to the effective lip-opening, everything else being equal. The six vowel features classify the Swedish long vowels as shown in Table 2.

In the consonant system the feature 'labial' should be used instead of [+anterior] [−coronal] to define the class of labial consonants. Labialized vowels are analogous to 'retroflex', i.e. [+coronal] vowels. Long (tense) Swedish vowels are accordingly diphthongized if they possess the features

[1] Lindblom and Sundberg (1969a) classified [ʉ] as 'velar' but expressed doubts as to the phonetic validity.
[2] The quality of short /ʉ/ is generally transcribed as [ɵ].

TABLE 2. *Swedish long vowels*
[æː] and [œː] are pre-r allophones of [ɛː] and [øː]

	Binary system										
	uː	oː	ɑː	æː	ɛː	eː	iː	yː	ʉː	øː	œː
Back	+	+	+	–	–	–	–	–	–	–	–
Low	–	–	+	+	–	–	–	–	–	–	–
High	+	–	–	–	–	+	+	+	+	–	–
Palatal	–	–	–	–	–	–	+	+	–	–	–
Round	+	+	–	–	–	–	–	+	+	+	+
Labial	+	–	–	–	–	–	–	–	+	–	–

'palatal' or 'labial'. These are the maximally 'close' vowels, compare Lindblom and Sundberg (1969a).

An alternative matrix may be set up with 'jaw closure' instead of the 'palatal' feature. The maximum degree of jaw closure is found in [iː], [yː], [ʉː], and [uː] which would be labeled [+closed]. With this solution one gains the distinction in actual tongue-palate opening comparing [ʉː] and [øː] whilst the distinction between [ʉː] and [yː] is reduced to one of labialization only. One then has to add the rule that labialization always determines the diphthongal element when present in the close vowels. Note the minimal distinction of [–back] separating [ʉː] from [uː] in either system. A third and rather different alternative system was suggested by Lindblom and Sundberg (1969a).

The variety of solutions possible in a system of interrelated physiological dimensions scaled according to binary principles is indeed a problem. One source of variability is that the number of possible combinations generated from a given ensemble is larger than the number of sounds to be encoded. Therefore there may result an ambiguity in feature selection. Two or more physiological parameters may contribute to one and the same acoustical and perceptual effect which may constitute a more natural candidate for the role of feature, at least in the sense of phonetic feature. Let us see what happens if we try to simplify the inventory of articulatory parameters by grouping together the features 'low', 'high', and 'palatal' to one single dimension assigning the value 0 for the most 'open' degrees [ɑː], [æː], and [œː] and the value 3 for the maximally palatal [iː]. Similarly the feature labial is added to that of rounding, as shown in Table 3.

A matrix of this sort is easier to comprehend than a multidimensional binary system. There are apparently three major classes within the system, the back vowels [uː], [oː], [ɑː] in which an increase in tongue height goes with increasing lip rounding (partially jaw dependent). The unrounded front vowels are differentiated by tongue (and jaw) height and the rounded front vowels are also differentiated by height and by extra rounding as a special feature of [ʉː], cf. Malmberg (1956) and Fant (1966).

TABLE 3

	uː	oː	ɑː	æː	ɛː	eː	iː	yː	ʉː	øː	œː
Back	1	1	1	0	0	0	0	0	0	0	0
High	2	1	0	0	1	2	3	3	2	2	0
Round	2	1	0	0	0	0	0	1	2	1	1

At this stage we might ask for the acoustic and perceptual correlates of these articulatory categories. The phonetic color is mainly dependent of F_1, F_2, and F_3 but it should be possible to find an optimal projection of this three-dimensional space on a plane. Pilot experiments now in progress at the Department of Speech Communication, KTH (Fant, Carlson and Granström) indicate that an F_1 versus F_2' plot would serve this purpose. F_2' is the frequency of the second formant in a two-formant approximation to the vowel. In mid- and back vowels F_2' is identical to F_2 and in high front vowels close to F_3.

A tentative F_1 versus F_2' plot of Swedish long vowels and some short vowels of specific identity have been plotted on a mel scale, Fig. 4. In this diagram we find evidence of a fairly even spread in the perceptual domain. The average distance between any of the sounds and its closest neighbor is 180 mels. The articulatory correlate of increasing F_1 is increasing jaw opening and a shift of the tongue towards a pharyngeal position. The articulatory correlate of the ordinate F_2' is a shift of the tongue away from the velum and towards the palate.

It can be seen that back vowels may be separated from front vowels by a line of the slope +45 degrees and rounded vowels from unrounded vowels with a line of −45 degrees slope. Therefore a rotation of coordinates as in Fig. 5 brings out the direct correlates to the main vowel classes. Back vowels are characterized by a distance between the first and the second formant lower than 400 mels. All unrounded front vowels lie close to a line of $M_1 + M_2' = 2,200$ mels and the rounded front vowels have an abscissa of $M_1 + M_2'$ less than 2,100 mels. The quantal steps in the ordinate comparing [iː, eː, ɛː, and æː] are of the order of 250–300 mels, whereas the quantal steps in the abscissa are of the order of 200–250 mels. Since we now have condensed the vowel space to a plane we have only two orthogonal parameters.

The abscissa ($M_1 + M_2'$) is twice the center of gravity of the spectrum,

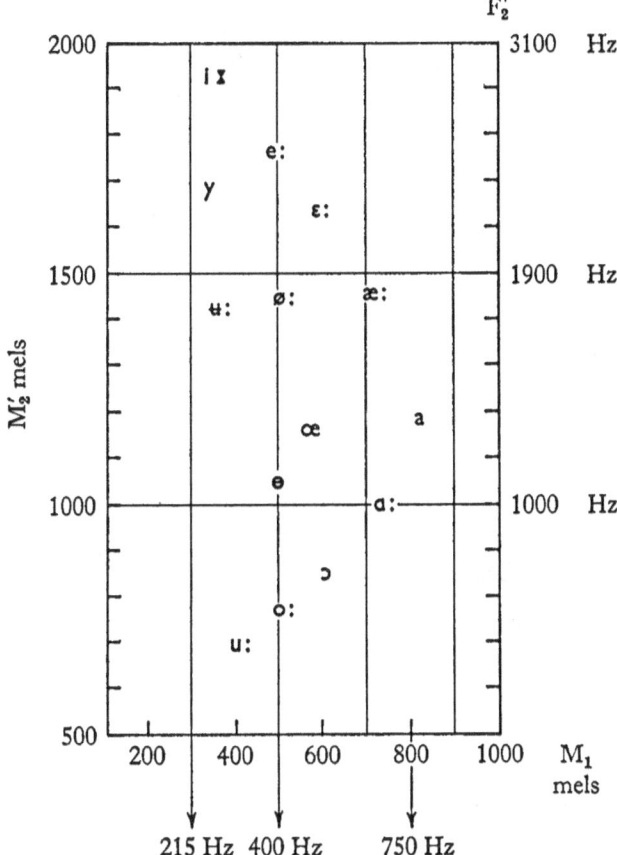

FIG. 4. Swedish long vowels and some short vowels in a M'_2 versus M_1 plot (mel scale). M'_2 is determined from an analysis-by-(two-formant) synthesis procedure.

giving equal weight to M_1 and M'_2, and will be identified with the negative of the old feature 'flat'. Labialization, velarization, jaw closing, larynx lowering will all lower the center of gravity whilst the ordinate, here referred to as the spectral feature 'spread', is a measure of dispersion. Note that it is related to but not identical to any of the old features such as [−compactness], [+diffuseness], or [−gravity]. The spectral spread is increased by moving the tongue from a pharyngeal to a palatal place of articulation. Five levels are indicated by the points [aː], [æː], [ɛː], [eː], [iː]. Note that increasing jaw opening increases in the first hand M_1 and thus makes the spectrum less flat and less spread. Fig. 5 would motivate a quantization of the long vowels in scales of 'flat' and 'spread' as shown in Table 4.

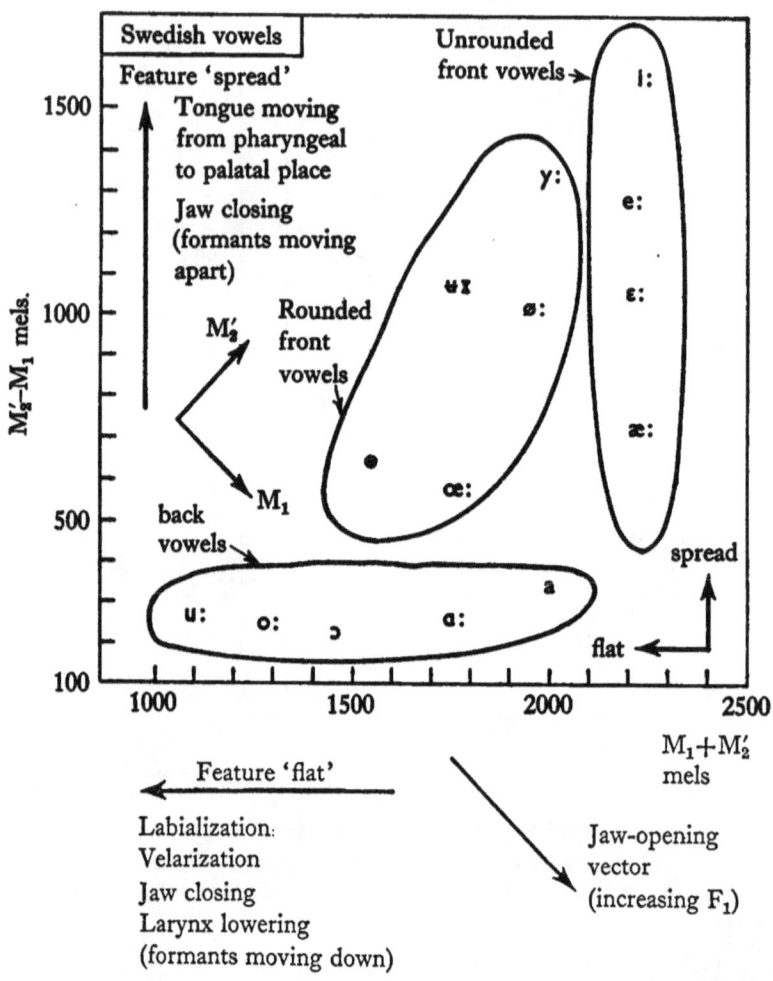

FIG. 5. Swedish vowels in a 'spread' versus 'flat' mel scale plot bringing out some orthogonal vowel categories (back and front vowels) and a tendency toward equidistant mel spacings.

TABLE 4

	uː	oː	ɑː	æː	ɛː	eː	iː	yː	ʉː	øː	œː	parameter
'spread'	0	0	0	1	2	3	4	3	2	2	1	$M_2' - M_1$
'flat'	5	4	2	0	0	0	0	1	2	1	2	$-(M_1 + M_2')$

Distinctive Features and Phonetic Dimensions 189

FIG. 6. X-ray tracings of Swedish vowels. (From G. Fant, 'The Acoustics of Speech', in *Proceedings of the Third International Congress on Acoustics, Stuttgart, 1959*, pp. 188–201, fig. 9, Amsterdam, 1961.)

These scales are absolute but can of course be reduced according to the principle of complimentary distributions. The progressing 'flatness' from [ɑ:] over [o:] to [u:] is the effect of rounding +velarization whereas the flatness of [ʉ:] is primarily a matter of small lip opening. As previously discussed, velarization does not appear to be involved in [ʉ:] but possibly an 'anteriorization'. The possibility of compensatory forms of articulation in the flatness domain are apparent. In the class of 'short', i.e. lax, Swedish vowels, the /ʉ/, phonetically [ə] is more 'velar' than the short [ø] (see Fig. 6). These facts support a perceptual rather than an articulatory feature basis.

It has often been suggested that articulatory descriptions of vowels actually rely on underlying perceptual classifications, Ladefoged (1967b). Our data indicate that the Swedish vowels are not arbitrarily spaced individuals in the space of physically producible sounds but show a clear organization in terms of linear sequences and a tendency toward equidistant spacings in an orthogonal perceptual space. This ordering appears to be a subset of a language universal system of maximal contrast. This idea was also expressed by Lindblom and Sundberg (1969a). Further work along these lines is continuing. Earlier work on mel scale mapping of Swedish vowels was published by Fant (1959).

References

Chomsky, N. and M. Halle (1968). *Sound Pattern of English*, New York.
Fant, G. (1958). 'Modern Instruments and Methods for Acoustic Studies of Speech', *Acta Politechnica Scandinavica*, 246.
  (1959). 'Acoustic Analysis and Synthesis of Speech with Applications to Swedish', *Ericsson Technics* 15, No. 1, pp. 3–108.
  (1960a). *Acoustic Theory of Speech Production* ('s-Gravenhage).
  (1960b). 'Structural Classification of Swedish Phonemes', STL-QPSR 2/1960, pp. 10–15.
  (1966). 'The Nature of Distinctive Features', STL-QPSR 4/1966, pp. 1–15.
  (1967). 'Sound, Features, and Perception', STL-QPSR 2–3/1967, pp. 1–14.
  (1968). 'Analysis and Synthesis of Speech Processes', pp. 173–277, in *Manual of Phonetics*, ed. B. Malmberg, Amsterdam.
Jakobson, R., G. Fant and M. Halle (1952). 'Preliminaries to Speech Analysis', MIT, Acoustics Lab., Technical Report No. 13.
Ladefoged, P. (1967a). 'Linguistic Phonetics'. Working Papers in Phonetics 6 (UCLA).
  (1967b). *Three Areas of Experimental Phonetics*, London.
  (1969). 'The Measurement of Phonetic Similarity', paper presented at the International Conference on Computational Linguistics (COLING), Stockholm.
Lehiste, I. and G. E. Peterson (1961). 'Transitions, Glides, and Diphthongs', *J. Acoust. Soc. Am.* 33, pp. 268–77.
Lindblom, B. (1967). 'Vowel Duration and a Model of Lip Mandible Coordination', STL-QPSR 4/1967, pp. 1–29.
Lindblom, B. and J. Sundberg (1969a). 'A Quantitative Model of Vowel Production and the Distinctive Features of Swedish Vowels', STL-QPSR 1/1969, pp. 14–32.

(1969b). 'A Quantitative Theory of Cardinal Vowels and the Teaching of Pronunciation', paper presented at the 2nd International Congress of Applied Linguistics, Cambridge, England.

Malmberg, B. (1956). 'Distinctive Features of Swedish Vowels: Some Instrumental and Structural Data', pp. 316–21 in *For Roman Jakobson* ('s-Gravenhage).

Peterson, G. E. (1968). 'The Speech Communication Process', pp. 155–72 in *Manual of Phonetics*, ed. B. Malmberg, Amsterdam.

Chapter 12
Notes on the Swedish Vowel System

Introduction

The purpose of this article is to summarize my views on the Swedish vowel system and to comment on the development of the theoretical framework. The Swedish vowel system is rather complicated and thus offers many possibilities of testing current ideas in linguistics, e.g. the feature system of CHOMSKY and HALLE (1968). One part of the problem is to describe the phonetic facts; the other is to discuss alternative distinctive feature representations within a phonological frame. These problems have recently received considerable attention in articles by FANT (1968a, 1968b, 1969) and by Lindblom and Sundberg (1969).

Phonetic facts

It is generally agreed upon that Swedish has nine long and nine short vowel phonemes. These constitute three groups: the back vowels, the unrounded front vowels, and the rounded front vowels, each comprising three long and three short vowels.

uː/ʊ	oː/ɔ	ɑː/a	back vowels
iː/ɪ	eː/e	ɛː/ɛ	unrounded front vowels
yː/ʏ	ʉː/ɵ	øː/ø	rounded front and mid vowels

The long/short distinction corresponding to the CHOMSKY-HALLE "tense/lax" feature is effective in stressed syllables only. The phonetic realization of this distinction lies in the close/open dimension, a longer/shorter vowel duration, and a shorter/longer duration of the following consonants.

The three-by-three matrix presentation above is not paralleled by an equally simple structuring of articulatory or acoustic facts. The symmetry is upset by the [ʉː] and its short counterpart [ɵ]. The [ʉː] is a front vowel and not a centralized back vowel as implied by the notation, whereas the [ɵ] is a midvowel. As pointed out by Malmberg (1956), the velar element

---

This article originally appeared in *Form and Substance*, edited by L. L. Hammerich, Roman Jakobson, and Eberhard Zwirner (Copenhagen: Akademisk Forlag, 1971). Reprinted with permission.

found in [ɵ] is not present in [ʉː]. Furthermore, the tongue height location of [eː] intermediate between [iː] and [ɛː] does not have a simple correspondence in the relation of [ʉː] to [yː] and [øː]. The [ʉː] can have the same degree of tongue height as [øː], whilst the phonetically distinctive element of [ʉː] is an extreme narrowing of the lips, which generally is realized as a diphthongal transition to lip closure and back to a more open terminal phase. This feature [ʉː] shares with [uː]. They are traditionally referred to as being "inrounded" whilst the [yː], [øː], and [oː] have a lesser degree of lip narrowing and are said to be "outrounded", referring to the protrusion of the lips. A diphthongal movement towards articulatory closure and back to a more open phase is also typical of long [iː] and [yː]. This is a matter of tongue body movement, whereas it is not always recognized that the main element of the [uː] and the [ʉː] diphthongs is a lip closing gesture. A closer examination of the few X-ray tracings available of the [ʉː], FANT (1969), and LINDBLOM and SUNDBERG (1969), reveals that the apex is generally somewhat elevated to provide a point of maximum tongue constriction well anterior to that optimal for a high F_2, whilst I have seen no trace of a "velar" component in the [ʉː] articulation. LINDBLOM and SUNDBERG (1969) have shown that it is possible to generate a synthetic [ʉː] from an articulatory position slightly posterior to that of [iː], i.e. in the direction towards [uː]. In view of the three-parameter model curves, FANT (1960a, 1968a) it is quite apparent that either the anterior or the posterior tongue articulation provides a lowering of F_2 relative to the maximum value at the midpalatal region.

The acoustic relations within each of the subsets of long and short vowels are shown in Fig. 1. Here the pre-r variants [æ] and [œ] of [ɛ] and [ø] are included. In these diagrams the ordinate is an effective second formant position defined by the preferred location of the upper formant of a two-formant synthesis. This effective F'_2 turns out to be equal to F_2 of back and mid vowels and approaches F_3 or a higher location in the [iː] region. This is of course a first order approximation only whilst relative intensity levels and the specific pattern of F_2 and higher formants account for additional perceptual attributes, which have not been investigated very well. However, these secondary pattern aspects are to a considerable degree predictable from the two-formant approximation, F_3 moving from a position close to F_2 in [ʉː], [øː], and [æː] to a position close to F_4 in the [iː] region.

The diphthongal glide of the vowels [uː], [ʉː], [yː], and [iː] serves an important function for maintaining appropriate acoustic-perceptual distinctions. As indicated in Fig.1 F_2 and F_3 move in separate directions for the labial and the palatal closing. This fact and the falling of F_1 in all phases of increasing closure add to the contrast between [uː] and [oː], [ʉː] and [øː] and between [ʉː] and [yː]. Thus, F_2 and F_3 are falling in the [ʉː] glide, whilst F_3 and to a minor extent F_2 display a rising transition in [yː] and [iː] glides.

These facts have only in the recent years become clear, FANT (1968a, 1969), FANT et al. (1969). An [ʉː] sampled at the very beginning will display a formant pattern rather close to that of [øː] and similarly, an [uː], if synthesized on the basis of a stationary formant pattern typical of that of the initial part of a natural [uː], is easily confused with an [oː]. It is interesting to note that rising F_3 of the [yː] diphthong is secured by the palatal constriction overriding the effect of the superimposed lip rounding, whilst the lowering of F_2 and F_3 of the [ʉː] diphthong as a result of lip narrowing is facilitated by the tongue palate passage being less constricted than in [yː] and [iː]. Also a point of alveolar or postpalatal tongue stricture of [ʉː] contributes to the overall low F_2 level required. The extent of the F_3 movement in [yː] is often greater than that found in [iː] which can be explained by a transition from a less open phase, where the lip stricture overrides the tongue stricture to an opposite state where the lip opening has a less influence on the formant pattern.

The perceptual theory advanced here is based on the two main dimensions F_1 and F'_2 of an equivalent two-formant synthesis. These two parameters or their sums and differences can be thought of as independent and orthogonal perceptual dimensions. Thus $-(F_1 + F'_2)$ can be thought of as an acoustic correlate of a generalized "flatness" dimension, whilst $(F'_2 - F_1)$ can be interpreted as a dimension of "spectral spread", see further the discussion in FANT (1969). The $F'_2 - F_1$ parameter thus separates the back vowels [uː], [oː], [ɔ], [ɑː], [a] from the rest of the system and, in addition, acts as the most efficient single parameter for delimiting the separate levels of tongue height within the front vowels. The vowel [ʉː] and its short counterpart [ə] have the common property of a greater flatness, i.e. smaller $F_1 + F'_2$ than the vowels [y] and [ø]. The flatness of the [ə] is a matter of lip narrowing and velarization, the flatness of [ʉː] is essentially a matter of an extreme lip narrowing. These facts support the third level of flatness suggested by MALMBERG (1956), which I have adopted in earlier feature discussions. It is of interest to note that some of FISCHER-JØRGENSEN's (1968) experiments on vowel perception support the notion of a psychological reality of the "spread" feature.

Linguistic facts

The [ʉː] vowel originates from a former [uː] vowel as a result of vowel shift in the 15–16th century. An additional back vowel took the place of the old [uː] in standard Swedish, whilst the vowel system of Swedish as spoken in Finland has one single vowel instead of our [ʉː] and [uː]. The shift of the corresponding short vowel [ʊ] to [ɵ] did not progress equally far.

Even before this vowel shift we had a rule of /k/ of the orthography being softened to a [ç] before all front vowels and this is still the main rule for pronunciation of /k/ before front vowels with the exception of [ʉː]. We do have [ç] in front of [ʉː] in Swedish words but they derive from a [tj] of standard orthography.

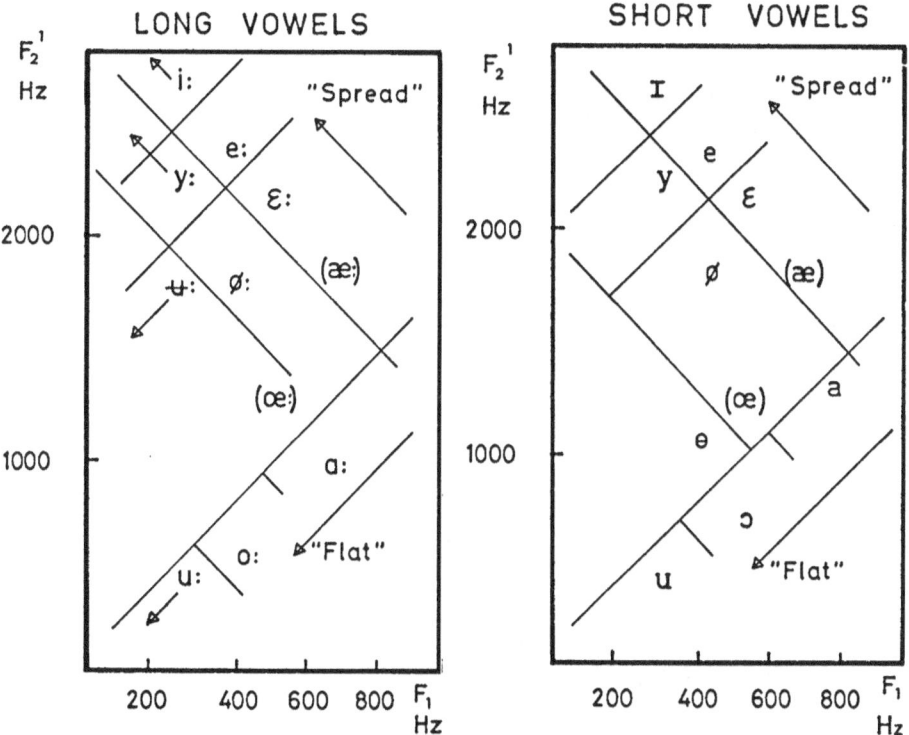

Fig. 1. Two-dimensional (F_1 and F'_2) representation of Swedish long and short vowels. F'_2 is an estimated perceptual mean of F_2 and higher formants.

The distinction between short [e] and [ɛ] is lost in central Swedish dialects and there is some tendency of the long [ɛː] merging with [eː] in some varieties of the Stockholm dialect as well as the pre-r [ə] merging with the pre-r [œ]. Indeed, as seen in Fig. 1, the differences are not very great.

The diphthongization already mentioned is a property of all long vowels with extreme low F_1.

Classificatory solutions

We shall next study some alternative solutions to a distinctive feature representation. Starting out with the JAKOBSON-FANT-HALLE (1952) feature system and allowing for three levels of compactness (F_1) and three levels on the flatness scale $-(F_1 + F_2 + F_3)$ besides two levels on the gravity scale $-(F_2)$ or $-(F_2 - F_1)$ we obtain the classification proposed by FANT (1960b).

Matrix (1).

	[u:]	[o:]	[ɑ:]	[i:]	[e:]	[ɛ:]	[y:]	[ʉ:]	[ø:]
grave	+	+	+	−	−	−	−	−	−
compact .	−	±	+	−	±	+	−	−	±
flat		±	−	−	−	−	±	+	±
tense	+	+	+	+	+	+	+	+	+

The compactness of each of [u:], [o:], and [ɑ:] is predictable from the flatness or vice versa. The [− comp] notation for [ʉ:] is likewise redundant. The system is equally well applicable to short (lax) vowels in which case the short correspondence of [ʉ:], i.e. [ə], receives the compactness value [±]. Diphthongization is predicted by

$$\begin{bmatrix} + \text{ tense} \\ - \text{ compact} \end{bmatrix} \rightarrow \text{diphthongizable}$$

If [+ flat] the diphthongization is made with the lips, otherwise with the tongue. The "k-softening" occurs as follows:

$$\begin{bmatrix} - \text{ grave} \\ \text{non } + \text{ flat} \end{bmatrix} \rightarrow \text{k-softening}$$

The next experiment in classification is concerned with the same type of features but allowing for binary distinctions only. This is evidently no problem for back vowels since we can assign the [− comp] to [u:] and the [− flat] to [ɑ:] leaving [o:] [+ comp] and [+ flat]. Within the front vowels the situation can be cleared up only by introducing a new feature. From the JAKOBSON-FANT-HALLE (1952) system we can borrow the feature "sharp" which is defined as palatal narrowing on the articulatory level and a high ($F_2 + F_3$) on the acoustic level. As suggested by FANT (1966),

Matrix (2)

	[u:]	[o:]	[ɑ:]	[i:]	[e:]	[ɛ:]	[y:]	[ʉ:]	[ø:]
grave	+	+	+	−	−	−	−	−	−
compact	−	+	+	−	−	+	−	−	+
flat	+	+	−	−	−	−	+	+	+
sharp	−	−	−	+	−	−	+	−	−
tense	+	+	+	+	+	+	+	+	+

In the system of corresponding short (− tense) vowels we are free to choose a [+ comp] specification of [ɘ]. The diphthongization rule now becomes slightly more complex

$$\begin{Bmatrix} + \text{ tense} \\ + \text{ sharp} \end{Bmatrix} \to \text{diphthong with tongue}$$

$$\begin{Bmatrix} + \text{ tense} \\ - \text{ compact} \\ + \text{ flat} \\ - \text{ sharp} \end{Bmatrix} \to \text{diphthong with lips}$$

What about the CHOMSKY-HALLE (1968) features? I have found, and it has been confirmed by HALLE, that their features do not suffice for dealing with the Swedish vowel system. The feature "covered", proposed for [ʉ:] is phonetically incorrect and cannot be used. The basic strategy of CHOMSKY and HALLE has been to define features on the articulatory level without paying much attention to their acoustic and perceptual correlates. There remains much work on the testing of the correlates and some ambiguities may call for revisions of the feature inventory, see FANT (1969). The choice of an articulatory level of feature definition conforms with the "generative" idea of primary levels in the speaking act, determining the shape of the events at lower levels closer to the receiver. By this principle a single acoustic-perceptual feature like flatness has to be translated to two or more articulatory features, such as lip narrowing and velarization.

My first attempt was to add to the CHOMSKY-HALLE feature inventory a feature "labial" for extreme lip closing. The feature labial when applied to vowels may be regarded as an extension of the round dimension to an extreme lowering of all formants and it also has a place in the consonant system as a substitute for the rather artificial [+ anterior, — coronal] encoding of the class of labial consonants. Otherwise the CHOMSKY-HALLE feature "back" is equivalent to the old "grave"feature. The three levels of compactness correspond to the [— high, + low], [— high, — low], and [+ high, — low] combinations. The solution then becomes identical in principle to that of Matrix (1) with flat substituted by "round" and "labial" and compact substituted by "high" and "low".

Matrix (3)

	[uː]	[oː]	[ɑː]	[iː]	[eː]	[ɛː]	[yː]	[ʉː]	[øː]
back	+	+	+	—	—	—	—	—	—
low	—	—	+	—	—	+	—	—	—
high	+	—	—	+	—	—	+	+	—
round	+	+	—	—	—	—	+	+	+
labial	+	—	—	—	—	—	—	+	—
tense	+	+	+	+	+	+	+	+	+

The diphthong rules

$$\begin{cases} + \text{ tense} \\ + \text{ high} \\ + \text{ labial} \end{cases} \begin{matrix} \rightarrow \text{diphthongizable} \\ \rightarrow \text{lip diphthong} \end{matrix}$$

are in principle those discussed in connection with Matrix (1).

The problem of deriving diphthongization in Swedish vowels from distinctive feature matrices was first approached by LINDBLOM and SUNDBERG (1969). They developed a set of articulatory features from a vocal tract model based on three tongue shapes, "palatal", "pharyngeal", and "velar", corresponding to [iː], [ɑː], and [uː]. The jaw opening was given two binary features, "close" and "open", and in addition a lip rounding, "labial" feature, was introduced. It turns out that their dimension "pharyngeal" operates as the negative of their "open" dimension and is redundant in this respect. Furthermore their "close" and "open" dimensions have the same classificatory function as the ternary compactness feature of Matrix (1) and the same as the CHOMSKY-HALLE "high" and "low" features in Matrix (3). The "palatal" feature operates as the negative of the JAKOBSON-FANT-HALLE "grave" feature and the CHOMSKY-HALLE "back" feature. The only new feature introduced by

LINDBLOM-SUNDBERG is the feature "velar" which is attributed to [u:] and [ʉ:]. They admit that the velarity of [ʉ:] does not fully stand up to phonetical tests but that it is rather to be regarded as a classificatory label for displaying phonological similarities with [u:].

LINDBLOM's diphthongization rule (in his work with SUNDBERG) that [+ close] vowels, i.e. vowels with minimum F_1 are diphthongizable, is identical to the rules stated in connection with Matrices (1) and (3). The labiality of the [ʉ:] and [u:] diphthongs LINDBLOM derives with reference to their "velarity" which as far as the standard pronunciation of [ʉ:] is concerned appears to be rather fictitious. In recent discussions I have proposed an alternative feature "palatal" referring to the location of the tongue in the front-back dimension close to that providing maximally high F_2. It is identical to the "palatal" feature of LINDBLOM and to the negative of the "back" or "grave" feature with the exception that [ʉ:] is labelled [− palatal] referring to a place of tongue constriction anterior to that of maximum F_2. The common denominator between [u:] and [ʉ:] is thus a nonoptimal tongue articulation for a high F_2. One can now, as before, state that long vowels with the highest level of tongue height are diphthongizable and that the diphthong is made with tongue if [+ palatal] otherwise with the lips. Also this "palatal" feature captures exactly the distribution of k-softening, i.e. [k] of the lexical transcript is pronounced as [ç] before a [+ palatal] vowel, whereas in LINDBLOM's systems the feature [− velar] must be added.

Instead of the CHOMSKY-HALLE "low" and "high" features for tongue height one could adopt WANG's (1968) suggestion of "high" and the moderator "mid" capable of producing four levels. The fourth level would enable the inclusion of the pre-r variant of [ɛ:] and [ø:] in the feature matrix as follows:

Matrix (4)

	[u:]	[o:]	[ɑ:]	[i:]	[e:]	[ɛ:]	[æ:]	[y:]	[ʉ:]	[ø:]	[œ:]
back	+	+	+	−	−	−	−	−	−	−	−
high	+	−	−	+	+	−	−	+	+	−	−
mid	−	+	−	−	+	+	−	−	−	+	−
palatal	−	−	−	+	+	+	+	+	−	+	+
round	+	+	−	−	−	−	−	+	+	+	+
tense	+	+	+	+	+	+	+	+	+	+	+

$\begin{Bmatrix} + \text{ high} \\ - \text{ mid} \end{Bmatrix} \rightarrow$ diphthongizable

$\{ + \text{ pal} \} \rightarrow$ diphthong is made with tongue

$\{ + \text{ pal} \} \rightarrow$ k-softening

$\{ - \text{ pal} \} \rightarrow$ diphthong is made with lips

Concluding remarks

I have attempted to demonstrate the inherent similarities of a number of alternative distinctive feature analyses of Swedish vowels. The minimum number of four features is obtained with the JAKOBSON-FANT-HALLE system if ternary levels are adopted for the compactness as well as for the flatness feature. The minimum number of features in a strictly binary system, five, is obtained with the JAKOBSON-FANT-HALLE system by utilizing a sharpness feature which applies to [i:] and [y:]. With the CHOMSKY-HALLE system one extra feature must be added, making up a total of six binary features. The additional feature can either directly refer to the extreme lip rounding of [u:] and [ʉ:] or to their nonoptimal tongue location with respect to high F_2. The former solution introducing a feature "labial" has the benefit of being useful in the consonant system also as a substitute for the rather questionable [+ anterior], [− coronal] classification of the labial consonants. The special "palatal" feature, on the other hand, would alone be sufficient for expressing the k-softening rule. The phonetic validity of this feature must be further tested before it can be adopted.

The diphthongization affects all long vowels with maximal tongue height. The diphthong is made with the tongue if the articulation is strictly palatal, otherwise it is made with the lips. This rule works well for its generative purpose but it is only partially supported by reasons of phonetic consequences, since it is quite feasible to produce a lip diphthong with any tongue height. In general, a tense articulation with narrow lips would tend to provide a lip diphthong and a tense articulation with the tongue in a palatal high position would be the natural prerequisite for a tongue diphthong. Moreover, an optimal contrast between the two types of diphthongs requires that the effect of the lip passage does not override the effect of the tongue passage and vice versa, i.e. there should be maximal closure at only one of the two places.

The palatal diphthong is rising and the labial diphthong is falling in terms of F_2 and F_3 which adds to the contrast between [y:] and [ʉ:]. In all diphthongs F_1 is falling which adds to the distinction between [u:] and [o:], between [ʉ:] and [ø:], and between [i:] and [e:].

In my view it is not likely that vowels are perceived by a strict decomposition in terms of phonological features. The tense/lax or long/short distinction has probably a direct counterpart in the human decoding and the diphthongization adds to the contrast of high vowels. In other respects human perception of a vowel probably operates with a direct identification of its approximate place in a multidimensional continuous parameter space. A two-parameter approximation, based on the features "spread" and "flatness" has been discussed.

Gunnar Fant
Tekniska Högskolan
Stockholm

REFERENCES

(1968) CHOMSKY, N. and HALLE, M.: *Sound Pattern of English* (New York).
(1959) FANT, G.: "Acoustic Analysis and Synthesis of Speech with Applications to Swedish", Ericssons Technics *15*, No. 1, pp. 3–108.
(1960a) FANT, G.: *Acoustic Theory of Speech Production* ('s-Gravenhage).
(1960b) FANT, G.: "Structural Classification of Swedish Phonemes", STL-QPSR 2/1960, pp. 10–15 (Stockholm).
(1966) FANT, G.: "The Nature of Distinctive Features", STL-QPSR 4/1966, pp. 1–15 (Stockholm).
(1968a) FANT, G.: "Analysis and Synthesis of Speech Processes", pp. 173–277 in *Manual of Phonetics*, Ed. by B. MALMBERG (Amsterdam).
(1968b) FANT, G.: "Den akustiska fonetikens grunder", KTH, Taltransmissionslaboratoriet, Rapport nr. 7, second edition (Stockholm).
(1969) FANT, G.: "Distinctive Features and Phonetic Dimensions", STL-QPSR 3/1969, pp. 1–18 (Stockholm).
(1969) FANT, G., HENNINGSSON, G., and STÅLHAMMAR, U.: "Formant Frequencies of Swedish Vowels", STL-QPSR 4/1969, pp. 26–31 (Stockholm).
(1968) FISCHER-JØRGENSEN, E.: "Perceptual Dimensions of Vowels", *Proc. of Seminar on Speech Production and Perception, Leningrad, Aug. 13–16, 1966*; publ. in Z. für Phonetik, Sprachwissenschaft und Kommunikationsforschung, Band *21*, Heft 1/2, pp. 94–98.
(1952) JAKOBSON, R., FANT, G., and HALLE, M.: "Preliminaries to Speech Analysis", MIT, Acoustics Lab., Technical Report No. 13.
(1969) LINDBLOM, B. and SUNDBERG, J.: "A Quantitative Model of Vowel Production and the Distinctive Features of Swedish Vowels", STL-QPSR 1/1969, pp. 14–32 (Stockholm).
(1956) MALMBERG, B.: "Distinctive Features of Swedish Vowels: Some Instrumental and Structural Data", pp. 316–321 in *For Roman Jakobson* ('s-Gravenhage).
(1968) WANG, W. S-Y.: "Vowel Features, Paired Variables, and the English Vowel Shift", Language *44*, pp. 695–708.

Chapter 13
Automatic Recognition and Speech Research

Introduction

The purpose of this article is to collect some thoughts on automatic speech recognition (ASR). At the Speech Transmission Laboratory we have very limited experience with actual recognition schemes but we feel a need to formulate research objectives and outline alternative approaches.

Pierce (1969) has recently challenged the community of automatic speech recognition workers by an article in which he expresses a rather critical view of the aims and methods of current work in this field. According to Pierce, most projects have a narrow scope and are based on primitive concepts, the practical value of ASR is limited, and the handling of the general recognition problem is beyond our present capacity. However, I do not believe the Bell Telephone Laboratories have given up their work in this field and the purpose of the challenge should be regarded as a stimulant for proper planning rather than a general discussion.

Indeed, most of the work reported up till now is concerned with limited inventory word recognition schemes that allow a tolerable level of accuracy for its master voice only and require special voice training. Some more sophisticated systems are speaker adaptive and some make use of linguistic and probabilistic constraints, but no system has yet been reported on that fully utilizes all of these constraints and in addition is designed for time-normalized, low bit rate, information preserving processing at lower levels.

The typical primitive approach is to sample speech intensity within a few frequency bands at regular time intervals and with two or only a few levels of amplitude. This quantized representation is then correlated for maximum match with the standard patterns of the lexical items. It is not profitable to introduce many amplitude and frequency levels since the lack of time normalization introduces gross matching errors anyway. The performance of such systems is rather low but they have the advantage that speaker adaptive func-

This article originally appeared in Speech Transmission Laboratory Quarterly Progress and Status Report 1/1970 (Stockholm, Sweden: Royal Institute of Technology, 1970).

tions as well as new lexical items can easily be added. No phonetic criteria are needed since a word is recognized as a single unit.

This type of recognition is similar to that utilized by a dog responding to simple oral commands. A decomposition of speech into a set of minimal phonetic categories and the handling of more complex sentences than single words is attempted in more advanced ASR-projects. Evidently it is hard to compete with the human brain and practical compromises have to be made in any design. This, however, is not the same as saying that computers cannot be taught to react in a way similar to that of human beings.

Future success in ASR depends on two factors, an increase in basic knowledge concerning speech and language, and the advance of computer technology. The need for research is unlimited and will continue to be so for decades to come. Meanwhile, we should test the status of this field now and then and evaluate ASR's practical applicability in man-machine communication systems. The objectives of ASR are thus in a wide sense the same as of speech research in general. Recognition algorithms are the image of synthesis-by-rule programs and ASR is accordingly just as much an organizing principle for speech research as a product of such research. At least this is how it should be. Primitive systems do not provide a feedback to the investigators' facts concerning why mistakes are made and how models should be improved.

The demands for very large computer storage space for "unlimited" recognition of connected speech are basically the same as those in automatic language translation. The practical applicability will depend on future cost reduction, miniaturization, and feasibility of handling large data quantities that will enable the necessary storage of all a priori knowledge from the separate stages of the speech communication process, the semantic stage included.

In addition to these academic views I want to emphasize the need for developing reasonably optimized special purpose limited inventory systems and partial solutions, e.g. the technique of recognizing some basic phonetic categories that can be utilized in aids for the deaf, such as supplements to lip-reading.

Previous work

It is not my intention to present a review of the literature. Readers are referred to the survey of Lindgren (1965) which provides a comprehensive presentation of ASR in relation to speech research. One of the most detailed recent surveys is that of Hyde (1968) who lists a large number of earlier contemporary projects and concludes his study with a general discussion. His review of separate projects is rather condensed and does not allow much room for evaluation. His discussion, however, is concerned with general principles and recommendations. These are well founded. I can accordingly agree with Hyde that "Feature abstraction is better than pattern matching in recognition at the acoustic level," "The speech signal cannot be directly segmented into phoneme units," "Time normalization by simply stretching or compressing one speech wave compared with another, is of rather limited value," "Probabilistic information must be used with caution," "Learning systems have a place in automatic speech recognition but cannot be valuably exploited until the basic principles of recognition have been determined," and most of his other statements.

The 1/1970 issue of STL-QPSR contains summary articles on recent Soviet work at the USSR Academy of Sciences, Institute for Mathematics in Novosibirsk (Zagoruiko, 1970), and at the University of Lvov, Ukraine (Derkach, 1970). The Soviet work on ASR is well organized and has produced interesting results but was not very well referenced in the earlier Western literature (Falter and Otten, 1967).

Models of recognition

In principle it would be feasible to design speech recognition schemes without any knowledge of the perception processes, providing the human production processes are sufficiently well known and a sufficiently large empirical store of data relating speech waves and message compositions have been collected.

However, even though our knowledge of the speech perception processes is rather limited it pays to formularize our concepts of various stages at the listener end of the communication into working models for practical recognition schemes. One such model is that of Bondarko, Zagoruiko, Kozhevnikov, Molchanov, and Chistovich (1968; see also Kozhevnikov and Chistovich, 1965), which recognize three basic stages, an acoustic data sampling stage, a phoneme recognition stage, and a word recognition stage. A somewhat more elaborate model is proposed here in Figure 1. It contains five successive stages of processing labeled

1. Parameter extraction,
2. Microsegment detection,
3. Phonetic transcript,
4. Word identification,
5. Semantic interpretation.

The main path toward higher levels of recognition is paralleled by a down-

SPEECH RECOGNITION

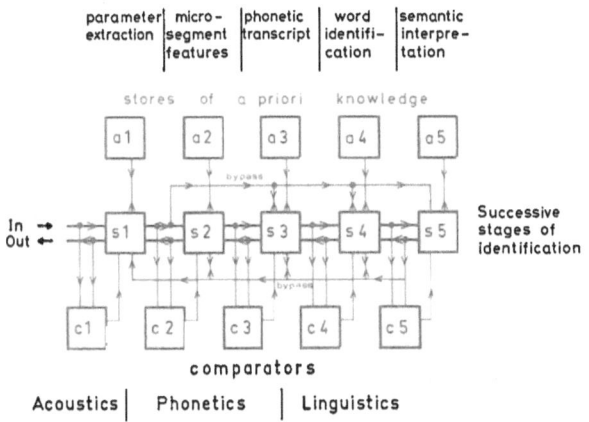

Figure 1. Block diagram illustrating successive levels and functions in a generalized speech recognition scheme.

stream translation path for enabling a testing at lower levels of tentative identifications at higher levels. A set of comparators marked c1, c2, c3, c4, c5 are introduced for this purpose. Each stage has its storage a1, a2, a3, a4, a5 of a priori information concerning inventories and constraints of the message representation at the particular level which provides reference data for processing and identification. Upstream and downstream bypass pathways are also indicated in the block diagram. These shortcuts would, for instance, provide evidence for identification of a speech sound or of a word directly from the lowest level. The downgoing bypass could enable a conditioning of lower centers to a state appropriate for testing a certain state predicted at a higher level. Multipathways in parallel and shortcuts appear to be a topological characteristic of the human brain also. Otherwise I do not claim that the block diagram of Figure 1 is representative of human perception. Its main purpose is to enable a discussion of recognition strategies but even for this purpose it is very incomplete, e.g. with respect to memory functions of shorter or longer span which is crucial for the recognition. The outgoing line would have some correspondence to speech production. In this sense the comparators would fit in a motor theory of speech perception although this is not strictly implied by the model. Reference patterns involved in a comparison should first of all be conceived of as belonging to a perceptual sphere (Fant, 1964).

The successive stages of a maximally ambitious recognition system could be given the following functions.

1. PARAMETER EXTRACTION

Sampling intervals should be of the order of 5–20 ms and preferably pitch synchronous in voiced intervals. Many different sets of parameters can be selected, such as

a. Short-time average amplitude in several frequency bands;

b. Short-time average amplitude and zero-crossing density in a few frequency bands or as a single overall measure;

c. Pole-zero spectral approximations with separate constants for voiced and unvoiced segments. Z-transform and Chirp-Z* variants (Rabiner, Schafer, and Rader, 1969);

d. Main spectral maximum locations and spectral slopes;

e. Spectrum described by an expansion into moments or other functions.

In addition the voice fundamental frequency F_0 should be tracked. Formant and pitch tracking has proved to be rather difficult to execute without errors. This is the main reason why formant vocoders have not yet been very successful. The a priori knowledge store a1 could contain vocal transfer constraints such as the normal relation between spectral energy distributions and formant frequency patterns to avoid erroneous formant number labeling in c.

The short-time memory in stage s1 should span over at least three successive sample points. Time differentials of parameter values should be included to enable microsegmentation in s2.

2. MICROSEGMENT EXTRACTION

Rapid changes in the speech spectrum and intensity induced by changes in the active source or sources or in the main characteristics of the vocal transfer function give rise to discontinuities that define boundaries of "microsegments" (see Fant, 1962, 1968). These minimal production units are not identical to phonemes but can constitute parts of phonemes. The "source," "manner," and "place" categorizations of such segments are essentially the same as for feature analysis in general whereas the typical "place" correlate is a spectral feature that often varies continuously across segment boundaries, e.g. from a stop burst to a following vowel. The situation is similar to when there is a shift from noise to voice source in the course of a normally voiced consonant following an unvoiced consonant. However, not all manner correlates give rise to sharp boundaries. An example is velum lowering well ahead of a nasal consonant in which case the appearance of the nasalization is gradual. Also, there is not always a continuity of place cues, e.g. the spectral energy goes from a fricative such as [s] to a vowel, such as [a].

---

* Frequency analysis along a $\sigma+j\omega$ line in the s-plane in order to sharpen formant peaks.

The output of the microsegmenter stage s2 is a sequence of segments classified as to "source," "manner," "duration," and "place of articulation" or if the segment place cannot be identified the cues are to be reconsidered at the next stage, s3. The memory span required is of the order of 4–7 segments. The a priori information contains vocal-tract physiological and acoustic constraints, including rules for speaker normalization. Spectrum "place" parameters should be selected according to established perceptual models.

3. PHONETIC TRANSCRIPT

The phonetic transcript stage, s3, converts the microsegment data to a representation in terms of a string of phonemes and superimposed prosodemes. Alternatively, the output of stage s3 is an equivalent distinctive feature matrix (Jakobson, Fant, and Halle, 1952; or Chomsky and Halle, 1968). The particular choice of feature is not very important as long as the phoneme is uniquely defined by the features. These need not be binary.

It should be noted that a microsegment description process is nonunique, being arbitrarily dependent on the choice of parameters and thresholds. There is also a speaker dependent variability to take into account. These variabilities are compensated for by the inherent redundancies. The algorithm for identification of a phoneme or of one of its distinctive features, i.e. "nominal" phonetic category should take into account such free variations.

The a priori knowledge storage a3 contains rules for the phonetic correlates of the distinctive features and includes the sequential constraints in terms of possible phoneme or feature sequences. The location of vowels within a string of phonemes and prosodic categories, such as stressed and unstressed syllables and tonal accents, should be identified first. Rules for coarticulation (Öhman, 1967 a, b), and reduction (Lindblom, 1963), and more detailed rules of segmental durations and structuring related to underlying sequences of phonatory and articulatory commands also enter the a3 storage. A memory span of about seven syllables is needed. An intermediate representation in terms of syllables might be advantageous. However, coarticulation effects are not limited to syllabic units and the initial identification of syllabic nuclei is accordingly more important than exact identification of syllabic boundaries.

4. WORD IDENTIFICATION

The segmentation and identification of a tentative string of phonemes and superimposed prosodemes as a sequence of words has to proceed according to linguistic rules. A primitive system was utilized in the study of Reddy and Robinson (1968; see also Zagoruiko, 1970). The concepts of modern generative grammar could be exploited in more sophisticated systems.

The a priori storage a4 contains the equivalent of lexical, syntactic, and phonological rules of the language. Probabilistic information should be added.* The output of stage s4 is a string of words properly identified and transcribed according to the particular lexical and syntactical conventions adopted. A print-out in ordinary spelling is one possible form of the output of s4. "Parts of speech" of the order of sentences might be bounded by reference to overall prosodic patterns (Öhman, 1967b).

5. SEMANTIC INTERPRETATION

The semantic interpretation acts as a support for proper selections at the s4 stage by the requirement that the decisions shall conform with the semantic sphere, e.g. the topic as judged from the prior history of the message.

The phonetic versus the engineering approach

When developing an overall synthesis strategy there are two extreme philosophies to choose between. One is the "phonetic" approach in which case one or both of the stages s2 and s3 of Figure 1 is incorporated. The other, by-passing s2 and s3 and directly identifying words on the basis of parametrical speech wave data, could be called an "engineering approach." Which should be chosen? An advantage of the common engineering approach is its general feature of simplicity. Phonetic decisions are avoided and one can operate directly on overall correlation functions which preserve distinctive elements from the initial learning process or from subsequent adaptive learning sessions. This argumentation is deceptive and has determined the approach in most research groups.†

In the extreme phonetic approach, on the other hand, phonemes are decoded on the basis of their distinctive features. This is graphically represented by a branching tree with nodes for each feature. It can be rightly criticized that an error in one feature will invalidate the recognition whereas the engineering approach with overall correlation functions would emphasize the most likely word in spite of local variations. However, the choice is hypothetical only, since a strict serial feature recognition system without parallel branchings to one and the same phoneme is of academic interest only. Practical phonetic schemes should employ nonexclusive algorithms (Reddy, 1967b), i.e. a many to one input-output relation.

---

* The overall gain is limited by incorrect identifications of very infrequent words. This risk may be minimized if reliability measures are computed already in stage s3, e.g. if probabilities of alternative phoneme strings have been determined.
† We have some limited experience with such systems.

Most adherents to the engineering approach fall for the temptation of using a simplified parametric representation which causes an initial information loss. Clipped speech is intelligible to a human observer thanks to the capacity of the human brain but is not equally intelligible to a computer. The amplitude distribution in a few filter bands has a limited capacity to define the speech message as experienced from the low performance of vocoders with too few filters. This is, of course, a matter of cost also and very limited vocabularies can be identified with a sampling of the overall speech intensity contour only. However, performance could be much improved by a more sophisticated sampling system reducing the initial information loss.

One drawback of the "engineering" approach is that speaker-dependent nonphonemic variations of parametric patterns might dominate the correlation functions. On the other hand, this fact could be used in a retrospect analysis of the causes of errors in the systems and according to the engineer, such an approach could contribute to the development of knowledge concerning distinctive elements in the patterns. This possibility is interesting and could be exploited for the benefit of the phonetic approach where a collection of knowledge for separating speaker-dependent variations from distinctive cues is a basic requirement.

The greatest problem in the engineering approach is to achieve a proper normalization in the time domain. It is quite apparent that a contribution to the overall correlation between stimulus and reference will be highly negative at intervals of overlap between a vowel of a reference word and a fricative in the same word uttered at a different tempo during the test. In the phonetic approach, on the other hand, the microsegmental structure will provide a natural segmentation which in spite of being nonunique provides an inherent normalization. However, we need more experience on the output and efficiency of such segmental procedures.

Various schemes for time normalization have been suggested. Schroeder (1968) has suggested a continuous method which provides information on both the pathway selected in a multidimensional frame and the time spent within each part. Velichko and Zagoruiko (1969) have used linear time normalization for more simple cases and a nonlinear system when the demands on the primary recognition are greater. The method involves the comparison of successive 14 ms samples within the reference and the stimulus starting from the beginning of each word. Successive pairs of stimulus sample and reference sample are selected by adding one time increment to either or to both, whatever gives the best match. The sums of the correlation functions along this pathway are compared for each pair of stimulus and possible reference words.

A proper identification of a sequence of microsegments labeled according to voiced/voiceless and other source and manner categories might suffice for a limited vocabulary recognition.

Distinctive feature theory

The distinctive feature concept is a very powerful tool in linguistic theory as well as in practical applications of speech research, but the relations between the two levels are not always simple. The basic principle implies that all members within a group of phonemes, e.g. all stop sounds, all voiced sounds, all nasal sounds, or all front vowels, have a feature in common in terms of the human production process and in terms of corresponding speech wave characteristics and auditory sensations. One and the same processing stage would accordingly suffice in an automatic recognition process for each of the distinctive features and the number of parallel processors is simply the number of features of the classificatory system. However, the variability induced by the context in a general sense can be considerable. A feature decoding must take into account what other features co-occur in the matrix column of the phoneme and which features occur in adjacent phoneme columns and furthermore the values of all prosodic descriptors. In extreme cases a direct identification of a phoneme is the simplest way of decoding its distinctive features and the latter are then of secondary interest only. This is the main reason why I have chosen to state that a representation in terms of distinctive features matrices is an alternative to phonemes at the output of stage s3 rather than an intermediate representation in an earlier stage. Instead, the microsegmental phonetic representation at the output of stage s2 serves as a set of cues for recognition of either phonemes or distinctive features in stage s3. However, phonetic and linguistic regularities, e.g. segmental constraints, are often simpler to state with reference to distinctive features than with respect to phonemes. In this sense it is the "classificatory" function of the feature defining a certain category of phonemes rather than its phonetic manifestation that is of importance.

The phonetic value of a distinctive feature can be regarded as a vector in a multidimensional signal space. The variability due to context shall be expressible by rules which define how the feature vector is changed when the conditioning elements are varied. A minimum requirement of phonetic reality of a feature would be that any two sounds in any context differing by one and the same feature only shall display a difference vector of the same sign along a common phonetic dimension.

The production correlate of the feature is a specific control channel of the speech mechanism. This idea of features pertaining to natural "biological" channels is, of course, strong as long as a clear cause-effect relation can be tested. The feature systems of Chomsky and Halle (1968) have not been followed up on the acoustic and perceptual level as rigidly as the Fant, Jakobson, and Halle (1952) system which emphasized the perceptual identity of features.

In a practical analysis scheme when several alternatives shall be tested for maximal likelihood it is convenient to contrast phonemes directly and not by the classificatory features only. Thus a choice between [l][r][d] can be optimized by defining differential features for testing each of the alternatives with respect to all other alternatives (Derkach, 1970). In general, a feature-by-feature pathway for going from one phoneme to another phoneme in the complex signal space may display a very uneven and long sequence of lines whereas the direct resultant vector may be of a rather small magnitude (Fant, 1966).

This is one consequence of the present trend in linguistics to define features as a set of convenient minimal sign for formulating rules of language regularities in the first place and as phonetic manifestations in the second place only. This situation reflects our great lack of systematic knowledge in general phonetics and the need to establish generative rules not only on the linguistic level but also on a "subphonological" level to derive all the conditioning rules and constraints of speech production, speech waves, and speech perception.

There does not exist any acceptable feature system worked out for applications in automatic speech recognition. The phonetic approach of Reddy (1967a, b) is interesting but rather "ad hoc." For limited inventory analysis one can choose a system that suits the particular lexical inventory. For more general purposes, as an alternative to the Chomsky and Halle (1968) or the Jakobson, Fant, and Halle (1952) systems, one could apply a conventional set of phonetic features ordered into four main groups.

I. *Manner features* (vowel, glide fricative, stop, nasal, lateral, r-sound);

II. *Source and secondary manner features* (voiced aspirated, tense);

III. *Consonantal place features* (labial, interdental, dental, alveolar, palatal, velar, uvular, pharyngeal, retroflex);

IV. *Tongue and rounding body features* (three back/front and four low/high levels labeled front, central, back; high, midhigh, midlow, low, and rounded/unrounded).

This set of features also applies to parts of the microsegmental description (Fant, 1968). For recent discussions on feature theory, see Fant (1969a) and a forthcoming article by Fant. One advantage of a conventional phonetic feature system is that the terminology is easier to comprehend and that a natu-

212 Features: Theory and Systems

ral articulatory category need not be defined by combinations of other more abstract features. The greater redundancy of this conventional feature set could be an advantage in automatic recognition.

Only + signs need to be used in the matrix. Empty spaces are, for the most part, fully predictable from the selection of plus signs and usually negative, [+stop] implies [−vocalic]. If not predictable the empty spaces are negative in an "unmarked" sense (vowels are usually [−nasal], stops and fricatives [−voice] if not otherwise noted). An example of feature encoding of an English sentence, "The cat saw the bird" is shown in Table 1.

Note that the consonants are here specified by a single feature only* in each

Table 1.

	ð	ə	k	æ	t	s	ɔ	ð	ə	b	ɚ	d
I. vowel		+		+			+		+		+	
glide												
fricative	+					+		+				
stop			+		+					+		+
nasal												
lateral												
r-sound												
II. voiced	+							+		+		+
aspirated			+									
tense												
III. labial										+		
labiodental												
interdental	+							+				
dental												
alveolar					+	+						+
palatal			+									
velar												
uvular												
pharyngeal												
retroflex											+	
IV. front				+								
central		+							+		+	
back							+					
high												
midhigh		+					+		+		+	
midlow												
low				+								
round							+					

of the categories I, II, and III and become coarticulated with the category IV feature of adjacent vowels. Coarticulation in the typical sense is thus the time-space combination of consonantal place features III and tongue body features IV which within certain limits appear to represent independent control channels.

I find the above proposed classification of features into four groups, pertaining to manner, source, consonantal place, and main tongue body and rounding more natural than that of Jakobson, Fant, and Halle (1952) or Chomsky and Halle (1968).†

Recognition strategies. Final words

It is not within the scope of this rather philosophical article to recommend any detailed system for speech recognition. Several principles have been mentioned and the general flow diagram of Figure 1 could embody an infinite variety of solutions. There are some points I would like to stress. The variability of the acoustic correlates of phonemes and distinctive feature with the immediate and grosser frame could imply that the problem is unsolvable since the recognition of any feature would require some knowledge of all other features in a certain area of the matrix. However, a pretty good guess can be made initially in stage s3 of some distinctive features and phonemes, e.g. vowels and fricatives. The number of phonemes within a certain frame is not easily determined in an early stage. This uncertainty is largely a matter of difficulty of consonant segmentation.‡

Thus enough of the fixpoints develop initially to set up the conditioning

---

* In group I [+vowel] can combine with [+nasal] or with [+r-sound]. The latter "r-coloring" can also be transcribed [+retroflex]. In group II two features may be needed, e.g. for the Korean stops. In category III "Retroflex" can combine with alveolars and palatals. The vowel system IV requires a maximum choice of three + arranged according to classical dimensions.

† I do not claim that the feature system proposed here represents a best choice. The novelty lies in the four-group classification of features. A feature system based on a muscular control model of the articulatory organs would have inherent advantages but is not sufficiently developed yet. An approach in this direction is the vowel model of Lindblom and Sundberg (1969). The relation of features derived from this model and other vowel feature systems is discussed in a forthcoming article by the author in STL-QPSR 2-3/1970. In my view there is a great need for investigations of the acoustic and perceptual correlates of articulatory features and to consider feature systems defined initially on the acoustic level and given production correlates in the second place only. A recent study of Swedish stop sounds, Fant (1969b) contributes to the understanding of cues-feature relations.

‡ The number of vowels and their durations should be determined at an early stage of analysis. However, unstressed vowels can be very short, one or two voice pitch periods in extreme cases.

factors for recognition of remaining phonemes and features. The stress and intonation pattern identification proceeds in parallel with the first identifications and constitutes an important subset of factors conditioning the inherent features. Sequential and combinatory constraints rule out some of the alternatives. The final output of stage 3 can be thought of as a specification of alternative phoneme sequences, each evaluated with respect to its probability. Grammatical and semantic constraints add further evidence for identification of words and whole sentences. Generative rules can then enable the check on a lower level of alternative sequences and constructs predicted at higher levels (see Fant, 1968).

References

Bondarko, L. V., N. G. Zagoruiko, V. A. Kozhevnikov, A. P. Molchanov, and L. A. Chistovich (1968). "The Model of Speech Perception by Man," publ. by "Nauka," Novosibirsk (in Russian).

Denes, P. and M. V. Mathews (1960). "Spoken Digit Recognition Using Time-Frequency Pattern Matching," *J. Acoust. Soc. Am.* 32, pp. 1450–1455.

Derkach, M. (1970). "Heuristic Models for Automatic Recognition of Spoken Words," STL-QPSR 1/1970, pp. 39–49.

Dudley, H. and S. Balashek (1958). "Automatic Recognition of Phonetic Patterns in Speech," *J. Acoust. Soc. Am.* 30, pp. 721–733.

Falter, J. W. and K. W. Otten (1967). "Cybernetics and Speech Communications: A Survey of Russian Literature," *IEEE Trans. on Audio and Electroacoustics* AU-15, pp. 27–36.

Fant, G. (1962). "Descriptive Analysis of the Acoustic Aspects of Speech," *Logos* 5, pp. 3–17. [Reprinted as Chapter 2 of this volume.]

Fant, G. (1964). "Auditory Patterns of Speech," STL-QPSR 3/1964, pp. 16–20.

Fant, G. (1966). "The Nature of Distinctive Features," STL-QPSR 4/1966, pp. 1–14. [Reprinted as Chapter 9 of this volume.]

Fant, G. (1968). "Analysis and Synthesis of Speech Processes," in *Manual of Phonetics*, ed. B. Malmberg, North Holland Publ. Co., Amsterdam, pp. 173–277.

Fant, G. (1969a). "Distinctive Features and Phonetic Dimensions," STL-QPSR 2-3/1969, pp. 1–18. [Reprinted as Chapter 11 of this volume.]

Fant, G. (1969b). "Stops in CV-syllables," STL-QPSR 4/1969, pp. 1–25. [Reprinted as Chapter 7 of this volume.]

Forgie, J. W. and C. D. Forgie (1959). "Results Obtained from a Vowel Recognition Computer Program," *J. Acoust. Soc. Am.* 31, pp. 1480–1489.

Gold, B. (1965). "Word-Recognition Computer Program," Massachusetts Institute of Technology, RLE, Technical Report 452.

Halle, M. and K. N. Stevens (1959). "Analysis by Synthesis," in *Proc. of Seminar on Speech Compression and Processing*, eds. W. Wathen-Dunn and L. E. Woods, Vol. 2, Paper D7.

Hughes, G. W. (1961). "The Recognition of Speech by Machine," Massachusetts Institute of Technology, RLE, Technical Report 395.

Hyde, S. R. (1968). "Automatic Speech Recognition. Literature Survey and Discussion," GPO (England), Research Department Report No. 45.

Jakobson, R., G. Fant, and M. Halle (1952). *Preliminaries to Speech Analysis: The Distinctive Features and Their Correlates,* Massachusetts Institute of Technology, Acoustic Laboratory, Technical Report 13 (7th ed. publ. by the MIT Press, Cambridge, Mass., 1967).

Kozhevnikov, V. A. and L. A. Chistovich (1965). *Speech: Articulation and Perception* (transl. from Russian), US Dept. of Commerce, JPRS:30, 543, Washington.

Lindblom, B. (1963). "Spectrographic Study of Vowel Reduction," *J. Acoust. Soc. Am.* 35, pp. 1773–1781.

Lindblom, B. and J. Sundberg (1969). "A Quantitative Theory of Cardinal Vowels and the Teaching of Pronunciation," STL-QPSR 2-3/1969, pp. 19–25.

Lindgren, N. (1965). "Machine Recognition of Human Language," *IEEE Spectrum* 2, Nos. 3 and 4.

Martin, T. B., A. L. Nelson, and H. J. Zadell (1964). "Speech Recognition by Feature Abstraction Techniques," Technical Report AL-TDR-64-176, AF Avionics Laboratory.

Martin, T. B., H. J. Zadell, A. L. Nelson, and J. F. Schanne (1967). "Continuous Speech Recognition and Synthesis," RCA, Technical Report AFAL-TR-67-210 (Oct.).

Öhman, S. E. G. (1967a). "Numerical Model of Coarticulation," *J. Acoust. Soc. Am.* 41, pp. 310–320.

Öhman, S. E. G. (1967b). "Word and Sentence Intonation. A Quantitative Model," STL-QPSR 2-3/1967, pp. 20–54.

Pierce, J. R. (1968). "Men, Machines, and Languages," *IEEE Spectrum* 5, pp. 44–49.

Pierce, J. R. (1969). "Whither Speech Recognition?" *J. Acoust. Soc. Am.* 46, No. 4 (Part 2), pp. 1049–1051.

Rabiner, L., R. Schafer, and C. Rader (1969). "The Chirp Z-transform Algorithm and Its Applications," *Bell Systems Techn. J.* 48, pp. 1249–1292.

Reddy, D. R. (1967a). "Phoneme Grouping of Speech Recognition," *J. Acoust. Soc. Am.* 41, pp. 1295–1300.

Reddy, D. R. (1967b). "Computer Recognition of Connected Speech," *J. Acoust. Soc. Am.* 42, pp. 329–347.

Reddy, D. R. and A. E. Robinson (1968). "Phoneme-to-Grapheme Translation of English," *IEEE Trans. on Audio and Electroacoustics* AU-16, pp. 240–246.

Reddy, D. R. and P. J. Vicens (1968). "A Procedure for the Segmentation of Connected 'Speech'," *J. Audio Engr. Soc.* 16, pp. 404–412.

Sakai, T. and S. Doshita (1962). "The Phonetic Typewriter," *Infor. Processing 1962,* Proc. IFIP Congress Munich, Aug-Sept.

Shearme, J. N. and P. F. Leach (1968). "Some Experiments with a Simple Word Recognition," *J. Acoust. Soc. Am.* 43, pp. 375–377.

Shearme, J. N. and P. F. Leach (1968). "Some Experiments with a Simple Word Recognition System," *IEEE Trans. on Audio and Electroacoustics* AU-16, pp. 256–261.

Teacher, C. F., H. G. Kellett, and L. R. Focht (1967). "Experimental, Limited Vocabulary, Speech Recognizer," *IEEE Int. Conv. Record,* Part III, pp. 169–173.

Velichko, V. M. and N. G. Zagoruiko (1969). "Automatical Recognition of 200 Oral Commands," *CS,* No. 37, Novosibirsk (in Russian).

Zagoruiko, N. G. (1970). "Automatic Recognition of Speech," STL-QPSR 1/1970, pp. 32–38.

Supplementary Bibliography

These selected publications in phonetics and audiology are not included in this volume.

1. General survey publications

Jakobson, R., G. Fant, and M. Halle. "Preliminaries to Speech Analysis. The Distinctive Features and Their Correlates," MIT, Acoustics Laboratory, Technical Report No. 13 (1952).

Fant, G. "Speech Communication Research," IVA (Royal Swedish Academy of Engineering Sciences, Stockholm) 24 (1953), pp. 734–742.

Fant, G. "Modern Instruments and Methods for Acoustic Studies of Speech," Acta Polytechnica Scandinavica 246/1958, 84 pp.; also published in *Proc. of the VIIIth International Congress of Linguists Oslo* (Oslo 1958), pp. 282–358.

Fant, G. "Acoustic Analysis and Synthesis of Speech with Applications to Swedish," *Ericsson Technics* 15, No. 1 (1959), pp. 1–106.

Fant, G. "Speech Analysis and Synthesis," KTH, Dept. of Speech Communication, Speech Transmission Laboratory Report No. 26 (1962).

Fant, G. "Phonetics and Speech Research," *Research Potentials in Voice Physiology* (New York, 1964), pp. 199–239.

Fant, G. "Analysis and Synthesis of Speech Processes," in *Manual of Phonetics*, ed. B. Malmberg (Amsterdam, 1968), pp. 173–277.

Fant, G. "Phonetik und Sprachforschung," *Handbuch der Stimm- und Sprachheilkunde, Band 2, Die Sprache und ihre Störungen*, ed. R. Luchsinger/G.E. Arnold (Vienna, 1970).

2. Speech analysis

Fant, G. "Undersökning av 10 sekunders standardfras," L M Ericsson protokoll H/P 1051 (1948), in Swedish.

Fant, G. "Analys av de Svenska vokalljuden," L M Ericsson protokoll H/P 1035 (1948), in Swedish.

Fant, G. "Analys av de Svenska konsonantljuden," L M Ericsson protokoll H/P 1064 (1949), in Swedish.

Fant, G. "Phonetic and Phonemic Basis for the Transcription of Swedish Word Material," *Acta Oto-Laryng.*, Suppl. 116 (1954), pp. 24–29.

Fant, G. and M. Richter. "Some Notes on the Relative Occurrence of Letters, Phonemes, and Words in Swedish," *Proc. of the VIIIth International Congress of Linguistics Oslo* (Oslo, 1958), pp. 815–816.

Fant, G. "Sound Spectrography," *Proc. of the Fourth International Congress of Phonetic Sciences Helsinki 1961* ('s-Gravenhage, 1962), pp. 14–33.

Fant, G. and J. Mártony. "Pole-Zero Matching Techniques," STL-QPSR 1/1960, pp. 14–16.

Fant, G. "Formant Bandwidth Data," STL-QPSR 1/1962, pp. 1–2.

Fant, G., B. Lindblom, and J. Mártony. "Spectrograms of Swedish Stops," STL-QPSR 3/1963, p. 1.

Mártony, J. and G. Fant. "Pole-Zero Matching of Spectra of [l]," STL-QPSR 1/1961, pp. 1–2.

Tarnóczy, T. and G. Fant. "Some Remarks on the Average Speech Spectrum," STL-QPSR 4/1964, pp. 13–14.

Shupljakov, V., G. Fant, and A. de Serpa-Leitão. "Acoustical Features of Hard and Soft Russian Consonants in Connected Speech: A Spectrographic Study," STL-QPSR 4/1968, pp. 1–6.

Mettas, O., G. Fant, and U. Stålhammar. "The A-Vowels of Parisian French," STL-QPSR 4/1971, pp. 1–8.

3. Speech production

Fant, G. "On the Predictability of Formant Levels and Spectrum Envelopes from Formant Frequencies," *For Roman Jakobson* ('s-Gravenhage, 1956), pp. 109–120.

Briess, B. and G. Fant. "Studies of Voice Pathology by Means of Inverse Filtering," STL-QPSR 1/1962, p. 6.

Fant, G. and B. Sonesson. "Indirect Studies of Glottal Cycles by Synchronous Inverse Filtering and Photo-Electrical Glottography," STL-QPSR 4/1962, pp. 1–3.

Fant, G., K. Fintoft, J. Liljencrants, B. Lindblom, and J. Mártony. "Formant-Amplitude Measurements," *J. Acoust. Soc. Am.* 35 (1963), pp. 1753–1761.

Fant, G. "Formants and Cavities," *Proc. 5th Int. Congr. Phon. Sci., Münster 1964* (Basel, 1965), pp. 120–141.

Fant, G. and B. Sonesson. "Speech at High Ambient Air-Pressure," STL-QPSR 2/1964, pp. 9–21.

Bjuggren, G. and G. Fant. "The Nasal Cavity Structures," STL-QPSR 4/1964, pp. 5–7.

Fant, G., J. Ondráčková, J. Lindqvist, and B. Sonesson. "Electrical Glottography," STL-QPSR 4/1966, pp. 15–21.

Fant, G. and J. Lindqvist. "Studies Related to Diver's Speech," STL-QPSR 1/1968, pp. 7–17.

Fant, G. *Acoustic Theory of Speech Production* ('s-Gravenhage, 1970), 2nd edition.

Fant, G. "Vocal Tract Wall Effects, Losses, and Resonance Bandwidths," STL-QPSR 2–3/1972, pp. 28–52.

4. Speech perception

Fant, G. "Comments by G. Fant to Paper D3 'A Motor Theory of Speech Perception,' by A. M. Liberman, F. S. Cooper, K. S. Harris, and P. F. MacNeilage," *Proc. of the Speech Communication Seminar Stockholm* (Stockholm, 1963), Vol. III.

Fant, G. and A. Risberg. "Auditory Matching of Vowels with Two Formant Synthetic Sounds," STL-QPSR 4/1963, pp. 7–11.

Mártony, J. and G. Fant. "Information Bearing Aspects of Formant Amplitude," *Proc. 5th Int. Congr. Phon. Sci., Münster 1964* (Basel, 1965), pp. 409–411.

Chistovich, L., G. Fant, A. de Serpa-Leitão, and P. Tjernlund. "Mimicking of Synthetic Vowels," STL-QPSR 2/1966, pp. 1–18.

Chistovich, L., G. Fant, and A. de Serpa-Leitão. "Mimicking and Perception of Synthetic Vowels. Part II," STL-QPSR 3/1966, pp. 1–3.

Fant, G. "Auditory Patterns of Speech," *Proc. of the Symposium on Models for the Perception of Speech and Visual Form, Boston, Mass., Nov. 11–14, 1964,* ed. W. Wathen-Dunn (Cambridge, Mass., 1967), pp. 111–125.

Fant, G., J. Liljencrants, V. Maláč, and B. Borovičková. "Perceptual Evaluation of Coarticulation Effects," STL-QPSR 1/1970, pp. 10–13.

Carlson, R., B. Granström, and G. Fant. "Some Studies Concerning Perception of Isolated Vowels," STL-QPSR 2–3/1970, pp. 19–35.

5. Speech synthesis

Stevens, K. N., S. Kasowski, and G. Fant. "An Electrical Analog of the Vocal Tract," *J. Acoust. Soc. Am.* 25 (1953), pp. 734–742.

Fant, G. and J. Mártony. "Quantization of Formant Coded Synthetic Speech," STL-QPSR 2/1961, pp. 16–18.

Fant, G. and J. Mártony. "Speech Synthesis," STL-QPSR 2/1962, pp. 18–24.

Fant, G., J. Mártony, U. Rengman, and A. Risberg. "OVE II Synthesis Strategy," Paper F5, *Proc. of the Speech Communication Seminar Stockholm* (Stockholm, 1963), Vol. II.

6. Audiology

Wedenberg, E. and G. Fant. "Auditory Training of Deaf Children," *Acta Oto-Laryng.* XXXVII, Fasc. 5 (1949), pp. 462–469.

Lidén, G. and G. Fant. "Swedish Word Material for Speech Audiometry and Articulation Tests," *Acta Oto-Laryng.*, Suppl. 116 (1954), pp. 189–210.

Mörner, M., F. Fransson, and G. Fant. "Voice Register Terminology and Standard Pitch," STL-QPSR 4/1963, pp. 17–23.

Fant, G. "Q-Codes," *International Symposium on Speech Communication Ability and Profound Deafness* (Washington, D.C., 1972), pp. 261–268.

INDEX

Abramson, A. S., 156
Acoustic analysis, 5, 18, 19
Acoustic correlates, 18, 25, 145–149, 166, 186–190, 192, 194, 197, 211
Acoustic theory of speech production, 6–12
Acute feature, 137, 145, 148, 150, 158
Affricates, 104, 180
Alveolar feature, 211–212
Alveolar sounds, 68, 121, 145, 183
Amplification systems, 68
Analysis-by-synthesis techniques, 15, 23, 26, 29
Anterior feature, 137–138, 172–173, 179, 184, 189, 198, 200
Anti-resonances, 13, 23, 24
Articulation. See also Place of articulation
 complex, 29
 sustained, 96–97
Aspiration feature, 211–212
Aspiration sounds, 27, 64, 112, 113, 115, 116, 121, 129, 130, 182
Automatic speech recognition, 6, 17, 25, 143, 151, 163, 166, 174, 202–214. See also Visible Speech
Average pronunciations, 34–35. See also Normalization

Back feature, 175, 176, 185–186, 198–199, 211–212
Barney, H. L., 42, 86, 167
Binary principle, 152–153, 174, 175, 185, 207
Borovičková, B., 164
Boundaries, 21–23, 153–154, 166, 207. See also Distinctive features; Sound segments
Boundary shift techniques, 168
Bursts, 64, 67, 113, 115, 116, 118, 119, 130, 135

Categorical response, 164–165
Chiba, T., 46, 88, 91
Child's vocal tract length, 7, 29, 46, 84–93, 98, 167
Chistovich, L. A., 120, 157, 166, 167

Chomsky, Noam, 137, 171, 174, 175, 176–179, 182, 183, 192, 197–198, 199, 200, 211, 213
Close feature. 58. 192. 198
Coarticulation, 30, 113, 121, 124, 167, 173, 182–183, 207, 213
Compact feature, 57–58, 137, 145, 148, 149–150, 158–159, 176, 187, 196–200
Connected speech, 19–21, 35, 61, 68
Consonantal feature, 149, 155, 173, 175, 176–181, 211–213
Consonantal sounds, 177
Consonants
 acoustic information on, 18
 categorical response to, 164
 and distinctive features, 148–149, 153, 155–156, 164
 English, 100–109, 156
 perceptual distance, 100–109
 and spectrographic analysis, 5, 12–14, 61–68
 Swedish, 34, 61–68, 100–109, 110–138, 145, 148–150
Context, 163, 168
Contextual bias, 152, 166
Continuant feature, 178–180
Continuant sounds, 12, 61, 63
Cooper. F. S.. 125
Coronal feature, 137–138, 172–173, 179, 184, 198, 200
Correlates, 152. See also Acoustic correlates; Perceptual correlates; Production correlates
Covered feature, 183, 197
Cues, 5, 101–102, 109, 130, 149–150, 152, 153, 165, 167, 168, 206

Danish, 126
Delattre, P., 125
Dental feature, 211–212
Dental sounds, 14, 28, 69, 101, 107, 118, 124, 133–134, 145, 212
Derkach, M., 211
de Serpa-Leitão, A., 165, 167
Diffuse feature, 137, 158, 187

Diphthongization, 95, 97, 116, 129, 184, 185, 193–194, 196, 199, 200
Discrete vs. continuous view, 21
Dispersion parameter, 57–58
Distinctive feature matrix, 207
Distinctive features, 143
  in automatic speech recognition, 143, 208, 210–213
  boundaries of, 153–154, 166, 206
  economy of, 153, 156, 159, 164
  independence of, 175–176
  invariance of, 163
  major class features of, 176–181
  nature of, 18n, 151–159, 162–164
  orthogonality of, 153, 175–176, 190
  proposals for
    Chomsky-Halle, 137, 171, 174, 175, 176–179, 182, 183, 192, 197–198, 199, 200, 211, 213
    Fant, 25, 143, 151, 155, 162, 165, 174, 186, 192, 193, 210
    Jakobson-Fant-Halle, 18, 58, 143, 151, 155, 162, 166, 171, 176, 196–197, 198, 200, 211, 213
    Jakobson-Halle, 155
    Lindblom-Sundberg, 184, 192, 193, 198–199
    Lisker-Abramson, 156
    Malécot, 156
    Malmberg, 56, 186, 192–193, 194
    Stevens, 138
    Wang, 199
  psychological reality of, 174–175, 194
Distributed feature, 183
Duration, 26, 155, 207

Edholm, Paul, 90
English, 42–45, 71, 86, 124, 156
Equivalent circuit theory, 6–8

F_0. See Voice fundamental frequency
Fant, G., 25, 67, 86, 143, 151, 155, 162, 163, 165, 167, 174, 186, 192, 193, 210
Filtering function, 23, 24, 92, 161. See also Transfer function
Fine structure, 5, 6, 61, 67
Fischer-Jørgensen, E., 130, 136, 194
Flanagan, J. L., 42
Flat feature, 138, 145, 148, 150, 158, 187–190, 194–196, 200, 201
"Formant, spurious," 38–39
Formant bandwidth, 5, 7–9, 97
Formant cavity relations, 88
Formant frequency, 7–9
  boundaries, 22
  of consonants, 66–67
  description of, 5, 23

and machine recognition, 143
and normalization, 167–168
of Swedish vowels, 36–59
Formant intensity levels, 12–13, 36–37, 42–45, 52, 68, 71–76, 168
Formant spread diagram, 58
Formant structure, 5, 6
Formant sum diagram, 58
Formant transitions, 67, 121–125
Form factor, 76–79, 168
F-pattern
  articulatory variables of, 11–12
  child's, 7, 29, 46, 84–93, 98, 167
  of consonants, 13, 121–125
  definition of, 5, 24, 84
  female's, 7, 29, 36–37, 44–46, 49–51, 56–57, 84–93, 98, 167–168
  male's, 7, 29, 36–37, 39, 44–46, 49–51, 52–56, 57, 58, 79, 84–93, 167
  and place of articulation, 132–134
Fricative feature, 26–27, 211–212
Fricative sounds, 61–63, 101, 102–104, 112, 113, 114, 115, 138, 180
Front feature, 211–212
Fujimura, O., 98, 167
Fujisaki, H., 168
Fundamental frequency. See Voice fundamental frequency

Glide feature, 26–28, 211–212
Glide sounds, 104, 167, 179, 180, 181
Glottal relaxation, 182–183
Grave feature, 137, 158, 176, 196–199
Gravity, center of, 167, 187
Gravity feature, 57–58, 187
Green, H. C., 18

Halle, M., 18, 58, 137, 143, 151, 155, 158, 162, 166, 171, 174, 175, 176–179, 182, 183, 192, 196–198, 199, 200, 211, 213
Harmonics, 76–79
Hearing defects, 68–71, 109
High feature, 175, 176, 185–186, 198–199, 211–212
h-sounds, 8, 63, 64, 112–113, 149, 180, 181–182
Hungarian, 71
Hyde, S. R., 203–204

Inherent features, 143n
Instant release, 179
Intensity, 6, 8–9, 23, 26, 66–67, 167
Interdental feature, 211–212
Interdental sounds, 107
Interrupted feature, 149
Intonation, 5, 118, 214. See also Voice fundamental frequency

Invariance, 163
Inverse filtering technique, 7-8, 26

Jakobson, R., 18, 58, 143, 151, 155, 158, 162, 166, 171, 176, 196–197, 198, 200, 211, 213, 155
Jaw closure feature, 185, 198

Kajiyama, M., 46, 88, 91
Kawashima, T., 168
Koenig scale, 48
Kopp, A. G., 18
Kozhevnikov, V. A., 120

Labial feature, 173, 183-185, 198, 200, 211–212
Labial sounds, 14, 28, 107, 121, 124, 125-129, 132–134, 138
Ladefoged, P., 174, 176, 190
Laryngeal cavities, 88, 92
Lateral feature, 26-27, 179, 211–212
Lateral sounds, 27, 63, 167, 180
Lax feature, 148, 150, 155-156, 176, 182-183, 192, 196-200, 211–212
Lehiste, I., 119, 124, 182
Liberman, A. M., 125, 165-166
Lindblom, B., 119, 162, 163, 165, 174, 184, 185, 190, 192, 193, 198-199
Lindquist, J., 163
Liquid sounds, 147
Lisker, L., 156
Locus theory, 125, 165
Long-time average speech spectra, 67, 71
Low feature, 175, 176, 181, 198-199, 211–212
l-sounds, 63-64, 104

Machine identification, 17, 29, 143. *See also* Automatic speech recognition
Maláč, V., 164
Malécot, A., 156
Malmberg, B., 56, 186, 192-193, 194
Manner of production, 5, 6, 26-27, 108, 109, 206, 207
 features, 137-138, 162, 211-212
Mel scale, 10, 47-57, 186-187
Message level, 161, 162, 163, 168, 173
Microsegment detection, 204, 206-207, 210
Mid-closure feature, 178-180
Mid feature, 199
Miller, G. A., 100-101, 108
Minimum perceptible differences, 42, 44, 48-49
Minimum redundancy, 19, 162, 163, 212
Motor theory of speech, 166
Multi-band-pass sampling technique, 61
Multidimensional boundaries, 166

Nasal feature, 26-27, 149, 176, 179, 211–212
Nasalization, 13, 21, 154
Nasal sounds, 13, 167, 180
Nicely, P. E., 100-101, 108
Noise, 13, 24, 26-27
Normalization, 18-19, 29, 51, 52-56, 167-168, 174, 207, 209

Occlusive feature, 26-27
Occlusive sounds, 111, 121, 129-130
Öhman, S. E. G., 118, 119, 124-125, 135, 163, 164
Open feature, 58, 185, 189
Ormestad, H., 109

Palatal feature, 183-185, 198-200, 211-212
Palatal sounds, 14, 28, 58, 63, 118, 124, 130, 133-134
Parameters, 5-6, 19-21, 26, 152, 165-167, 204, 206
Peak factor, 76-79, 168
Perception, 58, 59, 100-109, 164-167
 and distinctive features, 138, 156-157, 176
Perceptual correlates, 186, 190, 194, 197, 211
Perceptual cues, 167
Perceptual distance, 101, 104, 107, 154-155, 176, 186
Perceptual invariance, 138
Perceptual quantization effects, 167
Peterson, G. E., 42, 86, 119, 124, 167, 174, 182
Pharyngeal constriction, 58
Pharyngeal feature, 198, 211-212
Pharynx length. *See* Vocal tract
Phonemes
 boundaries, 21-23
 relation to sound segments, 5, 22-23, 25, 29, 154, 163
Phonetic distance, 164, 176
Phonetics, 25, 143
 vs. phonology, 152, 163, 172-174
Pierce, J. R., 202
Place of articulation, 26-28, 108, 115, 121, 132-134, 136-137, 206, 207
 features, 137, 162, 171, 211-213
Plain feature, 158
Pole-zero descriptions, 7, 13-14, 23-25, 136, 206
Potter, R. K., 18, 42
Production correlates, 27, 171, 192, 210-213
Production theory, 6-12, 125-129, 136
Prosodic features, 143n

Reddy, D. R., 211

Relational invariance, 152
Resonance bandwidth, 9
Resonance frequency, 7, 12, 24, 39
Resonator features, 26
Resonator theory, 129
Retroflex feature, 211–212
Retroflex sounds, 26, 28, 138, 184
Rounding feature, 176, 185–186, 211–213
r-sound feature, 211–212
r-sounds, 63–64, 104, 180
Russian, 90, 92, 126

Segment pattern features, 26, 28–29
Segment type features, 29
Semantic interpretation, 204, 208
Series analysis of features, 157
Shape factors, 76–79, 168
Sharp feature, 158, 197
Short feature, 145, 148
Signal level, 161, 162, 163, 168
Sine wave-vowel association, 59–61
Sonorant feature, 173, 175, 176–181
Sound features, 23, 25–29
Sound pressure, 6–7, 71–76
Sound segments
  boundaries, 5–6, 21–23, 24, 26, 29, 67, 120, 166, 206
  classification of, 25–29, 162
  duration. 6. 110–121. 174
  relation to phonemes, 22–23, 25, 29, 154, 163
Source features, 211–213. *See also* Place of articulation
Spectral energy, 4, 61–63, 135–138
Spectrographic analysis, 3–15, 17–30
Spectrum decomposition, 10
Spectrum shape, 10
Speech communication chain, 160–162
Speech defects, 109
Speech mode, 165
Speech synthesis, 14–15, 17, 19, 130–131, 136, 174
Speech writing, coding, 5, 6
Spread feature, 187, 194, 201
"Spurious formant," 38–39
Steinberg, J. C., 42
Stevens, K. N., 138, 165
Stop feature, 211–212
Stop sounds, 12, 14, 21, 61, 64–68, 101–102, 107, 110–138, 180
  perception of, 133, 135, 136, 138, 165
Stress, 116–117, 120, 192, 214
Sundberg, J., 97, 119, 184, 185, 190
Swedish. *See* Consonants, Swedish; Vowels, Swedish
Swedish Technical Alphabet, 32, 34

Sweep-frequency analysis, 4, 35, 56, 61, 68, 94
Syllabic feature, 173, 175, 177–181
Syllabic sounds, 178
Syllabic timing, 119–120
Syllable, 149, 155, 165, 207
Synthetic speech, 29, 51, 165, 168

Tempo, 116
Temporal contrast, 149, 157
Temporal distribution of cues, 153
Tense feature, 148, 150, 155–156, 176, 182–183, 192, 196–200, 211–212
Ternary features, 196
Tongue body features, 137, 171, 176, 183–185, 211–213
Tongue body movement, 39, 121, 126–127, 129, 136
Transcription, 19–21, 174, 204, 207
Transfer function, 6–8, 13, 206. *See also* Filtering function
Transient sound segments, 26–27, 111–112, 115. 121. 130
Transitions, 5, 26–28, 61, 63, 126–129, 132, 135–138
Two-formant model, 52, 99, 125, 186, 194

Uvular feature, 211–212

van den Berg, J., 74–76
Velar feature, 198–199, 211–212
Velar sounds, 28, 124, 130, 133, 138
Visible Speech, 3, 18, 21
Vocal cavity wall effects, 11, 127, 182
Vocalic feature, 148, 173, 175, 176–180
Vocalic sounds, 177
Vocal tract
  dimensions of, 7, 29, 36–37, 39, 45–46, 56, 57, 84–93, 96, 97, 98, 167–168
  model of, 12
Vocal tract transfer function. *See* Filter function; Transfer function
Voiced feature, 26–27, 150, 155–156, 173, 211
Voiced/voiceless distinction, 115, 118, 119–121, 130–131, 133, 150, 155–156, 173, 182–183
Voice effort, 76–79
Voice fundamental frequency, 5–6, 24, 26, 37–38, 51, 58–59, 76–79, 80, 97, 137, 206
Voiceless feature. *See* Voiced feature
Voicing, 26, 67, 114, 115, 116
  boundary of, 120, 132
Volume velocity, 6–7, 12
Vowel feature, 211–212
Vowellike feature, 26–28

Vowels
  categorical response to, 164–165
  defining, 155
  duration, 96, 116–117, 119–121, 192
  English, 42–45
  major class features of, 180
  Swedish, 9–11, 32–33, 35–61, 68, 94–99, 110–138, 145, 148, 157–159, 183–190, 192–201
  three-formant synthesis of, 98
  two-formant synthesis of, 52, 99, 125, 186, 194

Wang, W. S.-Y., 199
Word identification, 204, 207–208

Zeros, 7–8, 13–14, 23–25

www.ingramcontent.com/pod-product-compliance
Lightning Source LLC
Chambersburg PA
CBHW020651230426
43665CB00008B/390